T0265558

LONG RUN TO GLORY

LONG RUN TO GLORY

The Story of the Greatest Marathon in Olympic History and the Women Who Made It Happen

STEPHEN LANE

Essex, Connecticut

An imprint of Globe Pequot, the trade division of
The Rowman & Littlefield Publishing Group, Inc.
4501 Forbes Blvd., Ste. 200
Lanham, MD 20706
www.rowman.com

Distributed by NATIONAL BOOK NETWORK

Copyright © 2023 by Stephen Lane

All rights reserved. No part of this book may be reproduced in any form or by any electronic or
mechanical means, including information storage and retrieval systems, without written permission
from the publisher, except by a reviewer who may quote passages in a review.

British Library Cataloguing in Publication Information available

Library of Congress Cataloging-in-Publication Data
Names: Lane, Stephen (Educator), author.
Title: Long run to glory : the story of the greatest marathon in Olympic history and the women
    who made it happen / Stephen Lane.
Description: Essex, Connecticut : Lyons Press, [2024] | Includes bibliographical references and
    index.
Identifiers: LCCN 2023007881 (print) | LCCN 2023007882 (ebook) | ISBN 9781493073023
    (cloth : acid-free paper) | ISBN 9781493077601 (epub)
Subjects: LCSH: Women long-distance runners. | Marathon running—History. | Olympic Games
    (23rd : 1984 : Los Angeles, Calif.)—History.
Classification: LCC GV1061.18.W66 L3 2024 (print) | LCC GV1061.18.W66 (ebook) | DDC
    796.42082—dc23/eng/20230407
LC record available at https://lccn.loc.gov/2023007881
LC ebook record available at https://lccn.loc.gov/2023007882

♾️™ The paper used in this publication meets the minimum requirements of American National
Standard for Information Sciences—Permanence of Paper for Printed Library Materials, ANSI/
NISO Z39.48-1992.

For Jess

Alis volat propriis

Contents

In the greater game we strive not for winning,
but to extend our personal boundaries of who we are and what
we can be,
not as much to become faster but to become more.

—Lorraine Moller
Four-time Olympic marathoner—1984, 1988, 1992, 1996
1992 Olympic bronze medalist

Introduction

IN THE BEGINNING, IN CHILDHOOD, RUNNING IS JUST WHAT WE DO. WE run, we jump, we play—we cannot be contained. With age, some learn to curb that impulse, some find other outlets for it, and some of us find that we still need to run. It is still play, but also much more: our key to physical and mental health; our way of finding balance; a means of expressing who we are and what we can do; a challenge we seek; and an escape from the other challenges we face.

The marathon has long represented the ultimate running challenge—a heroic, mythical, Olympian test. For most of us, the goal is first to complete it, then perhaps to run it faster—first we race the distance, then we race the clock. For the few who are gifted enough, determined enough, and perhaps obsessed enough, the challenge is to stand among the very best in the world, to wear a laurel wreath or an Olympic medal. But even for those few, the challenge is ultimately against oneself—what separates the marathon from other Olympic footraces, at least in our imaginations, is that the winner is not simply the fastest but the one who can push their body to the furthest limits of human endurance.

Every Olympic marathon has its share of drama. The stakes are so high because the opportunities are so rare—one can go to the edge only so many times in a career, and few athletes are fortunate enough to be at their peak for two Olympic cycles. Further, the marathon is capricious—it allows no margin for error and offers no guarantees: even the strongest, fittest, smartest runners in the world may find themselves humbled, not by their competitors but by the race itself.

To call any marathon the greatest in Olympic history is to surrender to the very human and ultimately fruitless compulsion for ranking. Still, the book's title wasn't chosen lightly. Never before in history had a single Olympic marathon brought together such a transcendent collection of talent. To further succumb to our rankings fixation, each of the top four finishers has a fair claim to being the greatest distance runner of all time: Going into the 1984 Olympics, Grete Waitz had never lost a marathon she had finished; Joan Benoit's world record of 2:22 was nearly two minutes faster than the second-best performance in history; Ingrid Kristiansen was the fastest distance runner alive at any race short of the marathon (and would add the marathon world record to her collection less than a year after the Olympics); and although few knew it at the time, Rosa Mota was on her way to establishing a reputation as the greatest championship marathoner in history.

All four are legends in the running world, and it is a matter of good fortune and remarkable timing (for us as spectators) that all four lined up in the same race. Had they been born even five years later, each might have won gold in a different event. Men's distance-running talent was spread across five races—the 1500m, 3000m steeplechase, 5000m, 10,000m, and marathon. In 1984, women could only choose between the 1500m, 3000m, or marathon; the International Olympic Committee added the 10,000m for women in 1988 and the 5000m in 1992. Had there been a full slate of women's races in 1984, Kristiansen almost certainly would have run the 5000m or 10,000m, or both. Waitz also may have chosen the 10,000m—according to Jackie Hansen, one of the leaders in the fight to get the marathon in the Olympics, Waitz told her in 1983 that she thought the 10K was her best event. Further, if women had the same opportunities as men in previous Olympics, it is conceivable that Waitz, who ran the 1500m in 1972 and 1976, would already have won several medals in the 10,000m or marathon by 1984 and been happily retired by the time the other three came into the sport.

Had each been born ten years earlier, it is possible that we would never have heard of any of them. Without the Olympic marathon, they may never have found a stage worthy of their talents—and the millions who watched their race would have been deprived of the gift of witnessing such greatness.

Which brings up a second argument for the preeminence of this race: it was a historic first, a milestone in the movement for equity in athletics, and a race that was generations in the making. In 1896, at the first modern Olympics, a desperately poor Greek woman named Stamata Revithi sought to enter the first Olympic marathon, apparently in hopes of gaining employment with the Athens city government as a reward for her efforts; the local press nicknamed her Melpomene, the Greek muse of tragedy. Her petition was denied, but she ran the course anyway, the day after the men.

Outside of the Olympics, the lineage from Revithi to the marathoners of the 1980s is somewhat obscure, for a variety of reasons. Record keeping in races was spotty, even into the 1960s. The term marathon referred not to the precise 26.2-mile (or 42.195 kilometer) distance, but was a catchall for any long race. Until the 1980s, course measurement was an inexact art anyway; what counts as an "official" marathon is in the eye of the beholder. The records we do have show that a Frenchwoman named Marie-Louise Ledru ran a marathon in Paris in 1918, finishing in 5:40. Violet Piercy ran a race in London in 1926, in 3:40—although perhaps it was only thirty-five kilometers. Arlene Pieper, who owned a fitness studio in Colorado Springs, ran the Pike's Peak marathon in 1959, finishing in 9:16. If that seems slow, it is because the course runs up to the summit of Pike's Peak (14,115 feet) and back; for many participants, the race is more of a fast hike—experienced runners often hit the halfway point in about as much time as it would take them to run a full marathon on a flat course.

Even as late as the 1960s, the Amateur Athletic Union (the governing body of track and field in the United States) stipulated that the longest allowable race for women was 1.5 miles. The first woman to run an AAU-sanctioned road race as an official entrant (in defiance of the rules) was Julia Chase, a 19-year-old student at Smith College, who ran the 4.75-mile Manchester Road Race in Connecticut on Thanksgiving Day 1961. (An article in *Life* magazine referred to her as "a fetching entry in a man's field.") In 1963, Merry Lepper finished the Culver City Marathon in 3:37. In May 1964, Dale Greig ran a marathon on the Isle of Wight in 3:27. A month later, Millie Sampson ran 3:19 in New

Zealand—apparently after a long night of dancing and carousing—but athletics officials disputed her record: it wasn't an official race, they said; the course was short, they said; they seemed to want to say that they didn't believe a woman could run a marathon that fast.

Doubtless, the record has gaps: stories persist of a marathon organizer in Kansas who, in 1927, sent an emissary to recruit runners from the famed distance-running Tarahumara tribe in northern Mexico. When the chief of the Tarahumara learned that the race was only twenty-six miles, the story goes, he sent three teenage girls up to run it. But even if the record is incomplete, it is clear: opportunities for women to race any distance were limited.

The first women's Olympic marathon came about only through a years-long effort to correct the myopic failings of the sport's rule makers. Its eventual inclusion in the Olympics was a victory that belongs to many: talented, determined athletes whose achievements helped change societal attitudes toward what women could do; skilled advocates who navigated and manipulated the bureaucracies of the governing bodies of international sport; and the right kind of troublemakers—rebels who pushed their way into places they were told they didn't belong. Their efforts culminated in a race of shining beauty, an inspirational example of Olympian athleticism and grit. Both the athletes who contested the race and the pioneering generations who fought to make it possible have become icons and heroes. But they didn't set out to be. They only wanted to run.

PRELUDE

AMSTERDAM, AUGUST 2, 1928, 3:25 P.M.: *On the cinder track inside Olympische Stadium, nine athletes prepared for the final of the women's Olympic 800m. The Olympic flame—a new addition in 1928—glowed atop Marathon Tower, which rose above the stadium. The wide banked oval of the cycling velodrome circled the perimeter of the track, a moat between athletes and audience. Heat, dust, and smoke choked the air. Spectators craned their necks toward the start, looking down at the athletes through a gauzy haze.*

The 1928 Olympic Games was the first time in Olympic history that women were permitted to compete in track and field—"athletics," to most of the world—and the 800m was their longest race. Some viewed it with bemusement, some with excitement, some with disdain. Women's athletics was not universally welcomed into the Olympics: "Impractical, uninteresting, unaesthetic, and . . . wrong," said Baron Pierre de Coubertin, founder of the modern Olympics.[1] Only the persistent efforts of Alice Milliat, a French athlete and founder of the Fédération Sportive Féminine Internationale (FSFI), forced the hand of the IOC. Twice she petitioned Coubertin to include women's athletics in the Olympics; twice he dismissed her. So, she started her own: the first Women's Olympics, which Milliat and the FSFI hosted outside of Paris in 1922, included eleven athletics events and attracted thirty thousand spectators. The second edition, held in 1926 in Sweden, drew sixty thousand spectators, including Swedish royalty. Milliat's successful Women's Games were a threat to the IOC, which didn't easily tolerate rivals to its international sporting hegemony. But because the IOC had excluded women's athletics, they had no way to control the upstart FSFI. Their only means of containing the threat was to admit women to the Olympics, which they did—grudgingly: after originally agreeing to include ten women's events, they cut the number to five—to be included in 1928 only on an "experimental basis."

Germany's Lina Radke entered the Olympics as the 800m world record holder, a title she and Sweden's Inga Gentzel swapped back and forth in the months before the Games. The record had been 2:26 since 1922; Radke ran 2:23.8 in August 1927, Gentzel dropped it to 2:20.4 in June of 1928, Radke ran 2:19 in July. Gentzel was more than just a mid-distance star—she was also the Swedish record holder in the 200m and may well have run that instead, had it been included in the Olympic program.

Canada's Jenny Thompson had dominated her national championships, winning by nearly one hundred meters, and would have been considered one of the favorites, had she not sustained an injury in training just days before the race. Japan's Kinue Hitomi loomed as perhaps the most fearsome competitor in the 800. Leading up to the 1928 Olympics, she set world records in the 100m (broken by eventual 1928 Olympic gold medalist Betty Robinson of the United States), the long jump (5.98m) and triple jump (11.62m), the 400m (59.0—at a time when many track experts doubted women could ever break a minute), and 200m (25.8); she was also the top javelin thrower in the world. At the 1926 Women's Games, Milliat awarded Hitomi a silver cup as the best athlete in the meet. But it was Hitomi's misfortune that none of her strongest events were included in the Olympic program. She originally entered the 100m; a poor prelim kept her out of the final. Seeking redemption, she entered the 800 at the last minute.

With the crack of the starter's pistol, Thompson, running with her leg well wrapped, shot out of her sprinter's crouch and into the lead. Her coach advised a cautious start, but she preferred to run from the front and dare the others to keep pace. As Thompson rounded the first bend, Hitomi accelerated to join her, and the two ran shoulder to shoulder into the backstretch. In last place was Gentzel. By disposition, Gentzel was a front-runner, but she stumbled slightly off the line, and was buried by the other eight.

It is a cardinal rule of the 800m that a runner gets only one move, one all-out burst in her bid for victory; there's no reserve for anything more. Most athletes save that move as long as possible for fear of running out of steam before the finish. Gentzel made hers on the backstretch of the first lap, rocketing to the lead at the 200m mark. It was risky to surge so decisively so early, but Gentzel lacked the pure explosive acceleration of some of the others, the ability to separate from the pack in an eyeblink. She needed to burn out the kickers before the end, and after her start, a mid-race surge was her only path to victory; she wasn't running for silver. She pulled the field through 400m in 1:04.2—recklessly fast; in an ideally paced race, such a first lap would yield a final time around 2:10, or nine seconds under the world record.

Early in final lap, the field bunched together as the athletes gathered themselves for the finishing sprint. Gentzel still held the lead, but the strain of her early move was evident. Hitomi was on her shoulder, and Radke, who settled in mid-pack at the start, glided along in third. Radke struck on the backstretch and immediately gapped the field. Gentzel was left helpless; Hitomi reacted just a hair slowly, and by the time she got up to speed, Radke was away and not coming back. Radke cruised the last seventy-five meters, calmly looking back every few strides to ensure that Hitomi got no closer. Hitomi, holding on to second, also looked back—though with more urgency: Gentzel found some last reserve and made a final charge, and Hitomi held her off by only two-tenths of a second. The three medalists—Radke, 2:16.8; Hitomi, 2:17.6; Gentzel, 2:17.8—all shattered the previous world record; Radke's new mark stood until 1944. Five of the nine women set new national records. By any objective measure, it was one of the greatest races in Olympic history.[2]

It was also the last women's Olympic 800m until 1960. Fantastical accounts—some by journalists not even in attendance at the race—described multiple runners collapsing at the finish, or even mid-race. One writer had "only 6 of 11" competitors finishing. The false reports were used as evidence of a failed experiment—pretext to eliminate women's track and field after just one Olympics: "The experience of Amsterdam seems to have justified my opposition to allowing women into the Olympic Games," stated Coubertin. "Reaction so far has been hostile to repeating the spectacle."[3] The gates that Alice Milliat forced open were very nearly slammed shut. Only a "compromise" kept women's athletics in the Games, but their races were limited to two hundred meters and shorter. It would take generations for women's athletics to make progress beyond where it stood in 1928.

PART I

CHAPTER I

Kicking Down the Door

The Pioneer Era, 1966–1972

BOBBI GIBB HID BEHIND A FORSYTHIA BUSH NEAR THE TOWN GREEN IN Hopkinton, Massachusetts. Spectators and runners filled the streets, all waiting for the start of the 1966 Boston Marathon. Spirits were high: it was Patriots' Day, a New England-centric holiday, ostensibly to honor the battles of Lexington and Concord that began the Revolutionary War in earnest. In a less historical sense, it marks the end of the long, gray winter and the unofficial beginning of spring. Vendors hawked balloons and popcorn; Girl Scouts sold cookies. A handful of police officers worked crowd control, mostly keeping non-runners clear of the starting line. As high noon approached, race officials checked competitors into the starting corral, runner by runner, number by number, barking orders at the racers, at the crowd, at each other.

A range of emotions—nervousness, excitement, impatience, giddiness—rippled through the runners in the corral. Some waited silent and stone-faced; others couldn't stop moving, shaking their arms and legs, bouncing from foot to foot. In 1966, marathoners comprised a small tribe—only five hundred runners contested Boston, then the largest marathon in the world—and the corral also had the feel of a homecoming. Racers competed against the course, the clock, and each other, but they also felt themselves banded together, embarking on a collective journey.

Outside the corral, behind the forsythias, Gibb was scared. Not of the race itself—she'd traveled four days by bus from San Diego to be a part of it—nor by the distance—for her, twenty-six miles wouldn't even qualify as a long run. In that moment, she feared exposure, the glare of the public eye. Two hours earlier, her mother had dropped her off on the outskirts of Hopkinton, and since then, she'd tried to be as anonymous and unremarkable as possible. She wore men's Bermuda shorts she'd borrowed from her brother and a new pair of running shoes, the first she'd ever owned—boys', because no manufacturer made running shoes for women. She usually wore nurses' shoes in training. She tucked her blonde hair under the hood of her blue sweatshirt, found a hiding spot as close to the starting line as she dared, and hunkered down to wait. But sitting still proved impossible: her nerves were jangly, and she was still stiff from the bus trip, so she jogged up and down the side streets, away from the crowds, for forty minutes. Now, just before the start, she crouched back behind the forsythias and waited.

The starter's pistol fired, the crowd cheered, and the lead runners took off at a brisk pace. As the middle of the pack shuffled by, Gibb pulled her hood low and jumped out to join them. Normally, crowds made her uncomfortable—she liked to run alone, on secluded trails or an empty beach. But this experience, being surrounded by other runners, spectators lining the street on either side, was what she had come to be a part of—this strange celebration of human endurance and spirit she'd first witnessed with her father some years before. She was thrilled to be a part of it but nearly sick with dread—she was sure to be discovered. But, from the day she'd received the letter from the race director rejecting her entry, being discovered had become the point of her run.

As a child, Gibb and her friends and cousins ran wild in the woods around her Winchester, Massachusetts, home. The others outgrew it; she never did. Sometime around sixth grade, she noticed her friends beginning to change, and she saw, in her future, a trap laid for her. She was expected to go to college—her father, a chemistry professor at nearby Tufts University, encouraged her to explore the natural world, and she loved the idea of losing herself in books, formulas, and equations. But then what? Would she just fold herself up and put all that behind her for marriage? In her mother, she saw a bright, buttoned-up housewife whose own growth had been stunted, and among her mother's friends, she saw women who seemed to depend on alcohol or pills to get through the day. It was a future she wanted no part of.

Escape was her means of protest. She'd run with the neighborhood dogs through the woods—Artemis and her pack. She'd run with no sense or care of how far she'd gone and no plan for when to turn back, reveling in the joy, the freedom, the autonomy of being in motion, a sense of connection with nature, a feeling of oneness with the universe. And when she saw the Boston Marathon for the first time in 1964, it was as if she'd glimpsed the place she truly belonged. She'd found her tribe. She had to run it.

Her training plan was essentially to run farther and farther until she was sure she could cover the distance. Though she wore no watch and never measured her routes, she would run as much as thirty or forty miles in a day. That summer, she made a solo cross-country trip, driving into the afternoon, hopping out and running for hours, then camping in an open field. She arrived in San Francisco, drove down to the water, went racing into the ocean and running along the shore, then camped on the beach. The next morning, she turned around and headed back home to Massachusetts.

She planned to run Boston in 1965 until she took a bad fall and sprained both ankles a few weeks before the race. In January 1966, the 23-year-old Gibb got married and moved to San Diego, where her husband was stationed in the navy. There, she met some local runners, who explained to her that there was a process for entering the marathon, that all those people didn't simply congregate in Hopkinton and make their pilgrimage to Boston together—she needed to submit an entry form and undergo a required physical exam. That February, she wrote to the Boston Athletic Association requesting an entry and received a letter back from BAA president Will Cloney: per the rules of the Amateur Athletic Union of the United States, which sanctioned the race, women were not permitted to run the Boston Marathon, which was a men's division race. The longest race women were permitted to run was 1.5 miles, he explained, adding that he believed women were not physiologically able to run 26.2 miles and that the BAA could not take on the liability of having her in the race.

She was furious. She laced up her shoes and banged out the door and ran until she began to calm down. She ended up in Del Mar, about twenty-six miles from San Diego. It was late; she slept on the beach, and when she awoke, her anger had settled into determination. She had originally wanted to run Boston as a spiritual journey, to feel a sense of connection with the other marathoners. Now she would run not just for herself but to overturn such mindless, prejudicial nonthinking. If she could show the world that women could run a marathon, what other dumb assumptions might be proven wrong? What other constraints might be loosened?

The night before the race, Gibb called her parents from the bus terminal in Boston and asked them to come pick her up. They hadn't known she was coming home, and she hadn't told them she was planning to run the marathon. Her father was worried, angry, and wanted no part in her escapade. Her mother, who had tried for years to get Bobbi to stop all the running and just be a normal girl, tried yet again to convince her not to run. Bobbi tried to explain: this was about more than running. In the end, the elder Gibb relented and drove her daughter out to Hopkinton. When she dropped Bobbi off, she hugged her, pinned some money to her shirt for a cab ride home, and whispered a tearful "good luck."

Now, Gibb had done it. She was running down Route 135 toward Boston, with hundreds of others, just another runner in the pack. But she knew it couldn't last; she wasn't more than a mile into the race when she heard the whispers behind her: "Hey, is that a girl?" "Can't be, can it?" "Are you sure?"

Would they shoulder her off the road? Would the police swoop down and grab her, haul her off the course, and throw her in jail? She had only one weapon at her disposal: she turned around and smiled.

"It is!" "Hey, are you going to go the whole way?" Yes, that was the goal. "Way to go, girlie!" "I wish my girlfriend would run . . ." Now she was truly one of them, and together they set off down the road. The sun warmed the day. She wanted to take off her sweatshirt, but her long hair and black one-piece bathing suit would draw attention like a beacon, and she still feared that the officials would throw her out of the race. "It's a free road," her new companions said. "We won't let them."

The news hummed down the course like a current. Local radio began reporting her progress. Spectators pointed and cheered. When the route passed Wellesley College, famous for its marathon day "scream tunnel" of students wildly cheering on the passing runners, the crowd thundered for her like they had for no other runner. She rode their energy like a wave, up Heartbreak Hill, and from there, downhill to the finish. She began to feel that she really had done it—yes, she'd had to sneak into the race, but the pack had accepted her as one of their own, and she would prove that she belonged. The crowds grew thicker and louder as she descended Heartbreak Hill onto Beacon Street and into Boston. Governor John Volpe waited at the finish to congratulate her.

But the marathon always exacts a price. She'd had no water or food since she left Hopkinton. Her new running shoes had rubbed her feet raw, and blood soaked through her socks and squished in the soles; she wished she'd worn her comfortable, old, broken-in nurses' shoes. Her early adrenaline had long worn off, and she was barely running now. But she had to finish—whose point would she prove if she dropped out now? She limped around the final turn onto Boylston Street, and the roar of the crowd carried her home. She smiled, picked up her stride, and crossed the line in 3:21, unofficially 125th place out of the 415 men who finished the race, not to mention the hundred-odd others who had dropped out.

The official finishers, the men, staggered off to celebrate, commiserate, and swap stories in the afterglow of their day. By postrace tradition—since abandoned as the race has grown—they were all invited to the BAA postrace meal: beef stew, Dinty Moore. After shaking hands with Governor Volpe, Gibb had to face the press. "Why'd you do it?" "How do you train?" "Does your husband know?" She smiled, laughed, bantered, and tried to make them understand how simple it was: she loved running, fell in love with the marathon, and just had to do it. Then she limped back out to the street and hailed a cab back to Winchester.

Her street was crammed with cars. The press had beaten her home. They crowded in her kitchen, interrogated her parents; the phone kept ringing. She answered the same questions, posed for more photos—she even allowed herself to be photographed in a red polka-dot dress in the kitchen, making fudge. Well into the night, she finally got her postrace meal and crawled into bed.

Several days later, Gibb and her mother paid a visit to the famously foul-tempered codirector of the Boston Marathon, Jock Semple, in his "office" in a building attached the old Boston Garden—really more of a dark warren with rubdown tables, a steam room, several whirlpools, and a clanky old radiator on which Semple heated his lunch (usually a meatloaf or cheese sandwich) in the winter. They brought with them a gift of Scottish heather, which Gibb's grandfather grew in his yard, and returned the blanket a race official had thrown around her shoulders at the finish. Semple looked like an old bantamweight fighter—gray hair, gray sweatshirt, wiry muscles and sinew on a compact frame that had softened and thickened with age. He grew up in Scotland, working factory jobs and running races for the factory teams, before immigrating to the United States in 1921. In 1930, he hitchhiked from Philadelphia to Boston to run the marathon. He finished seventh and knew he'd found his place. He got a job as a locker-room attendant in Boston and devoted himself to the tiny, cultish running community—and especially to the marathon. He eventually became a trainer and sports masseur (his "real" job) and spent most of his free hours working races up and down the East Coast—largely unpaid. He saw the same runners each weekend, and they were his people—they trained hard, raced hard, and earned his respect. He and Gibb chatted for a few minutes and parted amiably, Gibb with an impression of Semple as a "very sweet guy."

Opinions differed. The Boston Marathon was sacred to Semple, and god help those who disrespected it. "The weirdies!" he'd cry: college boys who raced on a dare, untrained guys who tried to sneak to the front of the starting line to sprint out with the elites and get on camera, and anyone else who tried to make a spectacle of his race—they all became targets for his fury. Once, a weirdie in a full Uncle Sam getup, advertising something or other on his back, dared join the race; Semple ran alongside him, throwing cups of water in his face and berating him. Another year, in the midst of a downpour, he aimed a flying tackle at a runner in a full snorkel suit—and missed, landing in the mud. Then there was the time that a poodle had the temerity to wander out on the course; it became the target of a ferocious Semple kick—which, again, thankfully, missed. Semple ended up on his back in the road. In 1964, as athletes were loading onto buses to head for the start, Semple threatened to punch one man "right in the face"; and at the finish, he angrily shoved someone else he felt was encroaching too far into the runners' path. In 1965, he nearly got arrested for assault during the race—a sergeant from the Framingham Police boarded the press bus (on which race officials also rode, keeping tabs on the lead runners) looking for him. From then on, BAA president and marathon codirector Will Cloney stood in the well of the bus, right in front of the door, to keep Semple from charging out after yet another weirdie.

But in Semple's worldview, Gibb was no weirdie. They shared common ground: a reverence for the marathon and pleasure in the simple joy of running. He and Gibb understood each other, and even though she'd jumped into the race unofficially, he considered her one of the tribe.

***

In 1967, Gibb ran again and hardly made a stir. Instead, it was Semple and his temper who made history. He was already in an especially foul mood at the start—the weather that year was cold and drizzly, which made checking in the runners before the race that much harder, because many of them wore coats or ponchos over their number. Checking in each runner, one at a time, had delayed the start, making both runners and officials even more miserable. And shortly after the start, near the 2-mile mark, members of the press had started needling him: "Hey Jock, is that a girl?" "It is!" "With a number??" Perhaps, sensing a story, they couldn't contain their excitement; it is also possible that the guys on the press bus, for whom Semple's eruptions made for good fun and good copy, intentionally wound him up: "Hey Jock, there's a woman in your race!" Sure enough, there she was, and it wasn't Gibb, whom Jock had greeted with a smile that morning. It was another woman, this one with an official bib number pinned to her gray hooded sweatshirt.

Cloney and Semple both charged off the bus after her. She was running in the company of three men. One, 50-year-old Arnie Briggs, World War II veteran, had run Boston eighteen times, finishing as high as tenth in 1952. He now coached the Syracuse Harriers running club and was familiar to both Cloney and Semple. "You know better than this, Arnie!" Cloney shouted as he approached the group. "Leave her alone," Briggs shouted back. Semple, in a floundering rage, rushed out from behind Cloney, charged the woman, and grabbed for her number. He missed, managing only to tear the glove off her hand. He came back at her for a second go, shouting, "Get the hell out of my race and give me that number!" This time, he was met by a cross-body block from a third member of the group, hammer thrower and Olympic hopeful Tom Miller. Semple went flying off the course and landed in a heap. "Run like hell, Kathy!" yelled Briggs.

Kathy, or Kathrine—or, on her official entry form, K.—Switzer did so.

Switzer, 20, had long, brown hair and an easy welcoming smile that hid an intense competitiveness. She'd started running in high school to get in shape for field hockey and found that she enjoyed the sense of measuring herself against herself, of always trying to get better. At Lynchburg College she quit field hockey, feeling that too many of her teammates weren't as committed or competitive as she was. But she kept running for the joy of it: like Gibb, she found something sacred in it—"like touching god," she said. One day, the Lynchburg men's track coach, Aubrey Moon, saw her out running and asked if she'd join his team. He needed more milers to fill out his squad, and rules didn't expressly forbid a woman from running men's track. In the spring of 1966, she got her time respectably under six minutes and even scored a few points for the team. But the mile felt so short, and the track so restrictive. When a teammate of hers went up to run Boston, she was intrigued: "Did any women run it?" she asked him. Yes, he replied, and manfully admitted that Gibb had beaten him by more than twenty minutes.

That fall, Switzer, who was studying journalism and communications, transferred to Syracuse University and began running with Briggs, who was the campus mailman and a volunteer assistant coach for the track and cross-country teams. On long runs through the streets and trails around campus, Briggs regaled her with stories of Boston Marathons past—to him, the race was a hallowed event, its champions a pantheon of heroes.

Switzer loved his stories, but one cold February morning, with Briggs in the middle of a story she'd heard many times before, she stopped him.

No more talking about it, she said. Let's run it.

Impossible, he said. Women couldn't.

Gibb did, she countered.

He insisted Gibb jumped into the race halfway through, at Wellesley.[1] Switzer refused to run another step unless he acknowledged that Gibb ran the full race, and that she could, too. The challenge was set, but Briggs demanded that she prove herself first. They topped out with a thirty-one-mile run, at the end of which Briggs passed out. He was convinced—she was ready.

She sent in her entry, and did the required medical check in Syracuse; the doctor certified that K. Switzer was fit and healthy enough for a marathon. On raceday, Briggs picked up their numbers in Hopkinton. In the sleet and snow, Switzer wore a heavy sweatshirt with the hood up and pulled tight as they walked toward the start. Officials looked only at the number on her chest, 261, when they checked her into the corral. At the gun, Switzer and Briggs, along with Miller and John Leonard (the foruth member of their party), set off with a record number of more than seven hundred entrants in the 71st Boston Marathon.

Now, three miles into the race, she was rattled. Semple's attack was terrifying, but she couldn't shake the image of the old man crumpled in a heap on the side of the road. She feared that Miller, her boyfriend at the time, had killed Semple. To her great relief (and terror), the press bus roared past again, and she heard Semple scream, "You all are in biiiiiiig trouble!" But the bus didn't stop, and as scared as she was that somewhere along the course Semple would arrange to have her snatched out of the race, she ran on, determined to finish—so much so that she slowed her pace to a near-crawl, making sure she kept plenty in reserve. By the time she reached the finish line, the officials were gone, and the clock was off. Of the dozen or so people waiting for her, most were reporters. Her time—probably around 4:30—was unimportant.

She grew up during that race, she would say later. The press's aggressive questioning afterward—"Why Boston, and why wear numbers?" "What are you trying to prove?" "Are you a suffragette?"—only hardened her further. Originally, Boston had been just a personal challenge, an exploration of her physical limits; the reactions of Semple and the press stirred something in her: she would train harder and faster and become a serious competitive marathoner, racing not just to finish but to compete. Further, she would work to expand opportunities for other female runners. Why couldn't more women do what she did? For that matter, why couldn't women like her run in the Olympics? It was a crazy dream, for sure, but anyone—man or woman—who dreams of the Olympics has a little crazy in them. She finished the race, exhausted and shivering, but with a new mission: down the road, an Olympic marathon for women; in the short term, women just needed the opportunity to run.

Even as Switzer arrived at the dark, cold finish line, photos of Semple's attack were being readied for the newspapers. Semple versus Switzer transcended sport. What feminists tried to articulate in books and speeches throughout the 1960s the photos captured on a visceral level. On one hand, this was slightly unfair to Jock—he was an equal-opportunity madman with a gender-neutral temper. In his mind, she had cheated to get the number, and he had every right to take it back; she was just another weirdie using his race to make a spectacle.

On the other hand, Switzer was a diminutive young woman. In modern times, Semple would have been fired and perhaps prosecuted. Instead, he was back at the helm in 1968, and Switzer was banned indefinitely from AAU-sanctioned events. Rules were rules, and what Cloney had shouted at Briggs was correct: he should have known better. AAU bylaws stated that women were not permitted to run in men's division races, and Boston—by default, really, because the AAU prohibited women from racing more than 1.5 miles—was a men's division race. Races that violated this rule risked losing their official sanction; men who competed in races that violated the rules risked losing their eligibility for international competition—including the Olympics.[2] When Gibb jumped out of the bushes and ran the marathon, Cloney officially—and technically, truthfully—stated that Gibb "did not run in the Boston Marathon," she merely covered the same route as the official race while it was in progress. "No girl has ever run in the Boston Marathon," he insisted in 1966. Switzer, however, not only violated the rules, but she put the marathon's official standing at risk and potentially rendered the top runners in the international field ineligible for the Olympics.

As the 1968 Boston Marathon approached, the press couldn't help but pester the somewhat chastened race director: What if more women showed up? He had no problem, he said, if they'd done the training, "like the Gibb girl."

And Gibb was there again in 1968, joined by a thousand male entrants and several other women, who, like her, ran unofficially: Marjorie Fish ran with her husband—he with a number, she without; Elaine Pedersen ran with her boyfriend's number. No matter—Semple was on his best behavior, and besides, running with someone else's number made one, by definition, unofficial. Gibb won again—her third Boston title in what is now called the women's Pioneer Era—but the 1968 marathon was her last for a while. She'd resolved to keep coming back until she proved the point—that women could run, and run well. Mission accomplished, she felt: the marathon was no longer just a man's game.

***

Gibb passed the torch to Sara Mae Berman, who won Boston in 1969. Berman, nee Sidore, grew up in New Hampshire in the 1950s and was not an athlete—"girls didn't do that sort of thing," she said. But her parents did give her the freedom to roam, and as a teenager she would take the train from her home in Manchester into Boston to spend the day happily wandering the streets, occasionally shopping, mostly just soaking in the city. She graduated from the Rhode Island School of Design in 1958 and soon married Larry Berman, an astronautics major at MIT. Larry, still in college, was captain of the cross-country team, and Berman—"the dutiful little housewife," as she described herself—would sit on a blanket and watch him run loops around Jamaica Pond.

Three children soon followed, and she began to feel constrained, even indolent, just keeping house. Larry asked if she was happy with the shape she was in. Most certainly not, responded Sara Mae. Her first day running with him, she took off at a mad sprint and nearly collapsed after a block. When he finally caught up with her, Larry asked who told her to start so fast. Eventually, she built up her endurance to five miles, at which point Larry said, great, now run it faster. Despite her design school pedigree, Sara Mae shared a practical, engineering mentality with Larry, and they started interval sessions at MIT's track, parking their children in a playpen in the infield, letting their eldest play in the cinders. In 1964, she ran her first race, as an unofficial entrant. "The guys were fantastic—not one nasty comment," she recalled. The officials, "old fuddy-duddies," she thought, took longer to come around.

But they got used to her. Each weekend, if she wasn't racing herself, she was at a race with Larry, coaching the running club they cofounded, the Cambridge Sports Union—one of the first coed running clubs in the country. In 1965 and again in 1966, the Bermans attended the national AAU convention to petition for an increase in the longest women's distance race from 1.5 miles to 2. They were treated, according to Sara Mae, "very uncivilly"—accused of wanting to exploit and endanger young girls, shouted down by members of the AAU executive committee. They did get the maximum distance for women increased to 2.5 miles starting in 1967 but decided not to press their luck any further.

Gibb's run in 1966 planted a seed in Sara Mae's mind, but she and Larry recognized that she wasn't ready for a marathon. But by 1969, she had increased her mileage from sixty to eighty miles per week, and she and Larry had marked out the Boston course to the quarter mile; at that time, most road races had no mile markers, Boston included. Berman ran and won again in 1970, setting the unofficial course record of 3:05, and won a third time in 1971, the last Pioneer Division champion.

The ground had begun to shift under the AAU's feet. In December 1971, Nina Kuscsik, fresh off a victory at the New York City Marathon, made a proposal at the annual AAU convention to allow women to run marathons officially. Kuscsik had a gift for working through the Byzantine AAU bureaucracy, and she was treated much better than the Bermans were in 1965 and 1966. She convinced the AAU to increase the maximum allowable women's race to ten miles. The AAU also acknowledged that "some women" could be permitted to run marathons. Which ones? Those who had already proven they could run a marathon.

If the AAU's new rule traced a confoundingly circular logical path—fitting, perhaps, for an organization that oversaw track and field—it did launch a new era in women's running. At noon on April 17, 1972, the starting gun fired, and the first sanctioned women's runners in the Boston Marathon—all eight of them—took off with about twelve hundred men. Kuscsik won, one of her seven marathon victories that year, and set the first "official" course record of 3:10, still five minutes slower than Berman's 1970 time.

Though Berman had been unable to train all winter, she wouldn't have missed the first sanctioned women's Boston Marathon for anything. In the days leading up to the race, reporters kept badgering her to comment on female marathoners' great victory over Jock Semple, the arch-chauvinist. Berman scoffed. She had known Jock since the early 1960s, and although she did allow that it was wise to stay out of Jock's way on race day, she knew that, in his mind, the world did not divide so much along gender lines as between runners and weirdies. In the 1960s, he donated trophies to women's races, and once on a visit to his native Scotland, he donated £200 to the women's division of his local running club. "We loved Jock," she recalled. "If you did the work, followed the rules, and didn't cause trouble, he respected you—and we respected him." Now that the rules allowed women to run officially, Jock welcomed them—just as he had the unofficial women runners such as Gibb.

The next year, at the starting line of the 1973 Boston Marathon, Switzer stood among the official entrants. Jock walked up to her; she braced herself for the worst, but instead of his usual scowl, he was grinning. "Let's get a wee bit o' notoriety," he said, then put his arm around her, turned them toward the cameras, and planted a kiss on her cheek. If she was caught off guard, it doesn't show in the photos; they both seem at home in the moment: the annual celebratory pilgrimage from Hopkinton to Boston was about to begin, and each was exactly where they were meant to be. Their smiles are easy, genuine—Jock's with a hint of mischief. Their world had changed; his bit o' notoriety was a stubborn man's way of admitting that he had been wrong, of asking forgiveness, of acknowledging her rightful place in the marathon they both cherished.

CHAPTER 2

Proof of Concept

Crazylegs, New York, 1972

ON APRIL 19, 1897, TOM BURKE DREW HIS BOOT ACROSS THE DIRT road in front of Metcalf's Mill in Ashland, Massachusetts, and declared, "There's the starting line, gents." Moments later, he shouted, "Go!" and fifteen men set off down dusty roads, dodging horses and the occasional electric car. So began the first Boston Marathon. Over time, the race distance was lengthened from 24 miles to 26.2, the start was moved one town farther west to Hopkinton, and dirt roads became asphalt. Otherwise, the Boston Marathon—and by extension, the sport of road racing—changed little. The marathon of 1967 had more in common with that of 1897 than with the modern, mass-participation event of today. The number of entrants remained small; there were no official water stations; there were no mile markers—the seemingly arbitrary timing checkpoints, at spots like 2.4 miles, 9.5 miles, and 19 7/8 miles, were just convenient places for officials to stop. (For example, the 9.5-mile checkpoint was at a fire station where they could sit inside and get a hot drink on cold or rainy race days.) To the general public, the marathon remained more a curiosity than a sporting event, and running was something one outgrew by the time one left school. Marathoners, despite Semple's protests to the contrary, were the real weirdies.

Prior to World War II, track athletes were the elites of the running world: they were mostly college men, and a select group at that—one could only fit so many runners in one race on the track. College meets

25

got prominent coverage, and milers were stars. Marathoning was a different universe. The runners were mostly working class, and ethnic clubs in immigrant enclaves in big cities along the East Coast sponsored teams and paid for the best runners from the home country to come over to race—Irish and Finnish clubs vied for supremacy at the Boston Marathon. During the Great Depression, the best runners in the nation would hop freight cars to get to Boston—or, like Semple, hitchhike. John A. Kelley (The Elder), who won Boston in 1935 and 1945, and completed the race fifty-eight times (the last in 1992 at age 84), was typical of marathoners in the first half of the century, in that running was just something to do in the space between bouts of manual labor: "I worked here and I worked there," he recalled, "nothing permanent, nothing steady. Running was fun. It helped kill time."

In the late 1950s and early 1960s, more Americans began to turn to running, partly to combat a general tendency toward sloth that had taken root in American society. After the war, life had grown comfortable—too comfortable. By the 1950s, military officers were alarmed that they were forced to reject nearly half of the army's recruits for "general lack of fitness." On one common international test of youth fitness, only 8.5 percent of European kids failed, compared to 78 percent of Americans. In 1956, President Eisenhower created the President's Council on Youth Fitness. In 1958, H. Browning Ross, editor of the *Long Distance Log*, a magazine (really, a mimeographed newsletter in those early days) devoted to covering road racing in the United States, founded the Road Runners Club of America (RRCA) to promote road racing and look after that segment of the running population ignored by the AAU and its singular focus on the track. Jogging clubs popped up in cities, and the RRCA promoted run-for-fun events—short, two-mile runs that included women. Still, road racing remained a small and strange world—inclusive but insular.

And Americans remained relatively unfit. What became known as the running boom in the United States had its origins elsewhere. In the winter of 1962–1963, Bill Bowerman, the legendary University of Oregon track coach, took a trip to New Zealand, where Arthur Lydiard, the godfather of modern distance running, had hundreds of people—old, young, men, women—meeting on weekends for long, hilly "jogs," his term for slow, steady running. In Bowerman's first week, he could scarcely keep up with a 70-year-old cardiac patient, but, after just six weeks, he did a twenty-mile run with Lydiard. Bowerman returned to Oregon fitter, happier, and determined to preach this new gospel of jogging. At first, dozens, then hundreds, then thousands of the formerly sedentary joined Bowerman and his team for easy weekend jogs. In 1967, he wrote a book, *Jogging*, which laid out a program for beginners and included (at his wife's insistence) advice for women who wanted to run.

Meanwhile, the shockwaves of Gibb's 1966 marathon rippled outward from Boston. She was not the first woman in the postwar world to run a marathon, but Gibb made her mark on the oldest yearly marathon in the world, a true international race at a time when few existed, and she brought media attention to the Boston Marathon on a scale it hadn't seen in years. She said she ran to share the joy she found in running; women such as Switzer and Berman were inspired to try a marathon, others to simply try running—they phoned Gibb out of the blue, breathless, only to tell her they had just run around the block for the first time since they were children. Men, too, were inspired—some, who had scoffed at Gibb's achievement, were goaded until they put up or shut up; others figured, if Gibb could do it, maybe they could, too?

Although no one, least of all Gibb, would ascribe marathoning's increased popularity solely to her run, entrants in the Boston Marathon jumped from 540 to 741 in 1967—the largest single-year increase in the race's history. In 1968, the year after Switzer's altercation with Semple, entries jumped to more than one thousand. More than thirteen hundred runners signed up in 1969, and race organizers were overwhelmed; the whole race was still pretty much managed out of Jock's rubdown suite. In 1970, for the first time in history, the BAA limited entrants: runners had to provide evidence of having completed at least two races of at least ten miles in the past year or written testimony from a coach as to the runner's fitness and "conscientious" training. Sportswriters, as ever, tried to poke Semple by asking whether female runners—still barred by the AAU in 1970—affected the integrity of the race. "Everyone makes a big issue out of the women," he said, "but they run on their own. They're not the problem." The "potbellies with the 52-inch waists," on the other hand—these were the weirdies who were "spoiling a good race."

The sheer masses of entrants—most neither potbellied nor intent on spoiling a good race—were signs of the transformation underway. In 1968, only about forty marathons took place in the United States. In 1971, the *New York Times* ran a feature on Kuscsik—"Housewife Runs, Too"—and cited "the growing number of people on Long Island" doing marathons and "the almost constant marathon races . . . on weekends in Central Park, Prospect Park and Marine Park . . . Van Cortlandt Park . . . and several other parks and tracks on Long Island." To the uninitiated, "marathon" just meant "really long run"—which, to the really uninitiated, could have meant anything more than around the block; one assumes that the author of this article meant any race longer than a mile.

By 1972, there were well over one hundred actual 26-mile marathons—though most drew fewer than one hundred runners. Boston was still the soul of the sport, and Semple its guardian—irascible and downright hostile to those outside the tribe, fiercely protective of those in it. But another weirdie would harness the growth and change in marathoning for the opportunity it was, and transform road races into the modern, mass-participation spectacle they've become.

Like Semple, Fred Lebow was an immigrant. And, like Semple, he would devote his life to the marathon. When people talk about Lebow—friends, lovers, rivals, colleagues, or competitors—they do so with a smile. "My boss, friend, brother, mentor, and oldest boy," said Anne Roberts, who worked for years with Lebow. "The kind of guy you wanted to take care of," said Allan Steinfeld, his close friend and successor as director of the New York Marathon. "The P. T. Barnum of Running . . . a promoter," according to George Hirsch, former chairman of the board of New York Road Runners. Sometimes, it was a smile of exasperation: "I still don't know what he's up to and what he's not up to," said one board member of the New York Road Runners. Writer Jim Ferstle called him "the antithesis to the image of the purity of running." Not everyone in the sport appreciated what he did for running—or to running, as his critics would have it—but he became the sport's chief promoter, its pied piper, and helped bring millions of Americans into the running tribe. And although he was never an activist in the sense of devoting time and effort to the cause of equity for women in running, he created a stage for the best female runners and trumpeted their achievements with zeal. There would have been a women's Olympic marathon without Lebow, but the road to get there would have been far less interesting.

Born Fishel Lebowitz, he was hiding and on the run from the age of 14—first from the Nazis, then from the Soviets. Forced to flee his native Romania, he took up diamond smuggling to make a living, taking contraband across the English Channel to London. In the 1950s, he moved to New York and took up the slightly more reputable business of producing designer knockoffs in the garment district. He worked long hours but would still leave his factory office with a restless, pent-up energy. He tried tennis as a recreational outlet, but that gave him ulcers; he'd schedule a match but then couldn't show up, overcome by fear of losing. He started running only to gain an edge in tennis, but after his first run in Central Park, he dropped competitive tennis forever. Every chance he had, he went back to Central Park's reservoir loop. He even found himself cutting out of work early to jog. Running, he said, made him feel like "a horse that's been kept in a stall for a year and finally . . . let free."

Any similarity between Lebow's running and that of a horse ended there: he talked fast, thought fast, did everything fast—except run. In the beginning, he ran about ten minutes to the mile, nearly five minutes per mile slower than the best runners. Didn't matter; somehow running was different from tennis—it calmed him, and he found he enjoyed competing against no one but himself, trying to run farther and maybe a little faster. He found out about a group who did road races in the Bronx—they met in Macombs Dam Park, across from Yankee Stadium, because it had a public restroom where they could change. Out of the blue, Lebow dropped in on this group of working-class runners, guys who formed the core of the New York chapter of the Road Runners Club of America. His first race, eleven laps around Yankee stadium, he finished second-to-last, just ahead of a 65-year-old with a limp. He felt like an outsider, couldn't understand their talk of intervals and splits and drafting. They, in turn, didn't know what to make of him, a Manhattanite with a European accent, who sported a fashionable leather coat and a precise mustache.

He was an "interloper," according to Norb Sander, an early member of the New York Road Runners, who became a close friend of Lebow's. But he was a runner, part of the tribe, so they took him in.

In February 1970, Lebow ran his first marathon, in 4:09—a respectable showing, considering he had to dodge street traffic in the Bronx, not to mention the rocks that kids chucked at the crazy folks jogging through their neighborhood. Even before he finished, his mind was churning. He wanted to get these races out of the Bronx and into Manhattan—the "big time," he thought. Besides, Central Park would have less traffic because the city closed the streets to cars on the weekends. Fewer rock-throwing kids, too. In April, he pitched the local AAU chapter on his vision for the New York City Marathon, and promised he had "many wealthy friends" ready to sponsor it. The AAU was unimpressed. Nonetheless, in September 1970, Lebow and one not-so-wealthy friend, Aldo Scandurra, staged the first New York City Marathon in Central Park. They bought a few cases of soda to hydrate the runners and $10 watches for the top placers. Fifty-five runners finished; Gary Muhrcke, a firefighter from Queens, won in 2:31. It was a modest beginning, well short of Lebow's goal of two hundred runners, but he was hooked. In running he had found his home, and in organizing and promoting races, he found his vocation.

In 1971, he tried to spiff up the New York Marathon—he'd purchased a banner to go over the finish line, but he strung it facing the wrong way, and didn't realize it until it was too late to change it. However, he attracted 246 entrants—and even if the older, bigger Yonkers Marathon, which was often the site of the AAU national championship, was the most prominent race in the New York area, Lebow was getting noticed. In the spring of 1972, the legendary marketing firm Carl Byoir & Associates, handling the account of Johnson Wax, approached Lebow about putting on a women's marathon to promote their new product: a women's shaving gel called Crazylegs—which, said the whispers, was just men's shaving cream dyed pink. "You're crazy!" he retorted, informing them that there were maybe a half dozen women in the greater New York area capable of running a marathon. "How about a mini-marathon?" he asked. Miniskirts, legs, shaving gel, running—it all made sense to Lebow. In the space of a five-minute telephone call, the Crazylegs Mini

Marathon, a six-mile race through Central Park, now one of the greatest 10K road races in the world, was conceived.

A month later, in mid-April, he had no runners, no commitments, no promotional materials, only a looming June 3 race date. Nor had he demonstrated any real success attracting women to his races—only four women had finished the 1971 New York Marathon. He made a call to Switzer. She hadn't given up on the promises she made to herself after her marathon debut. In 1967, she'd gone back to Syracuse and had begun organizing races and fun runs for all comers: children, adults, seniors, men, and women. She'd gotten to know Lebow a little, and she wasn't surprised to hear from him—nor was she surprised that Lebow didn't yet have a plan for delivering masses of female distance runners on June 3. His style, she knew, might best be described as improvisational: he promised big, then counted on something—providence, luck, a talent for getting others to help out, his own indefatigable salesmanship—to help him deliver. He offered to bring her to New York and pay her expenses to help put together the race. An all-women's race in New York with a major sponsor? She might've paid him for the opportunity—Crazylegs might go nowhere, but in the short term, it would at least give more women a chance to race; long term, it might turn out to be a good step toward an Olympic marathon.

Working with Fred was a whirlwind. They stalked the Central Park Reservoir Loop for hours during the day, handing out race entries to any woman who would stop to talk. They cruised singles bars at night (Fred may have had an ulterior motive), where he would talk to young women, many of them smoking as they sat at a darkened bar, and try to persuade them to run six miles through Central Park. He hatched promotional ideas nonstop—some of which he ran by Switzer, some he didn't. One in particular seemed aimed more at the men marketing shaving gel than the women who might use it: Playboy bunnies. He recruited a half dozen young women from the Playboy club to line up at the start in full costume—high white boots, short shorts, bunny tails, and ears—to "race" Switzer and Kuscsik, the 1972 Boston Marathon champion, the day before the race. On race day, Lebow hung signs renaming the Central Park path on which the runners would start "Cheesecake Lane." Instead of pin-on race numbers, he printed bright white shirts with the race numbers stenciled on them—right below the word "CRAZYLEGS." Switzer could roll her eyes at the bunnies, but the shirts were a real problem. Athletes couldn't promote a corporate sponsor so brazenly without risking revocation of their amateur status—a detail Lebow either didn't know or simply ignored; rules were not his strong suit. Though the longest event for women in the upcoming 1972 Olympics was the 1500m, no doubt some of the women in the six-mile road race had Olympic aspirations, and Lebow's stunt put that in jeopardy. Plus, she felt they all looked a little ridiculous in matching shirts. But because the shirt bore their race number, they had no choice.

To some in the race, he'd gone too far. "I thought women were finally being allowed to run distance . . . finally accepted as something more [than] freaks," wrote Charlotte Lettis, who finished second in the race. "Then the perversion started . . . it was a freak show—a money-making, newspaper selling, shaving cream-pushing freak show," which "set women's athletics back into the . . . era of stunts and exploitation." Traditionalists in the running community, whatever their views on pink shaving cream or Playboy bunnies, were appalled by the circus-like atmosphere and what they viewed as crass salesmanship. But Lebow couldn't have cared less—he wanted running to be less self-serious, more lighthearted, even, god forbid, fun. Besides, his sponsor was thrilled.

Switzer found it impossible to stay mad at Lebow. She understood that he was a promoter first and a crusader for women's running second—or third or fourth. And Lebow had attracted seventy-two women to a single race—underwhelming by modern standards, but unheard of in 1972. To be a female runner was often isolating; Switzer had run races where she was the only woman. To see other female competitors was to have allies, and most likely you knew them by name; to take part in a race with more women than she could possibly talk to before the start was to feel camaraderie and competitiveness on a scale she'd never experienced. Further, the race earned a full column in the *New York Times* sports section, though sportswriter Gerald Eskenazi took pains to note that Switzer, who finished sixth, was having trouble with her eyeshadow, which "ran all over her face." Nevertheless, she considered Crazylegs "an inspiration." Despite the bunnies and the sideshow atmosphere, despite the fact that it was a six-mile race and not a marathon, Switzer saw Crazylegs as a way to "show the IOC that our request wasn't just about a few feisty women barging in on men's races."

Lebow's carnival barker's gleam brought attention to the sport, but as Gary Muhrcke observed, "The older running community didn't need all that." Running had been obscure, quiet, small—and the old guard, the guys from Macombs Dam and the Bronx, liked it that way. Lebow understood the sense of simplicity they cherished, but he wanted to share running with the world. He was part merry prankster, part dreamer, and a born salesman. He couldn't help but think big. For him, Crazylegs was proof of concept—you could have a great race, generate buzz, and have fun doing it. And he could see change on the horizon: road races were a marketer's dream, even if most marketers didn't know it yet.

In August 1972, Switzer was in Munich for the Olympics. Walking alone in the night, she looked up at the neon skyline towering over her, flashing the logos of all the Olympic sponsors, and she had her own glimpse of the future: women's marathoning needed that kind of visibility and global reach—something only major corporate dollars could bring. To her, Crazylegs became proof of a different concept: the right kind of sponsor, with the right message, could legitimize women's running, move it past the days of pranks and novelty acts, make it big. The IOC would want to hitch itself to that kind of star, would have no choice but to include the marathon in the Olympics. Like Lebow, she had a deep appreciation for running. And like Lebow, she could see that the sport was on the verge of bursting, and its future looked a lot more like Crazylegs than it did dodging traffic and rocks in the Bronx. For the sake of all runners, women especially, that energy had to be harnessed for something more than just generating buzz. Yes, running was a marketer's dream, but she had a different type of marketing and a bigger purpose in mind.

Interlude

Munich, September 9, 1972, 5:55 p.m.: *Forty-four years after the first women's Olympic 800m, six years after Bobbi Gibb first ran the Boston Marathon, and nine months after the AAU first approved "some" women in the United States to run marathons, nine women lined up for the longest women's race in Olympic history, the first-ever women's 1500m.*

Violence marred the Munich Games—in the early morning hours of September 5, eleven Israeli athletes and coaches were taken hostage by Palestinian terrorists; the hostages all would be killed before midnight on September 6. But the Games must go on, said Avery Brundage, president of the IOC, and after a one-day pause, sport returned to Munich's Olympic stadium. The crowd, perhaps eager to turn from grief and outrage to the celebration of athletic achievement, returned in force. The number of spectators routinely exceeded the stadium's 75,000-seat capacity by ten or even fifteen thousand.

On the night of the 1500m, the crowd buzzed with energy, and at the start erupted in a sustained roar. Berny Boxem of the Netherlands set an alarmingly fast pace, going through 300 meters in just over forty-five seconds—roughly ten seconds under world record pace. Her teammate, Ilja Keizer, strained to hold on to second place, the rest of the field in full flight behind. In last place, out of view of the camera, sat Lyudmila Bragina of the Soviet Union—the favorite, the world record holder, and a woman under more pressure than any other runner in the field: Soviet leadership expected—demanded—sporting excellence, measured in victories over the West. But if Bragina felt the pressure, or if languishing in last place concerned her, neither her stride nor her expression betrayed it.

When the Soviet Union rejoined the Olympic family in 1952, its leaders had more than sports in mind. For the Soviets, sports were politics continued by other means. Victory was evidence of the superiority of the Soviet system, and at least in women's athletics, the propagandists had a point. Athletes from the Soviet Union and Eastern Europe had equal access to the best training resources that their countries could offer; American female athletes were not even treated like second-class citizens in their own country: "Most of us feel that being second class would be a great advance," said Doris Brown, who

35

bowed out in the heats of the 1972 1500m. Not coincidentally, Soviet and Eastern Bloc athletes dominated the women's events at the 1972 Olympics.

Maria Romanova of the USSR, the head of the Women's Committee of the International Amateur Athletics Foundation, was largely responsible for the addition of the 1500m. In fact, she was responsible for the largest increase in women's athletics at the Olympics since the original five events were added in 1928. On her watch, the IAAF recommended the reintroduction of the 800m for 1960; the addition of the 400m and pentathlon in 1964; and the 100m hurdles, the 4x400m relay, and the 1500m for 1972; more important, she pushed the head of the IAAF, Lord Burghley, to threaten to start a break-away world athletics championship to rival the Olympics if the IOC didn't approve the new events. Romanova was a staunch advocate for women's athletics—walking the same path as Alice Milliat before her—but also a good Soviet soldier: more women's events meant more medals for the Soviet Bloc, and more evidence against the West. The very reason the 1500m existed as an Olympic event was for Bragina—or, if not her, someone else wearing the red-and-white kit of the Soviet Union—to win it.

The pace slowed over the next two hundred meters—sanity returned, briefly, before Keizer took the lead from her teammate and again tried to accelerate. But the energy wasn't there; the pace sagged again, and the field bunched—until, with 800m to go, Bragina slid out to lane two, eased up to Keizer's shoulder, then surged into the lead. Keizer gave chase, and they soon opened up a ten-meter gap on the rest of the field. But Bragina's stride quickened again, and Keizer could not hold on. The only drama on the final lap was whether Bragina would eclipse her own record. By the time she reached the backstretch, it was clear that she would; the remaining question was by how much. She finished, still pulling away, in 4:01.37, nearly four seconds faster than the record she had set in the semifinal—itself more than a second faster than the record coming into the Olympics. It was a near-superhuman display of strength, stamina, and speed, particularly in light of the near-suicidal starting pace. Perhaps, whispered some, her performance was literally superhuman—rumors of drug use by Soviet and Eastern European athletes were all around the Olympic village. Drug testing, however, was "immature."[1] Performance-enhancing drugs or not—and no concrete evidence ever directly linked Bragina to doping—it was hard for anyone watching her race to make a serious argument that women could not withstand the rigors of distance competition.

Incidentally, one athlete did collapse before the finish: West Germany's Ellen Tittel stumbled once, then twice, on the final lap before falling to her hands and knees inside the first curve. She was carried off on a stretcher: stomach cramps, she later said. Unlike in 1928, there was no outcry, no calls for the 1500m to be removed from the program. But Romanova retired from the Women's Committee; no further events were added to the women's athletics program until 1984. And although American women continued to languish behind most other countries on the track, the American road racing scene heralded a new, powerful movement for women's running.

CHAPTER 3

Party in the USA!

America, the 1970s

THE RUNNING BOOM BEGAN IN THE 1960S, GATHERED STEAM AT THE beginning of the 1970s, and exploded as the decade wore on. And just as Switzer and Lebow foresaw, running became a marketer's dream—largely because the new converts were, according to *Washington Post* writers Jane Leavy and Susan Okie, "white, white-collar, and well-off."[1]

In 1972, ABC televised the entire Munich Olympic marathon live—a broadcast first. And in a nod to the changing demographics of the running population, the network brought in a special guest commentator, Erich Segal, a marathoner (he'd run Boston nearly every year since 1955), Ivy League classics professor (he hit for the cycle, doing stints at Dartmouth, Princeton, Harvard, and Yale), and author of *Love Story*, the best-selling novel (and top-grossing film) of 1970. Millions of Americans tuned in on September 10 to watch one of Segal's former students, Yale graduate Frank Shorter, win marathon gold. America (white, white-collar, and well-off America, anyway) had a new hero, the right man for the time—a marathoner.

The new breed of runner was of the same generation that had taken to the streets in the 1960s, marching for civil rights and against the Vietnam War, believing they could change the world. As the 1970s slouched on, they took the streets again—this time wearing running shoes, hoping only to change themselves. If running seemed a poor substitute for protest, and self-improvement a poor replacement for trying to fix world's problems, the turn to running might be explained in part by a reckoning with reality: the world seemed to have grown more complicated, and its problems utterly unsolvable. In the early post-World War II world, Americans regarded themselves masters of their own destiny: they had survived the Great Depression and defeated fascism, and nowhere else on earth did the future seem so bright. But that future began to look dim; whatever -ism one had ascribed to in the 1960s, pessimism reigned in the 1970s. Nixon's presidency imploded, oil shortages crippled the nation, violent crime seemed rampant and inflation unstoppable. The Soviet menace loomed; the threat of nuclear annihilation brought with it existential dread, and whether one had supported the Vietnam war or marched to end it, the American exit was a humbling reminder of the limits of American might. For the white, white-collar, and well-off, running was an escape. "We jog," said Dr. Paul Milvy, professor at Mt. Sinai Medical School and member of the New York Road Runners, "while Rome burns."[2]

Running could offer some individual salve to a collective wounded pride, some sense of personal control at a time that the nation seemed to have none. Further, marathoning, with its link to a mythical, Greek golden age, radiated an aura of individual heroism. The legions flocking to the marathon couldn't match Shorter's pace, but in covering the marathon distance, they could (in their mind's eye, at least) don the garb of the classical hero. Of marathoners, Segal wrote, "Some are Lancelots, most are Don Quixotes. All are noble."[3] Lebow described a marathon for runners like him as a "particularly heroic physical accomplishment . . . at a stage or state in life when few if any opportunities for heroic physical accomplishment are in reach."[4] Jim Fixx, author of the best-selling *Complete Book of Running*, wrote, "If you run ten miles in seventy minutes, you know exactly what you have done . . . you can be sure you have behaved as morally as any angel in heaven could ask."[5] Thaddeus Kostrubala, who wrote *The Joy of Running*, described marathoning as "glorifying life, defying death in all its forms. Right in the snapping teeth of death, I dance and laugh."[6]

Some Americans tried new spiritual or psychological practices (many of which borrowed heavily from millennia-old religious practices) such as transcendental meditation, the Human Potential Movement, Gestalt Therapy, or Erhard Seminars. Running could mind meld with this new consciousness: Valerie Andrews wrote in *The Psychic Power of Running* that through running, "we reach a transcendental state that may enable us to connect with other forms of consciousness flowing through the universe." Joel Henning, in *Holistic Running*, wrote that running "progresses through stages of deeper meaning. . . . It is indeed a form of worship, an attempt to find God, a means to the transcendent."[7] "When I run the roads," wrote George Sheehan, "I am a saint. For that hour, I am an Assisi wearing the least and meanest of clothes. I am Gandhi, the young London law student, trotting 10 or 12 miles a day and then going to a cheap restaurant to eat his fill of bread. I am Thoreau, the solitary, seeking union with the world around him. On the roads, Poverty, Chastity and Obedience come naturally. I am one of the poor in spirit who will see God. My chastity is my completion in the true Eros, which is play."[8]

Not everyone bought in. Many viewed this new generation of weirdies as sybaritic and emblematic of what became known as the Me decade. "Few acts are more selfish than the jogger's waste of energy," wrote Herman Spitz in the *New York Times* in 1979; instead, he wrote, they should channel their need for exercise into something productive, such as mowing lawns for the elderly. "This will not, unfortunately, spare us from the tiresome, self-righteous sermons about mystic experiences. No doubt we shall soon hear from former joggers who, after mowing to the point of exhaustion, pushed themselves and their mowers through one more lawn, an extra effort that rewarded them with a glimpse of nirvana. We will know that their hearts still beat with the resonance of water pumps and their souls still shine with the glow of self-flagellation, but—considering the altruistic nature of their deeds—we will be able to bear their martyrdom with some degree of equanimity."[9]

The women's running movement had its moments of starry-eyed mysticism, but on the whole, it seemed more grounded and real than the more phantasmic evangelism of men's running. In prewar America, wrote historian Pamela Cooper, running had been "a denial of helplessness" for immigrants and the working class; for women in the 1960s and 1970s, running offered something similar.[10] Gibb ran (or kept running after childhood) as her own private protest against the path she saw laid out for her. Berman took up running as a way to combat the listlessness she felt as a college-educated housewife. Nina Kuscsik, perhaps the most dominant marathoner of the early 1970s and the driving force behind the AAU's sanctioning of women's marathoning, began running after her divorce, "a terrible ordeal," she said. "I had to do something to help my self-image," she said, "to know I was important."[11] She picked up a copy of Bowerman's *Jogging*; a year after her first run, she ran her first race: the 1969 Boston Marathon.

On the roads and trails, a female runner could feel a sense of strength and independence largely denied to her in other realms of society. Women's running was also a sisterhood, a movement, and part of an athletic awakening across all women's sports. The year 1972 was a momentous one: tennis star Billie Jean King defeated Bobby Riggs; more than a tennis match, it was The Battle of the Sexes. (Most male runners had lost that battle long ago—in her first marathon, Gibb beat two-thirds of the men in the race.) Also in 1972, Title IX legislation focused attention on the massive inequities in sport for men and women in schools—and mandated change. It took a while for the true ramifications of the bill to be understood, but its impact was massive: in 1971, 294,015 girls participated in high school organized sports; by 1978, the year of compliance for Title IX, 2,083,040 girls participated.[12]

Running, more than any other athletic pursuit, was the physical expression of the values of the reinvigorated women's movement. And because the roads were open to all, there were no fights over limited resources such as playing fields, tracks, or gym time. Once Kuscsik persuaded the AAU to open the gates, female runners were largely welcomed into the marathoning tribe by their male counterparts. Moreover, running was accessible—other than a pair of shoes, the runner required no equipment. It was a declaration of independence—one runners could make on their own terms, in their own way. The physical act of running could be difficult, and the courage to begin could be hard to muster. But because participants faced fewer constraints than those in other sports, it offered a clear and simple path to a sense of individual empowerment—something difficult to find for women elsewhere in their lives. If male runners fancied themselves "Siddhartha in a jockstrap," as writer Sam Merrill put it, women could be "Susan B. Anthony in a sweatband," according to Cooper.[13]

Lebow saw the connection—the running boom's new wealthier demographic, the women's movement, and his marathon. In December 1971, Kuscsik had convinced the AAU to allow women to run marathons officially, but the rule makers insisted that a women's race have a separate start from the men's. At Boston, in April, Kuscsik and one of the officials, Aldo Scandurra, who'd helped Lebow put on the first New York Marathon, drew a chalk line on the sidewalk next to the men's starting line on the road: instant separate start. But in October 1972, at the New York City Marathon, Pat Rico, chair of the AAU women's committee, was on hand to see that both the spirit and letter of the rule were enforced: she insisted that the women start ten minutes before the men. Sensing an opportunity, Lebow called newsrooms around New York, telling them something was going to happen at the start of the third NYC Marathon that they wouldn't want to miss.

And he delivered. When the gun went off, the six women on the starting line sat down and unrolled posters protesting the AAU rule: "Hey AAU, this is 1972—Wake UP," read one, "The AAU is archaic," read another. The women then waited the ten minutes until the gun went off for the men's start, got up, and joined the pack of male runners. Only two of the women finished: Kuscsik won, and Patricia Barrett finished second. The others never intended to run, or at least not the whole distance; Lebow had recruited them for the photo op. Jane Muhrcke, wife of 1970 New York winner Gary, ran about a half mile before stepping off to the side—she wasn't a runner, though she'd often babysit Kuscsik's children while Nina ran. (Muhrcke has made her own mark on the New York City Marathon: that year, she wove laurel wreaths for the men's and women's champions, as she's done every year since.) Lebow got his publicity—the *New York Times* splashed a photo of the sit-down strike across four columns of the front page of the metro section—and the AAU voted to abandon its separate-start rule.

***

If runners sought transcendence on the roads, they could find it; if personal transformation, they would have it; a political statement, they could make it. No matter their level of seriousness (or self-seriousness), runners found something they wanted. And many of them, male and female alike, wanted to have a good time. Running, though often solitary, offered community—something that had grown harder to find as American society grew more fragmented. Lebow declared that race directors weren't just race managers but "social and entertainment directors."[14] Americans, wrote journalist and historian Roger Robinson, invented the concept of road race as party: large, boisterous crowds, loud music, and free beer. Often, lots of beer. Organizers made a habit of ending races at, or at least near, a bar, and local bars jumped in to sponsor races and host after-parties. Tommy Leonard, barkeep of the Eliot Lounge in Boston and friend to running legends like Bill Rodgers, hosted the most important unofficial official Boston Marathon after-party—top runners, sponsors, and officials all could be found drinking and dancing through Patriots' Day night at the Eliot. Leonard also opened his doors for the traditional New Year's Day Welly to the Elly, a morning run from the halfway point on the Boston Marathon course in Wellesley to the Eliot, where a hair of the dog might cure whatever ailed a runner after New Year's Eve and an easy thirteen miles the morning after. And inspired by Shorter's Olympic win, Leonard started the Falmouth Road Race, now a bucket-list summer event, 7.3 miles between two bars on Cape Cod, part race and part festival. Road races were transformed from pilgrimages for a small (and skinny) tribe of devotees to parties with mass appeal.

In 1976, Lebow turned the New York City Marathon into the world's biggest party with the greatest possible mass appeal. He was no longer operating on a shoestring—Manufacturers Hanover, one of the largest insurers in the country, was his major sponsor. But he still worked best on a tightrope, seemingly happiest when a heavy shadow of doubt hung over his projects, or when trying to coordinate a nearly infinite number of moving pieces. He relished the underdog role, and when colleagues half-jokingly suggested that the marathon venture out of Central Park to tour through all five boroughs, he seized on the idea. He worked the politicians, the police, and the media, and recruited an army of volunteers. He made under-the-table payments to the best male runners—Rodgers and Shorter—to ensure a compelling race, and bribed neighborhood gangs in Brooklyn with T-shirts and jackets to act as security when the marathon passed through their turf. A week before the marathon, he realized he'd forgotten to set up water stations in Brooklyn and Queens; hours of last-minute phone calls ensured that there would be water on the first fifteen miles of the course. The day before the race, he noticed that the massive, exposed joints of the Verrazano-Narrows Bridge—his new starting line—could easily swallow a runner's foot and cause a gruesome injury. He and his team of volunteers worked long into the night taping sheets of plywood over them. During the race, he nearly got arrested after he screamed at crowd control officers on the Pulaski Bridge in Queens and singlehandedly started moving barricades to give the oncoming runners more space.

In the lead-up to the race, he had all five borough presidents at a press conference doing a short "race" against Shorter. Brooklyn President Sebastian Leone told the media, "It's been said that runners will run fastest through Brooklyn . . . I predict that's when they'll slow down and enjoy the sights." Donald Manes of Queens predicted, "When [the runners] get to Queens, I'm sure some people will quit the race and buy a house."[15] Lebow made the marathon a celebration both for and of the spectators who lined the streets; the city was the story in 1976, not just the race. At the finish, Dick Schaap of NBC reported, "Twenty-six miles, 385 yards, no one was mugged, and no one was hit by a taxi. For the city of New York . . . the marathon was a resounding success." More than two thousand people ran—the largest marathon in the world—and more important, hundreds of thousands of spectators felt they were as much a part of the race as the runners. The big-city marathon was born. Marathoning's center of gravity had shifted to New York.

By decade's end, the total number of runners in the United States had grown from 1 million in 1970, to 30 million by 1979, according to a Gallup poll.[16] Liz Elliot, president of the National Jogging Association, suggested any number that high included "people who jogged downstairs in the morning."[17] The professional classes streamed into running, "fueled by reports that running was good for the heart, that runners have better sex lives, that social contacts are improved at weekend races,"[18] suggested one television report.

No segment of the running population grew faster than women—though, to be fair, it was the segment with the most room for growth. In 1970, six women ran the first Road Runners Club national women's championship marathon in Atlantic City (as a private club, the Road Runners happily ignored AAU rules, which in 1970 still forbade women from competing in marathons); Sara Mae Berman won. In February 1974, the AAU hosted its first national women's championship marathon in San Mateo, California—Judy Ikenberry won (her second marathon victory in a month, having raced the Mission Bay Marathon in San Diego three weeks earlier), and twenty-seven women finished.[19] That April, Berman convinced the BAA to hold a press conference to tout the fact that forty-two women were entered the 1974 Boston Marathon. Small steps, to be sure; however, the growth of the sport could be measured not just in numbers of participants, but also in marathon times, sponsorship dollars, media coverage, and racing opportunities.

One such opportunity was the first women's international marathon, hosted by Dr. Ernst van Aaken in Waldniel, Germany, in 1974. Van Aaken had been an avid runner until a car struck him while he was out on a run, severing both of his legs. Unable to continue in the sport, he devoted himself to coaching, to the scientific study of running, and to the promotion of women's athletics. In the 1950s and 1960s, he pushed the German athletic federation to include the women's 1500m in the national championship and advocated for including longer events for women in the Olympics. He compiled scientific data refuting claims that women were harmed by long-distance running—to the contrary, he stated: women were the original endurance athletes. Out on the roads, his athletes backed up his research: In September 1967, 18-year-old 800m runner Anni Pede broke the world marathon record by eight minutes, running 3:07. By the early 1970s, when women were routinely breaking three hours—only for critics to argue that they had the unfair advantage of pacing off the men in coed races—van Aaken sought to create a women's-only marathon. In 1973, he hosted his first, and, in 1974, he invited teams from five nations, including the top American finishers from the

AAU championship to the first-ever international women's marathon, the Waldniel International Marathon.

One more American, a young Californian named Jackie Hansen who hadn't been able to compete at the AAU championship, paid her own way to Waldniel. She was a recent convert to the marathon—in fact, she had just won a collegiate national title in the mile, and still considered herself a track athlete. Still, from the time she watched some of her teammates run a marathon in 1971, she wanted to do one herself. Her coach, Hungarian émigré Laszlo Tabori, didn't think much of the idea; he thought the marathon was for athletes too old or slow for the track. But Hansen, whom Tabori called "the most stubborn runner he'd ever coached," insisted, and she won her first marathon in 1972, in a relatively pedestrian 3:15. She won Boston in 1973, defeating Kuscsik by thirty seconds. At Waldniel, she ran 2:56, finishing fifth behind three of van Aaken's runners and France's Chantal Langlacè. To Hansen, Waldniel was incontrovertible evidence of what happened when women had the types of opportunities elite men took for granted—their times got faster, and fields got deeper. In an interview after the race, she said women deserved more: they should have their own Olympic marathon.

She came home from Waldniel with two goals: become the world's best marathoner and get the marathon into the Olympics. She persuaded Tabori to focus her training on the marathon rather than the track. With her track-honed speed, she was soon what Kathrine Switzer referred to as "the next evolutionary step" in women's marathoning: "We'd always said that someone was going to come along who was track trained and would put the speed talent together with endurance training," Switzer wrote—someone who would send marathon times into freefall. Hansen was only one of several such someones: she broke the world marathon record just ten weeks after Waldniel, running 2:43 in Culver City. Four months later, Germany's Liane Winter ran 2:42 at the 1975 Boston Marathon; two weeks after that, her countrywoman Christa Vahlensieck ran 2:40 in Dulmen, Germany. In October 1975, Hansen became the first woman to finish under 2:40, going 2:38 in Eugene, Oregon. The women's world record had dropped nearly forty minutes in ten years, over which time the men's record had improved thirty seconds—and there, the record paused briefly to catch its breath. In May 1977, Langlacé ran 2:35, only to have Vahlensieck respond with a 2:34 in September.

In 1976, Hansen watched the Montreal Olympics, where she certainly would have been in the hunt for a marathon medal, come and go. But women still didn't have a path to the Olympics in anything longer than the 1500m. Hansen started writing letters and giving interviews to anyone who would listen. The IOC, unfortunately, did not. At the heart of the IOC membership's sense of privilege was the belief that they guarded the gates to a sacred arena, one that had been constructed and consecrated as a celebration of manly virtues. They'd only grudgingly admitted women into Olympic track and field in 1928, and as late as 1970, Avery Brundage, president of the International Olympic Committee, declared that maybe the Greeks had had it right in prohibiting women from the Olympics altogether. In certain academic fields, the saying goes, new ideas advance "funeral by funeral";[20] in the case of the IOC, this was quite literally true: Members were chosen for life, and although Brundage retired from the presidency in 1972, he was given the title "Life Honorary President" and remained an influential IOC member until his death in 1975. Unwilling to count on a sudden rash of mortality among the IOC leadership, Hansen spent the rest of the decade learning about the dizzying, interlocking alphabet soup of governing bodies—the IOC, the IAAF, the AAU, the United States Olympic Committee (USOC), and other national governing bodies—and began to build ways to influence them from the ground up.

***

Meanwhile, Switzer pursued other means of getting the IOC to listen. She understood that publicity and money sang an irresistible tune to the IOC—no matter their pronouncements about sacred and noble Olympian virtues. Road races could handle massive numbers of runners, and road race directors were welcoming to all—partly because road racing, traditionally the sport of weirdies, was more open and more fun, and partly because more runners meant happier sponsors. In 1974, when forty-two women at the Boston Marathon seemed a great accomplishment, the IOC felt that they could comfortably dismiss the entire women's running movement. But the sport was growing quickly, and if women's running grew big enough, and if it attracted enough media attention and corporate sponsorship, the IOC simply wouldn't be able to afford to keep the women's marathon out. Her vision may have seemed far-fetched in 1976, but she'd bring it to fruition sooner perhaps than even she expected.

In her 1967 run at Boston, Switzer had been put on the defensive, had run most of the race in fear of Jock Semple, and had been rattled by the press's aggressive questioning afterward. Ten years later, she'd learned to go on offense, to shape the narrative, and manipulate the media—to harness their power for her own ends. Shortly after working with Lebow on Crazylegs, she'd begun working in the PR department of AMF, a large sporting goods company. She served on committees for the Women's Sports Foundation, working on equity issues with other sporting legends such as Billie Jean King and Olympic medalists Peggy Fleming and Donna de Varona. And when the Women's Sports Foundation invited her to present to executives from a number of large corporations at a conference on sponsorship and media coverage in women's sports, she saw an opportunity.

Women's running, she said, would soon become one of the largest participatory sports in the world. Strong words, considering that only 141 women had run the 1977 Boston Marathon—less than 5 percent of the total entrants. But she could see rapid growth already happening and could feel bigger things coming: if companies such as Manufacturers Hanover were clamoring to sponsor events such as the New York City Marathon, companies looking to reach women could forge even stronger connections with their target audience by getting into women's running. The sport had the strength of meaning, of being bigger than just a sport.

Further, female runners were the right demographic for potential sponsors; when it came to women's sports, class mattered. From the beginning of modern organized athletic competition in the nineteenth century, country-club pursuits—tennis, golf, and even archery and swimming—acquired a veneer of acceptability that running, a working-class sport, lacked. In the early twentieth century, women were constantly told what running would do *to* them: masculinize them, harden their features; make them unattractive and leave them unable find a husband;

even render them infertile. As running changed from a working-class diversion to something between professional-class hobby and spiritual calling, so, too, did its perceived effects on women: by the 1970s, running was "a beauty treatment," according to Kathryn Lance, author of *Running for Health & Beauty*. "Everybody's Doing It," declared the cover of a July 1977 *People* magazine, under a photo of fashion model and *Charlie's Angels* star Farah Fawcett jogging with her then-husband Lee Majors.

It was no accident that cosmetics firms were early and significant sponsors of women's running: Crazylegs in 1972 was only the first; in 1977, Ohio-based cosmetics company Bonne Bell took over sponsorship of the Mini Marathon and turned it into a nationwide series of races. So, when Switzer made her pitch to a roomful of corporate executives, it was hardly surprising that Michael Williams, a vice president of Avon, sought her out during a break. He asked her to look at a proposal he'd received from Avon's Atlanta office: an international marathon, inspired by the success of van Aaken's Waldniel race. In a lunch meeting the next week, she pitched him not just a marathon but a series of races across the country. Avon was intrigued enough to greenlight the Atlanta marathon for the spring of 1978 but took a wait-and-see approach on the series—and Williams hired Switzer away from AMF at double the salary.

Tying together running, beauty, and cosmetics was, on the one hand, a step forward—better than being told running would make one a man. On the other hand, running for health, independence, strength, and a sense of identity didn't quite mesh with also running to live up to the impossible beauty standard that glossy magazines promoted. After the 1928 Olympics, when the IOC sought to eliminate women's track and field, IOC president Henri Baillet-Latour suggested that women be permitted to participate only in "aesthetical" sports—activities pleasing to the eye (of men). Fifty years later, running had become acceptable, even popular—but still, it seemed, women's sport had to be "aesthetical." Switzer understood the trade-off—she had to give sponsors what they wanted in exchange for the power and visibility that she needed. She'd make sure their message got out, but it would be harnessed to her own.

As the March 1978 race date approached, she threw herself into planning the marathon. "I knew," she said, "Avon would not be impressed with some rinky-dink draw a line on the road event."[21] She'd seen enough to know what she didn't want, and she knew that a women's-only event, organized by a woman, would bring with it the harsh glare of added scrutiny: she could emulate Lebow's sense of showmanship, but she couldn't afford to improvise or put out fires at the last minute, couldn't be seen running around screaming at police, volunteers, or sponsors on race day. She had to get the Avon International Marathon right—the day had to go smoothly, she had to exude calm professionalism, and the sponsors had to be thrilled. There would be no second chance.

She prepared long planning documents. Convened longer meetings. Checked and double-checked every detail, from course length to number of portable toilets. She wanted her race to feel welcoming to developmental runners: prerace running clinics, music, a festive atmosphere, expansive changing area, and high-quality T-shirts cut for a female body. She also wanted an elite field to demonstrate the quality of women's marathoning—14 of the top 25 marathoners in the world toed the line in Atlanta. She also wanted depth—78 women raced, an impressive number for an inaugural marathon in an era when few marathons outside of New York or Boston could attract even 50 women. She flew in van Aaken, the inspiration for the Atlanta race, as an honorary marshal. To further the aim of getting the marathon included in the Olympics, she invited officials from the IAAF and AAU, as well as Monique Berlioux, the executive director of the IOC—perhaps the highest ranking woman in international sport (though still not a voting member of the all-male IOC—she merely ran the office and negotiated TV rights). "I am most sorry to miss this occasion," wrote Berlioux, "which I am certain will prove very exciting and a positive boost to women athletes, who—you will forgive me for adding—are as much, if not better, suited physiologically than men to long distance running, although to date races for women have tended to be fairly short."[22]

However meaningful the actual race experience was, it also had to help sell cosmetics. Switzer highlighted all the benefits of running and trumpeted Avon's association with the marathon. "These women are so beautiful because they run!" exclaimed van Aaken in his address to the runners and spectators. She got coverage for the race in the major print media outlets, and all three national news networks had the race on the Sunday night news. And she made sure the story was about the Olympics: the *New York Times* included a quote from Lebow on the Olympics: "Today's results show the women are ready," he said.[23] *Sports Illustrated* devoted two pages to the race: four paragraphs to the running, the rest to the movement to include the marathon in the 1980 Olympics. Almost as if coached, the winner, Marty Cooksey, said, "I just came to do my best . . . and to show that it is good enough for the Olympics."[24]

By the end of the year, Avon was ready to put its full marketing weight behind Switzer's concept for a race series, which would culminate in another international marathon championship—to be held in Waldniel, to honor van Aaken. She consulted with Avon's international divisions in other countries and helped set up races in Japan, Belgium, and Singapore. Avon prepared a press conference to announce the Avon International Running Circuit. Switzer anointed Cooksey, the Atlanta champion, the official spokesperson for the circuit. At the press conference, Switzer had pioneers like Kuscsik talk about the early days of women's running (all of seven years ago) and even had Lebow there to lend his support to the cause. And, for a wee bit o' notoriety, she invited an old friend to be a special guest speaker: "the man who," she exclaimed, "in spite of himself, has done more for women's marathoning than anyone else in the world"—Jock Semple.[25]

Women's marathoning had an international presence, major corporate power behind it, and was one of the biggest stories in the sporting world. The pioneering marathoners of the 1960s and early 1970s—women such as Gibb, Switzer, Kuscsik, and Berman—had given way to runners such as Hansen, Vahlensieck, Winter, Cooksey, and a host of others, who elevated women's running to a new level. The stage was set. The sport awaited its first great star.

CHAPTER 4

A Star Is Born

Grete Waitz, New York, 1978

IN 1978, THE NEW YORK CITY MARATHON HAD TEN THOUSAND RUN-
ners, including more than nine hundred women. Lebow had a six-figure
budget to work with, plus an under-the-table budget to lure top talent,
and he attracted more national media attention than any other marathon
outside of the Olympics. And every year, he had to outdo himself—he
needed stories to feed the beast, stories that could break through the
clutter in the media capital of the world, stories with a weight and impact
worthy of what he billed as the largest sporting event on earth. He had
to build anticipation before the race, and he wanted eyeball-grabbing
headlines the day after. "Runner X wins in decent time" wouldn't do. He
needed records.

For 1978, he recruited a murderer's row of a women's field: Hansen,
the former world record holder; Vahlensieck, the current world record
holder; and Avon champion and new darling of the running media,
Martha Cooksey. Cooksey and Lebow announced that she would try to
be the first woman to break 2:30—an ambitious goal, given her relatively
modest 2:46 in Atlanta. In the buildup to the race, Bob Glover, the coach
of Greater New York Athletics, declared, "This may be the first women's
marathon in which they compete like men"—by which he appeared to
mean going out hard from the beginning. Brian Oldfield, a world record
holder in the shot put, media personality, and apparent expert on marathon tactics, chimed in: "Women have never raced like men before,"

53

he said. "They've never gone all out so they collapse at the finish. They always manage to jog back to their hotel rooms right after."[1] Leaving aside that men also tended to start conservatively and typically managed an easy jog after the race, or that women who went out aggressively were criticized for lacking tactical acumen, observers expected fireworks in the women's race.

On race day, temperatures warmed into the 70s; nonetheless, Cooksey started as advertised and established a massive lead. Vahlensieck and Hansen hung back, predicting, correctly, that Cooksey's early pace was unsustainable. She passed halfway in 1:14 and soon began to show signs of trouble. But neither Hansen nor Vahlensieck could catch her. Instead, gliding up to her shoulder was an unknown runner with her blonde hair pulled back in two tight pigtails. Her expression was calm and focused. Her feet ticked off the pavement like she was running across water, even in the latter half of the marathon. Cooksey hung on gamely for a mile or so, but her challenger eased away without a hint of increased effort or strain. Soon she had built a lead of nine minutes.

She was wearing a hand-lettered bib, number 1173—the elite entrants, such as Cooksey, all had low-numbered bibs, with an F prefixed before the number to designate the top women's runners in the field. Spectators flipping through the race program to find out who number 1173 was found no such number listed. Race announcer Toni Reavis, who followed the sport more closely than anyone—he even had a weekly radio show on running, *Runner's Digest*—could only tell the crowds that number 1173 was running well under world-record pace, and that he had no idea who she was.

She was Grete Waitz of Norway, and even if she was the picture of grace in motion, even as she made the final miles of the marathon look easy, she was going through her own personal stages of grief: "anger, frustration, depression, then anger again," she said afterward. Much of her wrath focused on her husband, who had convinced her to run in the first place.[2] She'd never run a marathon before, had never run longer than twenty kilometers (about twelve miles) in practice; now, twenty-some miles in, she wasn't sure she could finish. Spectators crowded the street, yelling and cheering, and her mind was foggy. She thought she was still winning, but she couldn't be sure, and she didn't know the course well; she was looking for trees—trees meant the park, and she knew the race ended in Central Park. She asked some of the men around her, "How far left?" They may have said three; was it kilometers or miles? Her husband, Jack, had shouted something, but she couldn't process it—maybe something about a record—and it didn't matter, anyway. She was too busy trying not to hurt. She'd run plenty of shorter races, and pain she was used to—quads burning, calves on the verge of cramping—but not everything, everywhere, all at once, and for such a long time. She wanted to stop and walk, but she was afraid she couldn't start up again; instead, she telescoped her world down to one stride at a time and focused only on getting to the finish line.

Thirty minutes before number 1173 crossed the line, Fred Lebow stood at the finish like an ineffectual modern-day Moses desperately trying to part the seas. In the lead car, he'd arrived at the finish just minutes ahead of the men's leaders—and found chaos. The police detail had been overwhelmed by the crowds, who swarmed onto the road. The runners hardly had space to get through to the finish chute, which was blocked anyway: the marathon's official auto sponsor, Subaru, had parked a car more or less on the finish line. A television helicopter swooped in low and kicked up a swirling mess of debris and dust into the faces of the crowd. Lebow screamed and shook his fist at the helicopter, rallied police and volunteers to make a channel through the crowds—just enough for the men's winner, Bill Rodgers, to squeeze through. By the time he had sorted out the men's finish and had yelled enough at Subaru's marketing rep to get the car moved—and lose the sponsorship deal—he had forgotten about the women's race. Some ten minutes after Waitz's victory, it finally clicked in Lebow's head that the top women should have been finishing by now. "Who won?" he yelled at anyone within range. "Who won?"

"Some blonde girl," someone said.

Waitz had finished in 2:32.29, more than two minutes faster than Vahlensieck's old world record. She doubled over, oblivious to the crowds that pressed in on her and reached out to pat her on the back. She made her way through a gauntlet of yellow-jacketed volunteers before a media scrum enveloped her. In halting English, she answered a few questions:

her background, her track career, her training; she taught them how to pronounce her name. Then the new world record holder threw her shoes at her husband and screamed at him "I'm never, NEVER doing that again!" The rest of what she said was, thankfully, unintelligible to the press—"Very hard words," Jack would say later, a twinkle in his voice. "I am glad there were no Norwegian speakers at the finish line." Then Grete and Jack escaped the chaos of the finish line and started the long, slow, painful walk back to their hotel. Twenty minutes later, a fellow Norwegian found them just sitting on a patch of grass in Central Park, about a quarter mile from the finish. Grete's legs hurt so badly she needed to stop and rest.

Waitz had gone into the race with little expectation for success, and she may have been unknown to the American running media, but her fellow athletes had some inkling of what was in store. The morning of the race, on the elite athlete bus out to the starting line on Staten Island, Vahlensieck sat near Jackie Hansen, American record holder and number two in the world. She leaned into Hansen's ear and pointed out Waitz: "She is our competition today." The day before the race, Vahlensieck's coach, Hans Martin Bresch, stated outright, "If Waitz can finish, she will win."[3]

Vahlensieck and Hansen, wearing bibs F1 and F2, had both dropped out of the race with foot injuries. No support vehicles were there to pick them up; they cut across the city to get back to Central Park, arriving in time to see Waitz finish. They sat on a hill, unnoticed, away from the crowd. Reavis's voice carried up to them, informing them that there was no sign of Vahlensieck or Hansen on the course, but an unknown woman was about to smash the world record. As Waitz crossed the line, tears welled in Vahlensieck's eyes. Hansen tried the usual words of consolation on her companion and rival: there would be better days, she would get the record back. But on some level, they both knew what they'd witnessed: the sport had just passed them by.

***

In Norway, Waitz had been one of the nation's most recognizable athletes since she was a teenager. Young Grete Andersen had been obsessed with running since age 12, when she found a dusty pair of track spikes lying around her home in Oslo. She put them on and sprinted along the grass strip in front of her apartment block, racing buses down the street. The next week, she went with her older brother to join the neighborhood athletic club. She was turned away—they did not accept girls—so she begged her parents to let her join a club across town, Vidar SC, which did. She loved the practices, but she wasn't very good. The longest event for girls her age was two hundred meters, and for two years, she consistently finished closer to last than first. She was all limbs, and lacked the power and coordination for sprinting. Her mother consistently dismissed her running—"Why bother?" she'd say. "You're not going to be a running star."[4] She insisted Grete take piano lessons, which Grete hated. The mother-daughter feud simmered—one wanting to raise a proper young girl, the other equally determined to be anything but. And what Grete found in running, she could never give up.

When she was fourteen, her coach sent her out on a longer run with a group of older boys—among them, a gregarious 18-year-old named Jack Waitz. She was nervous, and they were upset; the boys sized up her shy demeanor and gangly frame, and they concluded that they'd been given the task of babysitting for the day. They set off at a brisk pace and largely ignored her, talking and joking and waiting for her to fold. She hung on. They kicked up the pace; she gritted her teeth. Six hard miles later, they finished—with newfound respect for young Grete Andersen. They trotted off to change. She could barely walk, and she couldn't wait to come back to the next practice and do it again.

A few months after she began running with the older boys, she won her first race, a four-hundred-meter cross-country "distance" race for girls. At age 17, she was chosen to represent Norway in international competition in 1970, in an eight-hundred-meter race against other Scandinavian countries. "You're that good?" her father asked in surprise; her parents soon came around to the fact that running was here to stay—her stubbornness, if it didn't quite win them over, at least wore them down.[5]

She set her first national record in 1971, at age 18, and was anointed Norway's great hope for victory in European and global competition on the track—a heavy burden in a sports-mad country that tended to view silver as the color of defeat. After failing to make it out of the heats at the 1971 European Championships, she held herself together in the stadium, and through the media zone, and with her coach; then the teenaged Andersen cried alone in the locker room. At the 1972 Olympics, she again failed to make it out of her heat; members of the Norwegian press wrote that she owed an apology to the nation. She felt like public property and was ready to quit—sort of. She'd never give up running—it was her escape. But she could run on her own. She didn't need the scrutiny of competing for Norway.

By 1974, she and Jack were living together, soon to be married, and she was studying for a teaching degree. But she couldn't shake the need to prove herself as a runner—not to her fellow Norwegians, or to the media, but to herself; she needed to know how her best stacked up against the world's best. In 1974, she won a surprise bronze medal at the European Championships—the most prestigious and competitive meet outside of the Olympics. In 1976, leading up to Montreal, the Norwegian press touted her for a medal—likely gold, some writers gushed—in the 1500m. But Waitz knew better. She knew that the Soviet and other Eastern Bloc runners, who almost never raced in the West, were clocking unheard-of times. Worse, they "weren't eating the same thing for breakfast we were," as Jack put it.

Doping wasn't a new phenomenon, but it had become more widespread. And the cheaters were still far ahead of the testers—it is a cliché, even now, that drug tests are essentially IQ tests; the only ones getting caught were those who failed to cycle off drugs in time to test clean at competitions, or who failed to use masking agents properly, or whose national governing bodies failed to bribe the right people. Certainly, Eastern Bloc athletes weren't the only ones using drugs—Americans had been experimenting with steroids at least since the 1950s—but the Eastern Bloc countries had developed state-sponsored doping systems for their national teams and soon dominated women's athletics.

Waitz wouldn't cheat; she could only train harder. From 1974 through the 1976 Olympics, she didn't miss a day of training. She jumped her mileage as high as 125 miles per week, running twice a day. Her morning runs began in the dark, early enough that she could still make the commute—two bus rides and a subway trip—to her teaching job. At the end of the day, she'd do her second run or her workout—again in the dark during the long Norwegian winter. In blizzards, she'd run in rubber boots, crunching out a fast tempo through snow and slush. She once did a hard fourteen-kilometer run back and forth on the only patch of road that wasn't covered in ice—a stretch no more than four hundred meters long. Speed sessions in bad weather required some creativity—Norway had no indoor tracks. She would run in parking garages, or in an unused subway station near her house. She ran at a fast clip—Jack, whose best marathon time was 2:36, could hardly keep up; and their good friend, Knut Kvalheim, the Norwegian record holder at every distance from 1500m to the 10,000m, begged off, as he preferred an easier training pace. Grete's brother Jan, a medalist at the Norwegian championships, ended up doing many of her longer runs with her. She ran speed workouts so hard that they brought her to tears, but out-training the Eastern Europeans was her only chance to overcome their pharmaceutical advantage.

Even so, hers was a long-shot hope at best. She knew it, and the burden of her country's expectations left her emotionally drained, very nearly defeated before the race began. She found herself shaking, eyes welling up, just seeing the East Germans on the warmup track. But as she'd always done, she held it in—when she broke down, she broke down alone. For the Norwegian press she put on a brave face, answered their questions with a smile, and tried to temper their expectations. At the Montreal Olympics, she set a national and all-Scandinavia record, running 4:04—and failed to make the final. She returned home to Oslo to recuperate, get away from competitive track and field, and try to figure out what was next.

On an easy run with Jack, she overheard a young child, perhaps 6 years old, say to his playmate, "That's the lady that f—cked us over at the Olympics."

She still ran every day, usually twice a day. But she considered herself retired; for fun, she ran a fifteen-kilometer race in Sweden that fall and won by minutes. That winter, she mostly skied. Jack convinced her to try the track again. In 1977, she won the 3000m at the inaugural IAAF World Cup—a less grandiose meet than the name suggests: regional teams were comprised of athletes from Africa, the Americas, Asia, Europe, and Oceania, plus national teams from the United States, East Germany, and the USSR. The major powers didn't all send their best, and the 3000m was a fairly new event. The competition was somewhat thin.

In 1978, the first year Norway sent a women's team to the world cross-country running championships, she dominated the field, winning by thirty seconds. But the Soviet bloc didn't care about cross-country—medals on the track were all they cared about. The 1978 European Championships loomed that summer, and because Prague was the host, the Eastern Europeans would be even more intent on showing their superiority over the capitalist West. The Norwegian media touted Waitz again for gold. She knew better.

In her first event, the 1500m, she ran 4:00.55, which still stands as the Norwegian record—and finished fifth, behind two Soviets, a Romanian, and a Bulgarian. In the 3000m, she led with a lap to go; Svetlana Ulmasova of the USSR made up fifty meters in the last four hundred to take gold, and Romanian Natalia Mărăşescu took silver. Worse than after Montreal, the defeats hollowed her out; she'd always raced to test herself, to find her best—and to win. In a fair competition, she believed her best would give her a chance to win. But track was a rigged game—Eastern Bloc athletes swept every women's track medal at the European Championships, save four: silvers to Linda Haglund of Sweden in the 100m, Silvia Hollmann of West Germany in the 400 hurdles, and the British four-hundred-meter relay, and Waitz's bronze in the 3000.[6] She was a two-time Olympian, and she'd run faster than she'd ever hoped—and would never be good enough to beat the Eastern Bloc, would never live up to her country's outsized expectations. She was 25 years old and already the oldest woman on the Norwegian national team—her teammates called her "grandmother." Competitive running seemed to have nothing left to offer. Walking through the cobbled streets of nighttime Prague with Jack and Knut Kvalheim, she reached a decision. I'm done, she told them. I'm retiring—this time for sure.

Jack and Knut told her she ought to try a marathon first. Jack had thought for some time that it might be a great event for her, and if nothing else, it would be a challenge and a fine way to cap her career.

Knut suggested New York, the biggest and best marathon in the world. Grete shrugged. She wasn't going to go to New York alone, but it could be a nice vacation with Jack if they could swing it, one last trip abroad before she settled down as a teacher. She'd never run a marathon—never raced anything longer than 15K, never done a run longer than half the 42.2-kilometer marathon distance. But she allowed herself to be persuaded, if for no other reason than to put an end to Jack's pestering.

Knut called a friend at Finnair, which sponsored the New York Marathon, and Lebow extended an offer to pay travel and lodging for Waitz to race. But soon after, Patricia Owens, elite athlete coordinator for the New York Marathon, rescinded the invitation. Grete had insisted that they also pay for Jack to come over and, as a matter of policy, the New York Marathon did not pay for spouses. Owens barely thought to mention it to Lebow. But Lebow was the policy of the New York Marathon, and he realized that getting Waitz would be well worth the expense of flying Jack over, not because she would generate headlines—she was virtually unknown outside of Europe—or even contend, but because he thought she would likely go out too fast and blow up, and someone like Vahlensieck might get pulled along to a new world record. Just two weeks before the marathon, he agreed to fly her and Jack over. Before anyone thought of having official pacers in marathons, Lebow was using one of the best middle-distance runners in the world to help grease the path to a record.

The Thursday before the marathon, Grete and Jack arrived in New York and set out to make the most of their trip. Lebow hadn't scheduled her for any of the press conferences—he saw no reason to introduce the media to a runner he didn't expect to finish—so the Waitzes played tourist: they wandered the city, took in the sights, did some easy running. They sat on benches in Central Park and just watched people go by. At her one prerace obligation, a Finnair reception on Saturday afternoon, Lebow asked Waitz what her longest run had been in preparation. He wasn't sure he'd heard right when she said twenty kilometers—maybe she'd meant twenty miles? But no, she confirmed, kilometers. He walked away thinking that she probably wouldn't even make it halfway. Had he continued the conversation, he might have also learned that long runs weren't everything: she ran well over one hundred miles per week at a pace that scared off world-class men.

The night before the marathon, Grete and Jack treated themselves to a nice, expensive dinner: steak, ice cream, and a bottle of wine. The race hardly came up in conversation. For once, she was hardly nervous. She had done no real preparation for the race—in her mind she was already retired. New York was a lark, a vacation with a long run thrown in.

***

After the marathon, Lebow finally caught up with Waitz at her hotel, after she'd had a long nap and a shower. She still had to make it through the awards ceremony that evening, and he told her that she would be appearing on the *Today* show the next morning.

Not possible, she said—she didn't have a sub for her classes. Besides, she asked, what is the *Today* show?

Lebow insisted, then pleaded—she was the story of the race, and he needed her on TV. Jack finally called Grete's head of school, who allowed that it would be OK for the new marathon world record holder to return on Tuesday. After taping the show, Grete had one more request: Could Lebow get them a cab to the airport? Lebow picked up the phone and happily gave $20 to number 1173, the new face of women's distance running.

CHAPTER 5

Hat or Beer

Joan Benoit, Boston, 1979

In April 1979, Joanie Benoit was a 21-year-old senior at Bowdoin College in Maine, and her primary goal for the future was to run as much as she could for as long as she could. She'd dreamed of being in the Olympics since she was a child—originally, though, as a skier. At age 3, her parents told her she was too young to go skiing with her older brothers; she marched down to the basement, pulled out an old pair of skis, strapped them onto her feet, and "skied" down their snowy front lawn, falling every few feet. Point made, on both sides; her parents dropped her at her grandparents' and took the older boys to the mountain.

In elementary school, she played every sport she could, her mop of dark hair flying behind her tiny body, a nonstop athlete in the way only young children have the stamina to be. Year-round, she and her friends spent hours outdoors: in the winter, they skied and played pond hockey; in the warmer months, it was tennis and sandlot baseball. In the summer, if she wasn't in the middle of a neighborhood game, she'd be digging for clams, rowing a boat in protected coves along her beloved Maine coast, or playing at the beach. Sometimes she was just tearing through the woods with her friends or siblings. Idle time was an unknown concept. And there was running, too—she won pretty much every race she entered on school field days.

Sometime around fifth grade, things began to change. The week leading up to field day took on a new edge: the boys packed together, shouting about how they would beat the girls—prove that they were faster, stronger, better. For Joanie, sports had always been good fun, games about nothing more than trying to go faster, higher, farther for herself—her own little fulfillment of the Olympic motto. She could see something creeping into her world, an almost unconscious adherence to a new, unwritten code: children were no longer just children but divided into boys and girls, with different games and different clothes. Particular roles to play. New social groups. There were strange looks and whispered exclamations when girls did things like boys. Some sports were still OK—swimming, for example. Tennis was acceptable as well, though she couldn't help but notice that her friends toned down their aggression on the courts when boys were around. Girls and boys slipped into these new identities without thinking, without trying on the fit to see if it worked. It just sort of happened, and paths diverged.

Benoit made her most important childhood decision without a full appreciation of its significance: she decided not to give up on competitive sport. Staying true would exact a price—even as those around her celebrated champion female athletes, they still looked sideways at young girls intent on doing the work to become champion athletes. At times, she kept her athletic dreams and competitive nature under wraps to fit in, but she refused to bury that part of herself completely. To give up would have been to accept the amputation of a core part of who she was.

She played field hockey and basketball in high school, and in the spring ran track—any event from the 100 yards on up to the half mile, the longest race for girls. But she craved longer distances: running brought with it welcome solitude, a chance to tune out the world, turn her focus inward. She'd escape along the backroads to Fort Williams, an abandoned army base in Cape Elizabeth, wide open and hilly with a few small beaches and long stretches of rocky cliffs looking over the water. Early mornings and late evenings, it was almost deserted, which suited her—she started high school in 1970, just a few years after Gibb first ran Boston, and a girl out for a run on her own still drew stares; sometimes, when a car approached, she'd stop to walk, or step off to the side and pretend to pick flowers.

Skiing was still her passion. As a ski racer, she hurtled her tiny frame through the gates with reckless aggression, out to prove that she feared neither the mountain nor her older, stronger competitors. But in February of her sophomore year of high school, her recklessness got the better of her, and a nasty crash left her with a broken leg. She stewed, waiting for the cast to come off—track season began in March, and she had her sights on the state meet. Her doctor advised against running until she fully healed—summertime, he said. Her track coach concurred, telling her that even once the cast came off, her leg would take a while to get strong enough to handle the stress of daily training. Her parents wished she wouldn't run, but they knew how deep her stubborn streak ran and didn't forbid it. When her cast finally did come off in early spring, she began running on her own, her leg still so weak that she could only manage a slow, lopsided shuffle around the high school track. One day, a younger boy told her she shouldn't run if she was limping that badly; after that, she retreated to Fort Williams again, hobbling for miles all alone, barely able to drag her leg upstairs when she got home.

That spring, she made the state meet.

Next winter, she went back to ski racing but found she wasn't the same skier: she'd lost her fearlessness; without that edge, she realized she could never live up to her own standards of excellence. Everything she'd channeled into skiing—the aggression, competitiveness, and her Olympic dreams—she now channeled into running. By the time she graduated high school, she was the top runner in Maine and one of the best in New England.

In the fall of 1975, Benoit began college at Bowdoin, a small liberal-arts school just thirty minutes from home. It may have seemed a strange choice—Bowdoin didn't have a women's track team. But it was a top-flight academic school, and she was good enough to play field hockey for them. She loved the team aspect of field hockey. Running was something she'd mostly done on her own through high school, and she figured she could still run as much as she wanted in college. And, not for the last time, she seemed intent on proving—to herself above all—that she could do everything, and do it her way.

But collegiate field hockey was more intense than she'd imagined, and classes more difficult. She made friends in the dorm, joined a coed fraternity, had everything one needed for the ideal small-college life—except time for it all. Her schedule—running, classes, practice, schoolwork, repeat—didn't leave much room for eating, sleeping, or socializing. Still, running was the thing she couldn't give up. She'd joined Liberty Athletic Club in Boston, the oldest girls' track club in the country (started by a Lexington milkman in 1948), because Liberty's top girls traveled all over the nation to race against the best. On weekends, she'd catch the bus to Boston for races and try to keep up with her schoolwork on the ride down and back. And there was always another run to do—occasionally with guys on Bowdoin's men's team, often by herself—even in winter, in slush over her ankles, through snow or in icy rain that froze to her sweatshirt and in her hair.

Her indoor track times that first winter at Bowdoin were slower than what she'd run in high school. She was overcooked, trying to fit too much into each twenty-four hours, but she had her goals and, as she would admit later, goals often outweighed good sense. But by the spring of her freshman year, she shook herself out of her doldrums, and her results started to attract some attention—a fourth place at Penn Relays, seventh at the AAU nationals in the 3000m, first at the Falmouth Road Race. After her sophomore year, she dropped field hockey. For the first time in her life, running was her sole athletic focus.

Collegiate women's running was in its infancy—1975 was the first year of an official collegiate national championship, under the auspices of the Association for Intercollegiate Athletics for Women (AIAW). Coaches trying to build top-flight college programs started recruiting Benoit heavily, and Bowdoin still didn't have a team. For her junior year, the fall of 1977, she accepted a scholarship to North Carolina State.

Total student enrollment at North Carolina State was around seventeen thousand—twice the population of her hometown, Cape Elizabeth. She was pretty sure she was the only Mainer on campus. Back home, she'd run on her own, parachuting in to races with Liberty AC, then heading back up to Maine. In Raleigh, for the first time, she had a coach, Russ Combs, directing her practice each day. And she had teammates:

she ran with the team, ate with the team, traveled with the team, and even socialized with them—in fact, she knew few people at NC State outside of the team. In Maine, running had always been an escape for Benoit, a way to let go of all her other daily cares. In Raleigh, she had no separation between running and the rest of her life.

Further, her new teammates were on her level, perhaps even a notch faster. Julie Shea, who had set a national high school record in the mile, 4:43.1, arrived as a freshman the same year Benoit transferred in. In certain circumstances, training partners can push each other to heights neither could achieve on their own; other times, they grind each other to dust. Shea and Benoit could not have been more different in some respects: Benoit was a Mainer to the core; Shea was born and raised in Carolina, the daughter of a PE instructor at NC State. Benoit was a multisport athlete who was only just coming around to full-time running; Shea had set the national 10-and-under boys and girls mile record at age 9, running 5:35. But as competitors, they were similar: neither would give an inch. They were both one-steppers: first one of them would nudge slightly ahead of the other, almost without thinking; the other would match her pace, then nudge a step in front, also without conscious thought. Though neither intended for each run to become a race, their natural competitiveness got the better of them, and racing each other every day in practice dulled the sharp edge they needed for the actual competitions.

Combs, to his credit, recognized Benoit's need for space and saw, perhaps, not just a runner but a homesick kid. On weekends when NC State didn't have a meet, he allowed Benoit to travel home to races in New England. Good for her soul, perhaps, but not for recovery. That winter, she came down with a fever, which she did her best to ignore and train through. She tried to race that spring, but the bug persisted. She undertook her last race—the big three meet against Duke and North Carolina—with a 104-degree fever and landed in the infirmary. Mono. The doctors told her in no uncertain terms she had to shut down for the rest of the year. She thought she'd been miserable when she couldn't get away from running; turns out, not being able to run at all was worse. She was alone, wrung out, and homesick. She finished out her classes as best she could and went back to Maine to recover.

If there'd ever been a doubt, Maine was home. She felt connected to the place in a way she'd never find anywhere else—and certainly not in Raleigh. She was back on her beaches, her roads, with her friends and family—most of whom weren't runners. If running was her escape from the world, she realized she needed the rest of her world to be an escape from the pressures of running. She'd come home thinking that she was through with North Carolina State. But as she ran that summer, a sense of unfinished business nagged at her—a sense of failure that didn't sit well—and she knew that the team had a shot at a national title if she returned. In the fall, she went back, and she and Shea continued to battle, though with slightly more productive results: at the AIAW national championships, Shea finished second and Benoit sixth, leading NC State to a second-place finish. It was enough of a redemption, evidence enough that she could handle the rigors of big-time college athletics, and she transferred back to Bowdoin, home for good.

During her time in Raleigh, she'd learned a great deal about what worked for her and what didn't: she learned that the team structure, for all its benefits, wasn't the best fit for someone as independent-minded as she. She felt she had a strong enough sense of herself that she didn't need a full-time coach and that she was best served training on her terms; she was too naturally competitive to work productively with most training partners. And yet, she loved being on a team, loved the camaraderie—something that had drawn her to sports like field hockey in the first place.

By 1979, Bowdoin had begun to catch up with Title IX and had a women's track team. Benoit happily joined, but she was training and competing on a different level from her teammates in Bowdoin's fledgling program, and both she and her coach, Frank Sebasteanski, recognized that she needed challenges that small-college New England track and field couldn't provide. She'd scarcely landed in Maine when she was invited to run a major road race in Bermuda in February, featuring many of the top runners in the country. With Sebasteanski's blessing, she flew to Bermuda on Friday and prepared for the 10K Saturday morning. The sun and warmth were almost intoxicating—she felt stronger than she ever had, liberated from North Carolina State, released from the cold of the Maine winter, physically and mentally primed for a great race. She took off with the lead pack, and soon found herself in complete control, dominating the race, beating, among others, Julie Shea. It was a breakthrough of sorts, evidence that, while others may be faster, she was stronger and could outlast them at longer distances.

She felt nearly invincible, only a nagging soreness in her left heel reminding her that she was still human. Sunday morning, she woke up early to do a long run with Ellison Goodall, a runner from Duke. As it happened, the Bermuda race weekend included a Sunday marathon; Goodall suggested they run part of it. Despite that little twinge in her heel, Benoit set off with the main pack of marathoners, thinking she'd drop out when she got tired. Instead, she started getting more and more competitive. Soon, dropping out was unthinkable, and she found herself passing most of the field. She finished second, in 2:50.

The next morning, her heel was on fire. She limped around her hotel room, packing for her flight. Back home, she was met at the airport by some of her Bowdoin teammates, and they all piled into a car to drive to an indoor meet at Bates, another small Maine college and one of Bowdoin's arch-rivals. Her heel was a mess—she was in no shape to race—but Benoit had promised her coach and teammates she'd be back in time to race against Bates, and a promise was a promise. And it was just a track race. Her time was awful, she got beat—an utterly improbable result for Benoit at that level of competition—and could barely walk after.

She took a few days off, and her heel felt no better. She drove down to Boston and met with an orthopedic surgeon. Dr. Robert Leach listened to her story—nearly thirty-five miles of racing in two and half days, all on a sore heel—then took her to see another patient of his, who had just undergone surgery on both Achilles tendons. This, he warned her, was her future if she didn't take better care of herself. She went back to Bowdoin under strict orders: no running for at least a few weeks. It was not an easy time. She was a senior in college, and though she entertained more traditional postgraduation plans—her stock answer to the inevitable question was that she was thinking of going into teaching or law after graduation—she really wanted just to run. Twitchy because she couldn't run, angry with herself for overdoing it, and upset that she'd let down her team, she watched track practice, she said, "like a prisoner from behind tall bars."

For a brief time, though, Dr. Leach scared her straight. She rested—longer than she felt she needed—but also mapped out a new goal. Her Bermuda marathon, ill-considered as it was, had earned her a qualifying time for the Boston Marathon. And if she discounted the fact that she was limping for days after, running 2:50 had felt surprisingly easy. How fast could she run a marathon if she trained properly, and if she didn't race a 10K the day before? Even as she asked herself the question, she knew she'd have to find out.

Coming off the heel injury, her buildup to Boston was shorter than ideal. In March, she jumped her mileage up to one hundred per week. She lengthened her long runs and started running them faster—not exactly taking it as easy as she'd promised she would. In the weeks leading up to Boston, the marathon loomed almost like a final exam, and she only hoped she was prepared. In Bermuda, she'd started off slow, just out for a training run; she worried now about how well she'd handle running hard—racing—from the gun. But marathon training felt great, and her body responded well to the miles and the harder tempo.

By 1979, Boston boasted more than eight thousand competitors, including five hundred women. Benoit wasn't a complete unknown—she had a win at Falmouth, an all-American XC season, and a "world best" road 10K (admittedly, a fairly soft record in an event that hadn't attracted much elite attention; the track 10K record was ninety seconds faster) to her name. But she was not among the favorites in the international field, and she had no team counting on her, no rivals to race, no real measuring stick for what a good time would be for her, and no expectations beyond running hard and seeing what the day would bring.

The day brought a cold drizzle. Runners packed the Hopkinton High School gymnasium, which soon smelled of damp clothes, sweat, and liniment. Outside, runners jogged, hopped, went through their warmups, and shivered. By the time runners stripped down to shorts and singlets before the start, their sweatpants were sodden sponges. Benoit felt almost detached from the experience, an observer; in high school and college, before races, she got nervous and lethargic—almost sleepy—but today she felt an excitement, a sense of fun: ahead of her lay a long and difficult challenge, the kind of test she loved.

The lead runners started at a furious pace, as if they were trying to shake off the cold. Benoit, though she started several rows back from the front, found herself caught in the rush and came through the first mile in 5:42, or 2:29 pace, already well back of the lead. She eased off some, while Australia's Elizabeth Hassell led through five miles in 28:00—2:26 pace, a full six minutes under Waitz's six-month-old world record. The prerace favorite, Boston's Patti Lyons, had also wisely stayed off the early pace; she went by Benoit around mile 5 and took the lead as Hassell faded. Benoit tried to relax into a six-minute-mile pace—comfortably hard, she felt. The miles clicked by, and suddenly, around two-thirds of the way through, Lyons was in sight. They ran shoulder to shoulder for a mile or so, then Benoit, as she had done on so many training runs, progressively ratcheted down the pace.

Soon Benoit had the lead. She drifted up the hills, asking one of the men running near her when Heartbreak Hill was coming up. "You just went by it," he huffed. She drove on toward the finish and turned her focus inward: more than race plans, she trusted her body and ran how she felt. With three miles to go, she found her concentration broken momentarily by one of the many drunken revelers who lined the route from Boston College to the finish: a Bowdoin alum popped out of the crowd and ran with her, holding a beer in one hand, clutching a Red Sox cap in the other. Hat or beer seemed to be the choice he was offering—chug the one or wear the other. She took the hat, several sizes too big, and put it on backwards. She'd worn a Bowdoin track singlet to declare her loyalty to school and home; the Red Sox cap meant Boston would claim her as its own. She broke the tape in 2:35.15, a course record by more than seven minutes and a new American record.

Shivering, soaked, blue-lipped, Benoit made her way to the elite women's locker room—a makeshift structure in the parking garage of the Prudential Building. She stood barefoot under a jury-rigged shower behind a tarp while reporters shouted questions at her. Benoit shouted her own: "Does anyone have an extra pair of sweatpants?" Her clothing had been soaked through before the start in Hopkinton; she just wanted something dry to change into—even a towel to dry off after her luke-warm trickle of a shower. Benoit tried to respond to the reporters, but exhausted and freezing and thrilled, she had a hard time forming coherent thoughts. "I just did what my legs told me to do," she said.[1] Over and over, she kept shouting, "I can't believe it. I can't believe I'm here!"

Benoit eventually found some dry clothes, escaped the reporters, and joined many of her fellow runners at the Eliot Lounge. Tommy Leonard worked the bar, and she didn't pay for a drink all night as the raucous crowd of weary marathoners shouted congratulations and shared their own war stories from the race. She danced and celebrated into the wee hours of the morning.

Sometime in the more civilized hours of the morning, the new American record holder drove back up to her parents' home for a restorative meal and a quick load of laundry. She then headed back to campus, where she walked into the dining hall and received a standing ovation from her schoolmates.

That week, she was guest of honor at a reception hosted by the president of Bowdoin College. Sometime during the reception came a congratulatory phone call from a fellow runner—President Jimmy Carter. It was a blur of "yes, Mr. President. Thank you, Mr. President." There was something about coming down to the White House for an official dinner. She must have said yes; in the days after, she honestly couldn't remember.

If her graduation plan had been to run as long as she could before settling into a real job, a wonderfully long road now stretched before her, wide open and full of possibility.

INTERLUDE

SANTA MONICA, CALIFORNIA, AUGUST 5, 1984, 7:50 A.M.: *It is a gray morning at Santa Monica City College's stadium, a somewhat grandiose name for the sets of bleachers that stand on either side of the maroon track encircling a patchy grass field. The bleachers are full, save for a section set aside for Olympic officials and dignitaries, which is largely empty. Across the street, more spectators pack the top two levels of a parking garage. Flag bearers in white skirts and coats, one for each of the twenty-seven countries represented in the first women's Olympic marathon, line up on the track, facing the infield. Fifty athletes mill about behind them. A halfhearted breeze ripples the flags.*

A celebratory, excited buzz runs through the crowd. "For the first time in history," a voice says over the tinny loudspeaker, "We have an Olympic marathon for women." The announcement is repeated in French. The speaker introduces LAOOC Athletics Commissioner Bill Bedford. Halfway through the commissioner's remarks, the mic cuts out. Shouts of "We can't hear you!" and "Get closer to the mic!" are much more audible than whatever is being said over the PA.

Waitz leans over to tie her shoes, stands up, then leans over to check them again. She turns to one of her teammates to ask about the start—which way they go, how many laps, where they exit the stadium. Her teammates gesture: around once, twice, then out that gate, they say, pointing diagonally across the field. She nods; it isn't new information—she just needs reassurance.

Several countries down to her right, Benoit stands, arms crossed, holding a white painter's cap in her right hand. She seems to be half listening to the announcements, half to something her teammate, Julie Isphording, is saying to her, without really focusing on either. Her face has a look of part boredom, part impatience.

The flag bearers turn to face down the track, and the athletes line up in single file behind their respective flags for a short parade around the track—an opening ceremony in miniature. The crowd's buzz grows as the marathoners are introduced. Before the American contingent—they will be introduced last—Waitz receives the loudest cheer, to which she gives a tentative, almost apologetic wave. Her hair is pulled back and twisted into a bun to keep it off her neck. Her face is drawn, brow furrowed, jaw tight. Her eyes dart around

73

the stadium. She licks her lips, then blinks, as if trying to refocus, and chews on her lower lip.

When Benoit is introduced, the crowd erupts; she looks into the stands and waves with both arms over her head. With her short, floppy shock of dark hair and exuberant smile, she appears much younger than her twenty-seven years. Then the smile disappears, her face again becomes a still mask, and she stares straight ahead at nothing.

The procession makes a three-quarters circuit of the track to the starting line for the marathon. In the remaining minutes before the race, some athletes jog or stride out a little more briskly, as if trying to wake up their legs. Some just walk around, seemingly aimless. Many stop by the water coolers—taking a few sips, dumping cupsful on their heads, squeezing sponges of ice water into their hair and down their necks. The sun has yet to show, but when it burns through—and they are certain that it will—the heat will radiate not only from above but off the gray concrete underfoot. Most major marathons are run either in early spring or late fall; all year long, the competitors have imagined the heat of the Los Angeles summer, practiced for it, tried to adapt their bodies to it.

In these moments before the race, there is a lull, an ordinariness to their preparations. Each marathon is the same in some ways, and they've all been through it. There's a knowing, fatalistic dread—and a fear of the great unknown. They know what they're in for, what they are asking of their bodies, but at the same time, they can't be sure how their bodies will respond—what parts of their legs will hurt the worst, when the pain will start, and what kind it will be: the good hurt that comes with running fast and pushing your body to a place it has never been, or the discouraging pain and anguish of just not having what's needed on the day. There is an impatience to get going and get it over with, to put all the nervousness and anxiety to rest—and a natural desire to delay the inevitable as long as possible. A few athletes gather and chatter nervously, but for the most part, runners barely acknowledge one another—they nod briefly or avoid eye contact altogether. They will start together, they will run the same race, but the marathon is a place each of them goes to alone.

There is also a sense of the extraordinary history of the moment and the role they will play in it. Of the fifty, the majority know they have essentially no chance of standing on the podium after the race, but all of them understand *that there are bigger stakes. It has long been the unwritten rule for women's marathoning that, barring the risk of real injury, you finish the race—lest you give ammunition to those who would claim women are too delicate for marathoning. In this race above all, they carry the torch for women's running: a strong showing will further their cause; a poor showing overall could set back the sport for a generation.*

Waitz bends down slowly to tie her shoe again. She jogs stiffly around the curve of the track and back. Benoit stretches lightly, bouncing her fingers down to her toes.

"Two minutes! Deux minutes!" calls the starter. The fifty runners will be placed in four rows across the width of the track. It will be a walk-up start: they stand five meters behind the actual starting line until the starter calls them up to the mark.

Slowly, athletes walk or jog over to the line. Many stop at the water cooler one last time. Benoit and Waitz are among the last to make their way over. Benoit seeks out Waitz, shakes her hand, and wishes her luck. This will be the tenth time they have raced each other; Waitz has beaten Benoit nine times straight.

Benoit is in the front row, one of the first to be placed in her starting position. She exchanges a few pleasantries with the runners around her, but she seems to be trying to avoid them. She stares at the sky, into the crowd, at the ground, anywhere. Waitz stands off to the side as long as she can before lining up. She is in the second row, just behind and to the left of Benoit. It takes nearly five minutes to get the field lined up properly. Benoit fidgets with her hat—at the moment, she is wearing it backwards—her hair, number, uniform shorts. Waitz rocks slowly side to side, one foot to the other. The Finnish athlete next to her yawns. Waitz licks her lips. Mostly she stares straight ahead, but still her eyes dart around the track occasionally.

"On your marks!" yells the starter. There is a moment of hesitation among the field. Benoit stares down at her shoes and walks slowly up to the line.

Chapter 6

A World of (Limited) Opportunity

Waitz and Benoit, 1978–1979

After breaking the marathon world record, Waitz returned to Norway, still telling herself she was retired—no longer a competitive athlete, but just a runner, a teacher who ran every day. The media in New York had made a big deal about the record in 1978, but she didn't think much of it. She'd never cared much about times. Winning was the thing, and besides, the marathon was just a road race. Track was real running—it had the most important events, like the Olympics, and the best runners.

So, in December of 1978, when the sponsors of a New Year's Eve five-mile race in California called to see if she'd fly over to run it, she told them no. I'm retired; we're going on vacation, she said.

All expenses paid, they said.

Vacation plans took precedence, she said. She and Jack had planned a ski vacation with her entire family; it was hard enough getting the whole family together, and she wasn't going to cut out early for a race.

The sponsors called back: How about you do your vacation over here? We'll fly everyone over, get you a house—all expenses paid. Stay as long as you'd like, they said.

Hmm, she said.

That December, Jack, Grete's brothers, and her parents spent their vacation in the hills outside Palo Alto instead of in the Norwegian countryside. The New Year's Eve race was something new for Waitz. Typically, when she ran, she focused so intently that she hardly talked to Jack when he ran with her. Here, people in a race—a race!—were happily chatting with friends and people they'd just met; some were singing. Many in the crowd, and even some of the runners, were well into their New Year's celebration. Some of the top runners joined the party: they ran hard and ran to win, but afterward, happily mingled into the crowd. It seemed, culturally, a world apart from the sport of track.

Road races of all sizes and distances had sprouted across the United States. Some were small community affairs, some had bigger aspirations, and their organizers needed stars to generate headlines and attract crowds. Sponsors were still pouring money into races, and organizers could pay stars very (perhaps overly) generous travel expenses and honoraria for speaking at prerace events. Waitz found it all a little amusing. She still didn't think the marathon record was a major accomplishment—"I think she still would have retired," said Jack, "if not for that trip to California"—but it opened a whole new world to her.

In the United States, she was a star—but being a star on the road race circuit was different from what she experienced in Norway, where she faced incessant scrutiny and felt the oppressive pressure of her homeland's collective national expectations. In the United States, she and Jack could travel to a different race every weekend, all expenses quite generously paid, but remain largely anonymous outside of the races and the running expos. At races she was a public figure, quite literally on stage as a featured speaker or guest clinician, but the publicity was on her terms: after speaking and racing, she could retreat into the quiet, private life she built around herself—simple, orderly, organized around running, teaching, and Jack. While still teaching full time through the spring of 1979, she raced forty-two times in the year following "retirement."

In essence, the races were all trying to emulate the New York City Marathon. By 1979, it was the biggest marathon in the world, with more than eleven thousand starters. The New York City Marathon was the most exciting and important race outside the Olympics—at least to hear Lebow tell it. It was certainly the most important thing in his life, "the most important thing in the world," he declared, with at least some degree of seriousness. His excitement and energy were infectious, and his vision grand, but he didn't have time for the mundanities of life. He was the head of the New York Road Runners, which did more than just put on the marathon, but the marathon—the idea of it, of thousands of runners, of an entire city cheering them on—took over his life, impelled him and thrilled him. His beard grew scraggly and overgrown; it overwhelmed his once carefully groomed moustache. He eschewed his fashionable attire for a pair of old running pants and a race T-shirt, with a running cap perpetually askew on his head. His clothes hung off his body—he'd forget to eat if he didn't have a meeting over lunch or dinner to remind him. He hadn't scheduled a board meeting in who knows how long, and his record keeping was such that his auditors gave up, citing "inadequacies in the accounting records."[1] He'd rather spend hours with his volunteers, organizing race packets, or meeting with groups of runners, especially the regular, slow plodders like him. Even seemingly important details escaped his attention: in 1978, minutes before a press conference at City Hall, he hunched over his massive, display-sized map of the marathon course with a bottle of Wite-Out and a Sharpie, changing the date from October 3 to October 2, the year from 1977 to 1978.[2]

One thing remained unchanged: the sharp competitive streak that drove him. He wanted not only to have the biggest race, but the biggest stories—even absurd ones, such as his claim to have erected "the world's longest urinal" to accommodate the thousands of overly-hydrated, and still mostly male, marathoners who converged on the starting area in Staten Island.

Lebow could not have asked for a better story in 1978 than Waitz, the unknown record breaker. In the run-up to the 1979 New York City Marathon, she would not be so anonymous: a Norwegian television station sent a camera crew to trail her around New York, documenting her preparation for the marathon. And Lebow featured her in all the prerace press releases and put her front and center at press conferences. Though she was perfectly fluent in English, she spoke haltingly, carefully, guarded as always. But she was as patient and kind with members of the media as she was with fans and fellow runners, even the less-informed ones: Had she ever run the marathon, asked one reporter before the 1979 marathon. Yes—last year, she replied, with the gentle tone of the elementary school teacher she was. A better-informed reporter jumped in: Did she expect another record? Records talk was for others, she said. She'd be happy if she ran 2:35. She raced to win.

Chaos erupted at the start when thousands of runners surged off the line eight seconds before the gun went off, engulfing the field of elites; still, Waitz took four and a half minutes off her world record, running 2:27.33. She came through the halfway point just four seconds faster than she had the year before, in 1:14.51; she ran the second half in 1:12, which smashed the world record for the half-marathon by ninety seconds. Roberto Quercetani of *Track & Field News*, among the most widely respected track journalists at the time, called it "the most advanced achievement" in women's running and wrote that Waitz had "gone further than any other woman athlete" with her marathon record. The *New York Times* published an editorial, "2:27.33—and waiting," which noted that her time would have won the 1970 New York Marathon outright and would have beaten half of the male gold medalists in Olympic history. It held up her performance as incontrovertible evidence that the women's marathon belonged in the Olympics.

Waitz was less impressed. She was not a marathon rookie in 1979. She understood the race better, knew the New York course, and she was better trained for it—of course she should run faster. She didn't want a record, she wanted competition. "I was a little disappointed that Joan Benoit and the other girls didn't show up here," she said. "It is not good to be afraid of me. You can't be a better runner unless you are willing to be beaten. That's how I feel. If I am beaten, I say, 'OK, you're better than I am, but next time I try to beat you.'" More than winning, she craved the test that racing was supposed to offer. She needed a worthy challenger. And she had marked Benoit as the one.

***

Benoit had spent the months between her Boston Marathon win and the 1979 New York City Marathon feeling less like a worthy challenger and more like someone just trying to keep her head above water. In the days and weeks after winning Boston, her mailbox overflowed with congratulatory letters and requests. She fielded hundreds of calls—it seemed every running brand, road race, charity, and track club suddenly wanted a piece of her. Talent scouts from Hollywood sought her out. And final exams loomed. She'd been raised to be polite and wanted to be thought of as someone who was kind and giving of her time, but she also needed privacy and solitude. Benoit had always dreamed of the Olympics, of being among the best in the world. She'd recognized the obstacles she'd face and steeled herself to overcome them. Now, she confronted a different sort of obstacle. Maine and Bowdoin, remote and protective, had been a barrier between her and the voracious sporting-media-marketing industry that had grown up around running, but the barrier was crumbling. The phone calls were incessant, and the volume of mail overwhelmed her. For a moment, as she struggled to get ready for exams, she was ready to quit; she could imagine herself quite happily teaching or going off to law school and becoming an environmental lawyer, working to protect her beloved Maine coast.

But as overwhelming as the attention had been, she'd never let others dictate when she'd give up the sport, and she had unfinished business— she knew she could run much faster than she had at Boston. If she were going to throw herself completely into running, she'd have to work hard to manage her public commitments, to be polite and try to answer all the requests. She'd have to accept the trade-off—giving up some privacy—for pursuing her dream.

The tradeoff had its benefits. Pam Magee, head of marketing for Nike's women's division, had planned a racing trip to New Zealand and Australia for January and February, and Benoit jumped at the chance. Nike could pay "legitimate" travel expenses—essentially, it would pay for her room, board, travel, and incidentals, and she'd race, train, and be half a world away preparing, she hoped, for the Olympic trials that summer— in the 1500m, still the longest Olympic event for women. The trip was a rare opportunity. Running as a full-time career didn't really exist, especially for women. Bill Rodgers, who had just won back-to-back Boston and New York titles in 1978 and 1979, introduced a clothing line and opened a running store to capitalize on his running fame; Frank Shorter had his law degree. At major races, both received sizable under-the-table payments—in addition to aboveboard travel expenses or speaker's fees— something that often went only to the men.

Though her class had graduated in June, Benoit would graduate in December 1979—Bowdoin required that seniors spend their last two semesters on campus before graduating, and she'd spent the previous fall at North Carolina State, so she had a makeup semester to go. When Waitz won New York and called out Benoit by name, Benoit had final exams staring her down in six weeks, then graduation, then she'd be leaving her cocooned existence at Bowdoin—a place she'd come to think of as home. Then, just after the New Year, she'd *really* be leaving home and heading to New Zealand on the Nike-sponsored trip. Her life, her world, was in transition; her time and energy were spent getting ready for what came next and soaking up as much as she could of what she was leaving behind. She did plenty of running on her beloved back roads and trails in Maine, and hopped in some shorter races around New England, but a big-time marathon like New York was not a priority that fall.

In New Zealand, Benoit toured the islands and ran some low-key track races—even recording her best mile ever, 4:45, which went unnoticed because the young American phenom, Mary Slaney, finished over one hundred meters ahead, running 4:21.66 for a new world record. But that was all a buildup to her next marathon. On February 3 in Auckland, Benoit made her answer to Waitz: she ran 2:31—the second fastest time in history for women and four minutes faster than her American record from Boston the previous April. And she did it in nearly unbearable conditions: high humidity, temperatures in the 80s without much shade anywhere on the course; the men's winner, Dick Quax, was more than two minutes off his best. Casual observers of the sport missed the significance of the race, and it made barely a ripple in the media, but Benoit knew what she'd done.

From the beginning of her career, Benoit made it a habit to view more accomplished runners as markers, as her own private challenge. She studied their style, followed their results, used them to motivate her. In high school, she looked to older runners in the state. In her first year in college, she measured herself against runners such as Charlotte Lettis, whom Benoit considered a legend and nearly unbeatable; Benoit still counts a 1976 mile against Lettis as one of her greatest races: she lost, but broke 5:00 for the first time. She needed to test herself against the best, and although she was much more guarded than Waitz about saying so, Waitz was her ultimate test in the marathon.

If the two were ever to challenge each other in a high-stakes race, it didn't appear the Olympics would be the place. Waitz had already decided not to bother with the 1980 Games, convinced (correctly, as it turned out) that the field would be tilted even more drastically in favor of the dopers. Benoit knew her 1500m speed was no match for the world's best—she couldn't even hope to make the American team in so short a race. And in the end, it wouldn't matter how fast she ran the 1500: the United States boycotted the 1980 Moscow Olympics to protest the Soviet Union's invasion of Afghanistan. Although each may have wondered if there would ever be an Olympic marathon for women, that prospect seemed so dim as to be something best left aside for the time being.

But Switzer, Hansen, and a host of others had just launched what would be a frantic, yearlong race against the IOC's decision-making calendar to add the marathon by 1984. The course ahead was littered with obstacles: global geopolitics; the IOC's slow-moving inner workings; the intransigence of the Los Angeles Olympic Organizing Committee; and the vestigial ignorance of the sport's decision makers. But they were marathoners. Persistence in overcoming obstacles was a prerequisite; setbacks, dejection, and suffering in pursuit of a goal were all old friends.

CHAPTER 7

Victory

Hansen, Switzer, and the Alphabet Soup, 1980–1981

THE FULL PROCESS FOR ADDING NEW OLYMPIC EVENTS WAS SUPPOSED to go something like this: representatives from a national governing body (in the case of the United States, the AAU) would propose to the IAAF, the international governing body for athletics, that a new event be included. The proposal would be taken up by the IAAF Technical Commission (IAAFTC), which would then make its own recommendation, which would then be approved by the IAAF Executive Committee, then voted on by all the IAAF delegates. The president of the IAAF would then take the proposal to the IOC Program Commission (IOCPC), which would take its recommendation (yea or nay) to the IOC Executive Committee. The Executive Committee would have its own vote but would rarely contravene the recommendation of the Program Commission. The Executive Committee would then forward the proposal, with its recommendation, to the full body of the IOC for final approval. To give host cities ample time to plan, the full Olympic program was supposed to be finalized four years in advance, at the quadrennial Congress of the IOC, which typically coincided with the Summer Games. In the case of the women's marathon, then, if the marathon were to be included in the 1984 Los Angeles Olympics, approval would have to come at the Moscow Congress in 1980.

In 1977, Hansen and Nina Kuscsik persuaded the AAU to pass a resolution in support of a women's Olympic marathon, and to make a proposal to the IAAF to add the women's marathon to the Olympics. Ollan Cassell, director of the AAU and an IAAF vice president, said, "There's no question that the IAAF supports longer races for women . . . [we] pushed for it and tried to get it on the Olympic schedule."[1] How hard they pushed, Hansen had no way of knowing—their proposal simply disappeared somewhere in the sporting bureaucracy. There may have been valid reasons why the marathon proposal went nowhere: IOC rules required that an event be contested in twenty-five nations—which, in practice, was interpreted to mean it was part of the national championship program in those nations. Further, the IOC required that the event be part of the sport's global championships, but in the case of track and field, there was no world championship meet until 1983; the Olympics had always served as the world track and field championship. So, the IOC then looked to continental championships, such as the European or Asian Championships, or even Britain's colonial vestige, the Commonwealth Games.

The women's marathon met none of these requirements, but Hansen sensed that something else was holding back progress. Both IAAF and IOC leadership seemed dismissive of women's marathoning. Some members of the IAAF and the IOC still held long-disproved notions that women couldn't (or shouldn't) run the marathon for health reasons or clung to the belief that the marathon was, with its echoes of mythic heroism, the ultimate expression of the manly virtues of strength, will, and fortitude—and so, they felt, it should remain. Further, the IOC continuously worried about over-bloating the Games, and the marathon seemed an easy place to draw the line. All she knew for sure was that working through the committee structure and hoping the men in charge saw the light wasn't enough. Her patience ran low. She needed to bring more pressure.

She had no seat at the table, but she began to build a strong network of allies, and in 1979, they took the step of creating an official organization, the International Runners Committee. Among the founding members were Hansen; Jeff Darman, president of the Road Runners Club of America; Joe Henderson, an influential running writer, and editor of *Runner's World*; New Zealander Arthur Lydiard, godfather of distance coaches; and runners from around the globe, including Eleonora de Mendonça of Brazil, Sarolta Monspart of Hungary, Lynn Billington of England, and Michiko "Miki" Gorman of Japan. They had worldwide representation. They had influential members of the running world. They lacked money—until a rapidly ascending running shoe company named Blue Ribbon Sports, which happened to employ Hansen's husband, Tom Sturak, offered support. The Blue Ribbon founders viewed themselves as outsiders and rebels, and they didn't think twice about aiming their company's guerrilla tactics at the biggest figures in the running world, whether that meant rival companies such as Adidas, or powerful institutions such as the IOC. Blue Ribbon was beginning to make a name for itself—though the name was changing. By the time Blue Ribbon signed on to back the IRC, the company's name was Nike.

Nike was relentless, moved fast, and played to win. When Pam Magee, who oversaw women's running for Nike, asked Sturak and Hansen a simple question—"What would it take to get the job done?"—she mostly meant, how quickly can we make this happen? Nike had a "do things first, ask permission later" kind of culture; eventually, Magee would have to run her offer by her boss, Nike marketing chief Rob Strasser, but she was certain he'd greenlight it: it had a whiff of rebelliousness, and it promised a fight, which Strasser would love.

On the spot, Hansen didn't quite know how to answer, but eventually they settled on a plan: Nike would run ads in all the major running publications in support of the marathon. It would create a survey—really a bit of push-polling—to ascertain support for the women's marathon. And it would fund the IRC. By the end of 1979, the IRC was mailing out a quarterly newsletter and sending representatives to all major meetings of the international governing bodies to lobby major delegates and representatives in person. Members of the IRC courted allies and sources—moles, some would say—on important committees at the IAAF and IOC, to keep them informed and press their case. Nike also committed—or threatened—to help put on women's distance races (5000m, 10,000m, and marathon) at any "substitute Games" in 1980.

Hansen and her allies weren't the only group lobbying the IAAF and IOC. Switzer's Avon International Running Circuit had grown faster than even her most optimistic projections. Though the original circuit was merely six cities in the United States, all with major Avon offices, soon Switzer found herself consulting on races around the globe, as Avon's international divisions clamored for races of their own. She helped with races in Belgium, Japan, Thailand, and Malaysia; strategically, she pushed for races in Germany, France, and Spain, which had key figures in the IAAF and IOC who could help swing a vote for the marathon. She helped put on a race in Brazil—and positively gushed in her praise for the head of Brazil's Athletics Federation, who could influence a raft of South American votes in the IAAF and IOC.

Avon was a global behemoth; Nike was an up-and-comer with growing influence in the running world. They were soon joined by another major international corporation: Japanese cosmetics giant Shiseido. It essentially copied every detail of Switzer's operation to put on what it called the Tokyo International Marathon in November 1979. And Shiseido invited Adriaan Paulen, the head of the IAAF, and Marea Hartman, chair of the IAAF's Women's Committee, to attend. Paulen not only attended, but he surprised the crowd with a brief speech, in which he stated, "The days are long since past when doctors and athletic leaders were worried about the medical advisability of women athletes competing [in the marathon]. . . . Thanks to such races as the Waldniel Marathon . . . and this inaugural race in Tokyo, the great impetus of women's long-distance running continues, and the movement will gather more and more support."

Weeks after the Tokyo Marathon, John Holt, the IAAF general secretary, wrote to Arpad Csanadi, the head of the IOC's Program Commission, with "a very strong request to have the women's Marathon in 1984." Csanadi, from Hungary, cut an imposing figure: an ex-footballer with a powerful build and sharp eyes set under a shining bald head that called to mind a bird of prey. He looked the part of a dour Communist apparatchik, but he was amiable and politically deft. Because the Soviet bloc nations had yet to produce any competitive women's marathoners, Csanadi could expect significant pressure from political allies to keep the marathon out. He also had great personal respect for precedent and was inclined to ensure that the marathon jumped through all the proper hoops before inclusion in the Olympics. But he was also of an open mind and finely attuned to shifting winds. Holt cited the Avon International Marathon in Waldniel and Shiseido's Tokyo Marathon as evidence of dramatic growth and noted that "the number of finishers [as a percentage of entrants] is always much higher than the men." He concluded by writing, "There is no doubt that the Los Angeles Organizing Committee (LAOOC) would welcome this event, as confirmed by Mr. [Dick] Sargent [chief of operations for the LAOOC] at meetings held with him recently in Monte Carlo."[2]

He may have overstated the LAOOC's support. After meeting with Sargent in Monte Carlo, Holt followed up, reiterating the IAAF's interest in a women's Olympic marathon. Sargent responded, "As stated formally to the Program Committee of the IOC, the LAOOC would like to be in the position to respond favorably to all federations with their requests for expansion of their sport in the 1984 Olympics. However, any expansion in the number of athletes participating . . . would be an extreme burden on us. . . . No sport is being singled out, we are simply requesting all sports to assist us by resisting expansion. I trust that you will understand our position."[3] In a letter to the U.S. governing body for track and field (what had been the AAU was now TAC, The Athletics Congress), Sargent wrote, "We have advised Dr. Csanadi that the LAOOC certainly is not against women competing in the marathon in the 1984 Olympic Games, and that a possible reduction in some other area would be a means to accomplish this so as not to increase the overall number of athletes participating. We thank you," he added, "for your offer to assist."[4] Harry Usher, the vice president of the LAOOC, said that the number of athletes at the Games, "is getting out of hand." He complained that there was "a lot of pressure to put in more events for women, to put in a women's marathon," which didn't just mean more athletes—"you increase the trainers and other people that must accompany them," he added.

***

Though the LAOOC technically had no formal say in the program for the Games, it did, as Holt explained to Switzer on a run in the summer of 1979, "have a lot of leverage." They had caught the IOC in a moment of extreme weakness. To the spectating public, the Olympics retained much of its mythic grandeur; to athletes, the Olympics still represented the pinnacle of sport. But with each passing Olympiad, the reputation of the Games took another hit. The 1968 Mexico City Games were marred by a government-initiated massacre of peaceful anti-Olympics protesters, followed by violent house-to-house fighting and mass arrests, just days before the opening ceremonies. The Munich Games were disrupted by the hostage taking and murder of eleven Israeli athletes and coaches. Twenty-nine African countries boycotted Montreal in 1976, and because of a venue construction spree that went massively over budget, the city was left with a $1.5 billion debt.

LA had lost Olympic bids for 1976 and 1980; rumor had it that, in 1974, just before the vote on the 1980 Games, President Nixon tried to swing votes away from Moscow and to LA by offering IOC members bribes of, among other things, moon rocks. But in 1978, as the IOC prepared to vote on the host city for the 1984 Olympics, Los Angeles must have felt good about its odds: it was the only city left with a bid. After the Montreal debacle, several cities withdrew their preliminary bids, and LA's lone remaining rival, Tehran, pulled out as the government of Shah Mohammed Reza Pahlavi began to crumble and calls for revolution escalated. Despite there being no other option, three IOC members voted against LA, and six abstained.

At last, Los Angeles had "won." But Mayor Tom Bradley turned down the IOC. According to Olympic rules, the IOC signs an agreement with the government of the host city, stipulating that the city, not the IOC, assumes all financial obligations for the Games. After witnessing the Montreal debacle, Bradley refused to sign. The IOC had no plan B, no other potential host cities, and no money to put on the Games themselves—the IOC had had to borrow money just to get through the years between the 1968 and 1972 Olympics.[5] Members of the Los Angeles Olympic Organizing Committee offered to negotiate with the IOC as a separate, private entity—to operate as the Olympic host in place of the City of Los Angeles—and although the members of the LAOOC were wealthy, they too refused to assume exposure to a potential Montreal-sized debt. The United States Olympic Committee stepped in to guarantee any debts, and at last, the Games could go on: the LAOOC had sole responsibility for organizing the Games, and the City of Los Angeles was indemnified. The signing ceremony took place at the White House, though President Carter conspicuously avoided the ceremony.

The games before the Games—the yearslong push to prepare a city to host the largest sports festival ever staged—could begin. The LAOOC had financial guarantees from the USOC, ready access to the sporting infrastructure of Southern California—public beaches and marinas, venues like the LA Coliseum, the fabulous Forum in Inglewood, the Rose Bowl, Dodger Stadium, Santa Anita racetrack, several city and county convention centers and smaller arenas, and the facilities of dozens of area colleges and universities—as well as proximity to first-rate airports and the extensive freeway system, and all the benefits that the entertainment capital of the world could offer.

"We are treating this as a business," declared Usher.[6] And if the business had an operating principle, it could be summed up in a single word: No. Peter Ueberroth, the tanned, fresh-faced president of the LAOOC, had been a travel executive. He had a bit of a striver in him, and liked to say he'd built, from nothing, the largest travel services firm in the world outside of American Express. When he was vaulted from near-anonymity to the head of the LAOOC, he tried to project an air of California cool. It covered the mind of an autocrat. "Control is his life force," said Patty Patalano, who worked for Ueberroth both at his travel agency and during the Games.[7] Authority, Ueberroth was fond of saying, is 20 percent given and 80 percent taken. "Peter is very high on a desire to . . . be the guy calling the shots," declared LAOOC board member Lee Aurich.[8] According to Kenneth Reich, a journalist for the *Los Angeles Times* who covered the LAOOC extensively, Ueberroth insisted that he or Usher personally sign off on any expenditure more than $1,000—even if the budget had already approved it.[9] He liked to try to tell the director of food services exactly what could and couldn't be served. And yet, "If anything was extremely well planned and premeditated and calculated to the nth degree, that is certainly news to me," said Patalano. "We really made up an awful lot as we went along," said Usher. The organizing committee, he said, was "a crisis management environment."[10] Planning, said Michael O'Hara, another LAOOC board member, "was often seat of the pants."[11]

"Peter loves to say no," said Conrad Freund, LAOOC treasurer. Further, declared Reich, "He would say something one day and flatly deny it the next, sometimes abusively. It was hard to discern when he was telling the truth . . . he had an unpleasant habit of flatly denying things that turned out to be true." To be fair, that is part of the job of a person in Ueberroth's position when addressing the media. But if, to outside appearances, the LAOOC suffered from a lack of long-term planning, and its president had a casual relationship with the truth and a near-pathological need for control, it's little wonder that John Holt and the rest of the IAAF leadership wondered whether the American house was in order.

In response to the knee-jerk no from Sargent, Holt helped bring political pressure: the Board of Supervisors of Los Angeles County (which includes not only the city of LA but other large cities such as Pasadena, Compton, Long Beach, and Beverly Hills) passed a resolution requesting that the women's marathon be added to the Olympics. He enlisted the support of Sheldon "Shelly" Saltman, president of 20th Century Fox Sports and a major player in Los Angeles sports, promotion, and media. And he had Jon Wigley, IAAF Communications Officer, write to Jackie Hansen to suggest that "if the IRC wants to act as a positive pressure group, it might like to start in its own backyard with the Los Angeles Organizing Committee."[12]

The IRC had cultivated strategic relationships with a number of officials in the USOC and The Athletics Congress, the organization that had replaced the AAU as the national governing body of track and field. Among them was Bob Giegengack, the energetic, excitable, chain-smoking coach of the Yale track and field program, who spoke "like Elmer Fudd with a Brooklyn accent," according to fellow Yale track coach Mark Young. Calvin Hill, who starred on Yale's football team (before going on to the NFL) and did some track on the side, once allowed that he'd have been much better at track if he'd practiced more—but, he said, "I just liked to listen to Giegs talk."

Giegengack was on the USOC and the IAAF technical committee, and he'd become one of the staunchest advocates for the women's marathon. He kept the IRC informed on where things stood with various committees; the IRC, in turn, kept Giegs up to date on where they encountered resistance. After Sargent's blanket no, Giegs went on the attack. After an LAOOC board meeting, Giegengack cornered Sargent and demanded to know their plan for the women's marathon; he was told, in essence, to be patient. In April, during a presentation by Harry Usher at a USOC meeting in Colorado Springs, Giegengack put the USOC on record demanding that the LAOOC support for the marathon. Giegengack took the floor, and said, in regard to the LAOOC's position on the women's marathon, "The Athletics Congress has been let down . . . the United States Olympic Committee . . . has been injured." Nearly shouting, he added, "I therefore would like to put a resolution to this body, to the effect that we instruct the Los Angeles Organizing/ Olympic Committee to enthusiastically support the addition of the Women's Marathon, and to so express our enthusiasm to the Secretary of the IAAF." To a chorus of shouted "Seconded!" and raucous applause, his resolution was approved.

Don Miller, the head of the USOC, became personally involved. He had brokered the deal between the LAOOC and the IOC, and he had guaranteed the LAOOC's debts. On July 3, just two weeks before the beginning of the IOC meetings in Moscow, at which LAOOC was to make a formal presentation to the IOC, Miller wrote to Ueberroth, reiterating the demand in Giegengack's resolution, and asking for assurances that the LAOOC would support the marathon in their meetings in Moscow. "Please be assured," wrote Ueberroth, "that we will"—he underlined we will—"enthusiastically support the addition of this event."

The growing popularity of women's marathoning—with athletes and sponsors—brought its own kind of pressure, just as Switzer had foreseen. In April 1980, Adriaan Paulen made his case to Csanadi and the program committee at the IOC's headquarters in Lausanne. The IAAF, said Paulen almost apologetically, "had been overtaken by the situation."

The growth of women's marathoning had been so fast, he said, that "If the event had to wait until 1988 for inclusion . . . a great opportunity may be missed." He stressed that an unofficial world championship, Shiseido's Tokyo International Marathon, had already occurred—with the tacit approval of the IAAF leadership. Csanadi countered, saying the marathon still had not been contested in any continental championships. "The Olympic Games," he said, "could not be used in this regard as an experimental field." Csanadi noted that Paulen "was asking for it to be made an exceptional case," to which Paulen could only agree. It would be, said Csanadi, "a dangerous precedent."

Other members had reservations regarding the medical effects on women. Konstantin Andrianov, a member from the Soviet Union, argued that "inclusion of the women's marathon would be a grave step, as women would undergo great pressure." The committee recommended "not to accept the women's marathon at this stage, pending receipt of medical information." This, Paulen had been expecting, and he had a counter prepared: At an Avon-sponsored reception during the IAAF meetings in March, Switzer had distributed a report that contained the latest medical research on the salutary effects of marathoning on women. He had a statement from the American College of Sports Medicine from late 1979 stating that women should not be denied the opportunity to run for medical reasons. But the Program Commission would want to hear from FIMS, the Federation Internationale de Medecine Sportive—the medical arm of the IOC. By mid-June, Paulen forwarded a letter to the IOC from the chair of FIMS's scientific commission, which read, "There is ample evidence that women have excellent pre-conditions for endurance exercise. . . . Long distance running is not harmful for women if proper training is provided."[13]

In July, at the IOC Congress held in Moscow in conjunction with the 1980 Olympics, Ueberroth urged (enthusiastically, one hopes) "the IOC to reach an affirmative determination on this matter [of the marathon] as soon as possible." But the IOC membership probably wasn't in the mood to listen to American entreaties on any subject: in response to the Soviet invasion of Afghanistan in December 1979, the Carter administration began discussing a boycott of the 1980 Moscow Games unless the Soviets withdrew. Lord Killanin, head of the IOC, met with both Carter and Soviet leader Leonid Brezhnev—to no avail. Carter suggested moving the Games to Greece, an impossible ask just six months before the Games. Peter Ueberroth, believing that he could broker a deal, offered to meet one-on-one with Brezhnev; the Soviets politely declined. In the end, the United States was joined by over sixty countries in boycotting the Olympics. IOC members were furious, believing that the U.S. government had pressured its allies into boycotting. The Moscow meetings were held under an anti-American pall, and most IOC members, especially those from the Eastern Bloc, were in no mood to add a history-making event to an American Olympics.

Nonetheless, the IAAF gamely made its pitch for the marathon at the IOC's Executive Board meetings: Paulen once again stressed that an unofficial world championship had already happened in 1979 and added that "the development [of the marathon in international sport] could only be handled if the event was fully accepted, or control might be lost." He brought up the medical report from FIMS, which Csanadi acknowledged as "positive." Fred Holder, the IAAF treasurer, stressed that "development [of women's marathoning] could not be stopped." Csanadi still felt that 1984 was "too soon." Paulen pleaded; the IAAF delegation was thanked for its presentation and escorted from the room.

"There was a good case for the marathon," stated IOC's outgoing president, Britain's Lord Killanin.

Csanadi recommended "no decision at this time . . . pending . . . the experience of the championships in 1982 and 1983."

"Athletics," responded Killanin, was "the most important sport in the Games."

Executive Committee meetings often feel precisely choreographed, with IOC members speaking in carefully coded terms, dancing around direct confrontation; if Killanin's response seemed opaque, it was, in essence, a reemphasis of Paulen's main argument—itself a clever nod to the history of Olympic track and field and designed to prey on the IOC's existential insecurities. No body of international law assigned to the IOC in perpetuity the exclusive right to stage the world's foremost athletic spectacle. The Olympics are the Olympics only because throughout history, the IOC was able to choke off or co-opt potential rivals before they could grow. Alice Milliat and her Women's Olympics had threatened the IOC's hegemony in the 1920s, and that threat led to the first women's track and field events in the Olympics. Paulen drew a direct line from Milliat to the success of women's marathoning.

Although no one had explicitly threatened to create a separate Olympic-type event with the women's marathon, the possibility existed that if the IOC didn't act quickly, the marathon would become something like soccer, which was so big that it wasn't really interested in having its stars compete in the Olympics—FIFA, soccer's governing body, preserved its own control over soccer's biggest and most prestigious tournament, the World Cup. Switzer's Avon marathon series had impressive corporate backing and had received glowing coverage in the media. Lebow had built up the New York City Marathon into what was perhaps the biggest single sporting event in the world, when one added up runners and spectators. And he was just the type of promoter who might poke the IOC by declaring his marathon a "world championship" for women—he was already openly, publicly mocking the IOC's outdated, slavish devotion to the rules of amateurism. Shiseido's Tokyo marathon, in its first year, had drawn either 500,000 or one million spectators (depending on Paulen's tolerance for exaggeration). And Nike had already offered to promote women's long-distance events at any alternate "Olympic-style" competition. The underlying message was fairly simple: the IOC had better act before, as Paulen said, it was overtaken by events.

By the end of the Executive Board meetings, Csanadi, though representing the interests of the Soviet Bloc and defending the turf of the Program Committee, softened his stance enough to allow for a neutral-sounding resolution—namely, that the entire IOC session should "decide for or against the women's marathon, without a recommendation from the Executive Board." Given the mood of the IOC delegates in Moscow, Csanadi's ploy was likely strategic: had the marathon proposal been put to a vote by the full session, it would have been defeated. American representatives, rather than arguing in favor of the marathon, instead pushed for a delay in voting—the official reason given, to accumulate more scientific information, was an excuse. The case for the women's Olympic marathon lived to fight another day.

***

As if to emphasize the IAAF's fears, Switzer had one more card to play: to highlight the lack of a women's Olympic marathon, she'd scheduled the 1980 Avon International Marathon in London to take place on the day of the Moscow Olympics closing ceremonies. To host a major marathon in the middle of London, to close down the streets, was an audacious ask, but Switzer prevailed on city officials. "We have only done this before for the queen," said Sir Horace Cutler, leader of the Greater London Council. But for Switzer, the theater of it—runners (in Avon shirts, of course) streaming over Westminster Bridge with Parliament in the background, going by the Tower of London—was irresistible.

Other parts of the course, admittedly, were a graveyard—the run-down wasteland of the Docklands section was particularly bereft. It wasn't New York but the crowd matched or exceeded that of a European championship or Commonwealth Games marathon, especially where it mattered. Spectators stood five-deep at the start, in leafy green Battersea Park on the Thames. They jammed the finish area, on the already narrow King Street, which funneled runners toward the finish line in front of London's ornate, imposing Gothic-revival Guildhall. Switzer hired a team of British rugby players to keep the crowd behind barriers and the road clear for the runners. As New Zealand's Lorraine Moller rounded one final corner and into sight, en route to an Avon Championship record of 2:35, the crowd's roar echoed off the stone facades hanging over the street. A British pipe band in full regalia struck up a martial tune. Church bells pealed in the distance, as if it were coronation day. In the packed Guildhall courtyard, revelers cheered for runners but mostly seemed just to celebrate the occasion. The whole day took on the feel of a victory party.

And it was all captured live on television. Because of the American Olympic boycott, NBC Sports had a massive programming hole to fill. Switzer convinced the network to broadcast her marathon. NBC, the BBC, and a host of other international outlets gave the women's-only marathon a global television presence, a platform from which to make their case one more time. "No Olympic marathon for women yet," exclaimed the announcer, "but we hope they get it!" The race had world championship atmosphere, and the broadcast touted it as such. The field contained 250 runners from twenty-seven countries and five continents. It was held in London, which happened to be where the home offices for the IAAF were located. It drove home Paulen's point: it was time to act.

Under threat, the usually sclerotic IOC can move quickly. In February of 1981, at the meetings of the IOC Executive Board in Los Angeles, the question of the women's marathon—which wasn't supposed to be decided until September by the full IOC—came up again. The nine members of the Executive Board, plus their various retinues, plus Monique Berlioux, executive director of the IOC office, gathered at the Century Plaza Hotel. Switzer had flown in as well. She'd done all she could, but even so, she thought, there's still a chance that things could go sideways. She stalked the lobby and ballrooms, buttonholing IOC members one last time, giving her talking points once again, asking them to please try to convince the skeptics. They smiled and headed off to the meetings. She paced the lobby, on the outside looking in.

Berlioux once referred to the IOC as "une chambre d'enregistrement," or a rubber stamp, meaning that whatever the Executive Board decided would be approved, and that the president of the IOC would, along with one or two trusted allies, decide before any Executive Board meeting what decisions the group would make; it is unlikely that the board would have taken up the question of the marathon if key members hadn't already decided on the outcome.[14] In fact, Hansen had already been tipped by her sources that approval of the marathon was coming. Csanadi, perhaps sensing the shifting winds, stated that the PC "were not against the women's marathon," simply "not ready to take a definitive stand." He did, however, note that accepting the marathon "would be contrary to the rules and criteria" of the IOC. The new president of the IOC, Juan Antonio Samaranch, reiterated Paulen's support for it and added that the LAOOC "were anxious" for the marathon to be added. He canvassed the nine men in the room for their opinions. After six other members voiced their support, he added his own. Only Vitaly Smirnov, of the Soviet Union, argued for further delay.

It was left to Berlioux to make the announcement. The most powerful woman in international sports, who was in the process of negotiating a revolutionary new television revenue for the IOC, who was known as the power behind the throne—but who was not a member of the IOC and had no vote—could not keep a note of triumph from creeping into her voice: "It was not an easy decision, but an important one," she said before declaring that the executive board had approved the women's marathon for the 1984 Olympics.

In the hotel ballroom after Berlioux's announcement, Switzer took her victory lap. If she had a bit of a strut as she made the media rounds, a hint of a preen in front of the cameras, it was well earned. In her first marathon, she'd felt shaken to the core: she'd been attacked by Semple, harangued by the media, then banned by the AAU. But she'd turned the tables on all of them. She'd made a friend out of Semple and used him to promote her races. She'd made her Avon series headline news around the world and made the quest for the Olympic marathon the main storyline at each of them. And she'd brought the national and international governing bodies of the sport around to her side—cajoling, flattering, and educating athletics officials around the world as she set up Avon races in their home countries. She'd been a tireless promoter for the women's marathon—a self-promoter, her critics would say unkindly. But she'd popularized, even glamorized women's running, and here, in the ballroom, the spotlight was rightfully hers.

Hansen, like Switzer, had planted herself at the hotel, but she avoided the media. Although she'd known the decision was coming, part of her marveled at how quickly the IOC had reversed itself: ten months earlier, the Program Commission had shut the door on the women's marathon for at least another Olympiad; the IOC's disregard for its own rules was evidence of near-panic on the part of its Executive Committee. But in celebrating the victory, she had to swallow her frustration at how long she'd worked for this moment: two Olympic cycles and nearly ten years of her life, including the prime of her running career. Moreover, she had unfinished business. She'd come to town not solely to witness the announcement but to start pushing the IOC to add a women's 5000 and 10,000 meters to the Olympics.

For Hansen and Switzer, the announcement was the culmination of years of work. For Waitz, Benoit, and any who aspired to challenge them, it marked a new beginning. The race for Olympic gold would attract a new generation of competitors to the marathon and bring a new sense of urgency and intensity to women's marathoning. To the usual pressures of elite athletics, it added the weight of history. It would drive them all to new heights, but in the three-and-half years from Berlioux's announcement to the 1984 Olympics, the greatest marathoners in the world would travel a long, grueling road.

PART II

INTERLUDE

SANTA MONICA, CALIFORNIA, AUGUST 5, 1984, 8:05 A.M.: *"And there we go! The first women's Olympic marathon,"* says Al Michaels on the ABC television broadcast.

At the gun, most of the runners ease off the line as if waking up slowly. A few jump out front, not so much a racing tactic as an effort to stay out of the crowd of tangled legs and arms; fifty people circling the track together can be hazardous. Monica Regonesi of Chile, Marie-Christine Duerbroeck of Belgium, and Japan's Akemi Masuda—unknowns to the television audience, not among the favorites—lead the first laps; Kathrine Switzer, doing commentary along with Michaels, has researched them all and provides biographical details on their training programs and race history.

The main pack is unconcerned about the early deficit, which will grow to more than sixty meters. Waitz establishes herself on the outside of lane 2 and makes no effort to set the pace. Benoit is on the rail, lost in the churn of bodies, just one runner among fifty. "The favorites are trying to seek each other out in that crowd," says Marty Liquori, 1968 Olympic miler and the third member of the broadcast team. "I'm sure the strategy of Grete Waitz and Joan Benoit is to not let . . . their competition get more than 10 yards," he adds. "They're all going to be going for the gold medal—they're not going to be running conservatively . . . they're all going to go for bust and hang on to the pace as long as they can."

Rosa Mota of Portugal also surges off the line to get clear of the others, but halfway through the first lap, she looks behind her, as if to mark the position of the serious medal contenders, then settles and lets the pack swallow her. Mota is tiny even for a marathoner—Benoit looks tall by comparison—with short, dark hair. She began training seriously as a teenager, running through the streets of her hometown of Porto; "Go back home and help your mother!" people would shout at her. In 1975, at the age of 17, she won her first national title, in the 1500m. Throughout the rest of the 1970s, she was Portugal's best distance runner. Like Benoit, Mota's strength is her endurance. Her best times in shorter races are much slower than those of runners such as Waitz, who was well behind the best of the Eastern Bloc runners. In a world where the longest women's race was the 3000m, Mota had never made an impression on the international stage; like so many others in the field, the inclusion of the marathon in the Olympics was career changing. Both Waitz and Benoit view her as a serious threat in this race: the heat suits her, and she is at her best under pressure, a crafty competitor with the ability to keep her wits about her, even in the biggest races.

Just behind Mota and to her outside runs Ingrid Kristiansen. Kristiansen, energetic, emotive, and outgoing, squints at the runners around her—often she appears to be grimacing, but it's just that she won't wear her glasses while she runs. She had been a world-class cross-country skier—she made the formidable Norwegian team as a teenager and represented her country at the world skiing championships, but she had never been able to make the leap from very good to one of the best. The marathon has opened a new world to her. Kristiansen believes she can be the best marathoner in the world, and she is favored by many for gold. She is by far the fastest runner in the field—the world record holder for 5000 meters—but she lacks the depth of marathoning experience that Waitz and Benoit possess. She is just two years younger than Waitz but seems very much the little sister; in preparing for this race, she has worked on her mental strength as well as her physical, trying to solve her tendency to defer to Waitz in big races.

They are the four favorites, around whom the pack revolves in a swirl of color. The Norwegians wear singlets with a red upper, a blue band, and a white midriff; the Swedes, blue and yellow—but the colors tend toward the lighter end of the spectrum in a nod to the anticipated heat. For most events, the American track and field uniforms are red, but the marathoners wear a light gray. The New Zealanders had always worn a distinctive all-black kit with a silver fern; this day they are wearing white.

Collectively, their first laps have the feel of a continuation of the procession rather than the beginning of the race. The leaders go through 800 meters in just under 3:00, with the pack five seconds behind. They hit the first kilometer—the first of 42—at around 2:40 pace for the marathon. After two and a half laps around the track, they exit onto the streets of Santa Monica, to begin a winding journey through greater Los Angeles, toward the Coliseum and the finish line, twenty-six miles away.

CHAPTER 8

The Enemy Within

Waitz and Benoit, 1980–1981

FOUR MONTHS BEFORE MADAME BERLIOUX'S ANNOUNCEMENT, TWO days before the 1980 New York City Marathon, Waitz went ice skating at Rockefeller Center. Jack stood rinkside, shoulders hunched, arms crossed: if she caught an edge and fell, or twisted a knee, or bruised or broke something—he could imagine the worst. After the race, he could understand—but a foolish risk to take before, he thought. Grete, for once, was less anxious than Jack. In her fishbowl life in Oslo, she was always wary that the press or the public would somehow disapprove of their great Olympic hopeful enjoying herself too much; she hadn't been skating in Norway since she was a teenager. In New York, she was an anonymous celebrity: in two days millions of New Yorkers would cheer her name, but off the marathon course she was just another tourist in the city. So, for a few carefree moments, she let down her guard and twirled around the ice with her brother.

Two days later, in the cold and wind, she again broke the world record, running 2:25. She passed the first five miles in 27:00, or 2:21 pace—this on the slowest part of the course, up and over the Verrazano-Narrows Bridge. She finished four minutes, or roughly three-quarters of a mile, ahead of second place. In three marathons, she'd taken more than nine minutes off the pre-Grete record, and New Yorkers had adopted her as their own. "Sometimes I felt like I was running in my hometown and not New York," she said after the race. Afterward, she and Jack enjoyed a quiet dinner before the nighttime awards ceremony; the next morning, she did her now-familiar 6 a.m. appearance on the *Today* show.

***

"Three marathons. Three world records," wrote Amby Burfoot, running's premier journalist and the 1968 Boston Marathon champion. "Grete has also run numerous odd-distance road races in places like Los Altos, Falmouth, Lynchburg, Gainesville, Los Angeles, and Bermuda. She has won every single one of them. She has set course records in every one. She has set world records. No one has ever been close to her. Her smallest margin of victory was the 44 seconds by which she defeated Jan Merrill last summer at Falmouth."[1]

And she won four consecutive world cross-country championships from 1978 to 1981, another unprecedented feat. If a meaningful record on the roads existed, Waitz had it. In July 1980, she became the first woman to break 31:00 for 10K on the roads, running 30:59.8 at the New York L'Eggs Mini-Marathon.[2] (Her victory was almost dashed—and her time not recorded—when a garbage truck that Fred Lebow used to pace the leaders hooked a hanging overhead wire that went from the finish line banner to a lamppost. Truck pulled wire, wire pulled down lamppost, finish line became obstacle course, and the timing system briefly went off-line—all in the seconds before Waitz finished.)

"A lot of guys—Frank Shorter, myself—we did a lot of things well," said Bill Rodgers, the four-time Boston and New York winner. "But we never dominated."[3] No one ever had like Grete.

She'd grown up in a state-subsidized, working-class apartment block—three rooms, plus kitchen and bathroom—with her parents and two brothers. Both parents worked full-time, her father in a factory, mother at a grocery store. When she told friends from the neighborhood that she was a runner, they asked how she made a living.[4]

Every morning, no matter the weather, Waitz was out the door at 5:30 for 12–14 hilly kilometers. She kept a meticulous training log, recording mileage, workouts, weather conditions, any other important details, save one: she refused to note her pace.

"They are not so fast," Grete would say of her morning miles.

"She will not admit how hard she trains, but ask anyone," replied Jack.

"Don't run with her in the morning," said Norwegian 5000m record holder Arne Kvalheim. "She runs too fast. 5:45 [per mile] right out the door." Even allowing for some exaggeration—as fishermen talk fish, runners talk about training pace—Waitz trained faster than many elite men preferred to train. Arne's brother, Knut, another world-class runner, would confirm after training with her in the leadup to the Euros in 1978: "The hills were especially bad," he said. "I felt that I was really running to keep up. She has the ability to push herself very hard when she gets tired. To me and most runners I have known, it is too uncomfortable. But that seems to be her way, like . . . Prefontaine."[5]

Pain is the body's way of telling the mind to cease whatever it is doing before irreparable harm is done. It is a messenger, one whom Waitz knew well—and made a habit of ignoring. Running didn't hurt her the way it did the average person—not running hurt more—but the intense grind took a mental toll. Anticipating the burn of especially hard workouts might bring her to tears. Stinging ice and snow in the predawn of Norwegian winters might give her pause but couldn't keep her inside. Her body might ache in the dark of the early morning, she might feel like an 80-year-old rather than an elite athlete in her prime—these were days she'd stay in bed for a beat. But always, she got out the door.

In a marathon, "so many things can go wrong," said Waitz. "It's not like a 10K . . . you're more in control for 6.2 miles than for 26.2." But training harder, conquering physical pain and discomfort—that she could control. It helped quiet her doubts, helped legitimize her decision to be a runner. Waitz hadn't yet officially quit her teaching job, only taken consecutive leaves of absence—as if she still weren't convinced running would be enough. To push the body a little bit further than before, a little deeper into the pain cave than she'd ever gone before, meant that the body was capable of more than before, that she was getting closer to some final verdict of her worthiness, to some goal that remained always just out of reach, just past the finish line of her next race.

Waitz hardly talked when running. Even training with others, she was apart—not even Jack could experience this world the way she did. He might point out wildlife he noticed in the woods, or the sunrise—and might occasionally pull her back from oncoming traffic. She focused only on the run and the goal: to be the best. As a marathoner, she was.

Was it enough?

Back in 1974, Jack suggested she forgo the 1500m at the European Championship and run the 3000m instead—it was a new event, and her prospects were much better, he thought; Grete refused—she'd rather race the 1500 against the best than win the 3000 against a weak field.[6] After her third New York win, and her third world record, she said, "if I knew I could have a chance to win the 3000 [on the track]—and if I know there will be no drugs—it would mean so much more to me than winning the marathon. I would like to beat the best."[7] By 1980, the 3000m was no longer a second-tier event; in Waitz's mind, the marathon still was.

Just after running 2:25, in the midst of a three-year stretch of dominance unmatched in the history of distance running, Waitz began working with a new coach, Edward Stolba, an émigré from Czechoslovakia. Her workouts got harder, faster, more intense; she was pushing at the far margins now of what her body could handle, but worse than pain was doubt: it was like a pebble in her shoe. A little bit of doubt, of wondering if others were working harder, or if others were naturally more talented (and therefore could only be beaten by working even harder), could be a healthy motivator—but doubts had a way of festering, self-perpetuating, becoming corrosive.

She had plenty of confidence—it sustained her competitive edge: she couldn't be consumed by a desire to beat every other runner in the sport unless she believed she had the ability to do so. Her doubts went deeper, to the core of her identity as an athlete. She needed to believe that all the hard work, all the pain and suffering, would be worth it. More than believing that she could become the greatest, she needed to believe that the journey would be worth the cost. A single race, a single accomplishment, was transitory—gone as soon as it happened, never sufficient recompense for everything she went through on the way. The journey itself had to be worth it. Being a runner had to be worth it.

Stolba took a radically different approach to training from what Grete and Jack had cobbled together in previous years. He focused on speed, strength, and technique—trying to lengthen her stride and develop more of a kick. "Grete's aerobic box is full," he insisted. "It's hard to believe that she's become number one in the world without any special technique training," Stolba said, almost shaking his head. "People here are great believers in doing what is natural, but they know nothing about biomechanics and training systems." Her path to 1984 had not yet been mapped out; she and Stolba wanted two options open. "I have to decide," she said, "which I am—a track runner or a road runner."[8] Both the 3000m and the marathon would be contested for the first time at the 1984 Olympics. She couldn't realistically train for both, and she still yearned for a chance to prove herself on the track—if she knew the playing field could be leveled.[9]

What, after all, did she have to prove on the roads? When she stepped to the line, the rest of the field knew—even if, as true competitors, they would never say so—that there would be two races that day: Grete's, for another record, and theirs, for second place. Parts of that, she enjoyed: the sense of control over the field, knowing they were all looking to her, that the others in the pack wouldn't dare make a move until she did. She awed her peers, and to the media and spectators, she was the face of the sport. To sponsors and race directors, the expectation of another record was the story that would sell the race—absurd an expectation as that was. What should have been a supreme achievement, the rarest of accomplishments—a new record!—was the bar she had to clear in every race. The joy, she said, in breaking records, was overtaken by the pressure she felt: every time out, she had to be a better version of herself. And her doubts about the relative quality of road racing generally, and marathoning in particular, only intensified the pressure.

Once, on the bus out to the start of the New York City Marathon, she leaned over to Jack and said, "I hope the bus breaks down."

But she accepted the crushing expectations, the doubt, and the attention as all part of the job—part of the trade-off. She was still partly the 12-year-old girl racing buses down the street and wouldn't ever let go of the joy she found in running. And although she was a born introvert, naturally shy, she handled the public demands of being a star with disarming grace, as if she were talking to a class full of unruly students. Races were a way for her to share her love of running with everyone in the running community, a way to express the inarticulable meaning that running had for them all. She forged a deep connection with the running public, with the shufflers, with young runners, even with those who'd never run a step in their lives but still came out to crowd the barricades when she raced by.

But the connections she made went only so far—and as deeply beloved as she was, she didn't form many friendships, particularly among her running peers. An interviewer once asked her what she did during her down time: Dancing? "No," she said, "I don't go dancing." Sightseeing? "I saw the Empire State Building once from a cab." The interviewer asked if she'd seen the most popular movie in the theaters, which happened to be about running: "*Chariots of Fire?*" Waitz seemed confused. When it was explained to her what it was, she said, "No, I haven't seen that." What do you do, then? "When I am not injured, I run." Back in the 1970s, when her track teammates nicknamed her Grandmother, it hadn't just been in reference to her age. Hers was a different sort of lifestyle from that of her fellow runners, even her teammates from Norway: Waitz lived quietly, kept only a tight circle—Jack, her family, a few friends—around her, and kept others firmly at a remove.[10]

From the moment the Olympic marathon was announced, Waitz became the odds-on favorite, but she knew that the marathon itself was like another competitor; sometimes the body was up to the challenge, sometimes the marathon demanded too much. Anything could happen in a marathon, even if, so far, it seemed like it never did to her. Under Stolba's eye, she pushed herself harder and harder, as if seeking in the training itself what she had yet to find in other runners: competition worthy of the name, rivals of such ability that they would elevate the challenge of the race, legitimize it, turn it into something more than just Grete against the clock. But in her quest to push against the limits of her own potential, to beat back against the doubts that plagued her, she balanced on a very precarious edge.

***

Waitz could at least take comfort in her results—she was getting faster. Benoit wondered if her career was winding down almost before it got started. She'd begun 1980 on such a high. The trip to New Zealand had started so well: after new best times in the mile and the marathon, she felt fitter than she'd ever been. Days later, she cut her trip short. She'd come in from a run, hopped in the shower, and felt something under her arm. It had been sore—a bruise perhaps, or just a little collateral damage from the marathon? The more she poked it, the more worried she got—under the skin, she could feel a lump.

Benoit hated doctors. Not personally—her brother was a doctor. But she hated seeing them. Seeking medical care was, to her, an admission of weakness. Besides, doctors usually told her to rest. But the lump didn't go away, and fearing the worst, she flew home. In Maine, she received a favorable diagnosis: a hydroma—a water sac, basically; benign—no urgency to take it out. Her doctor told her she could wait on surgery, so she returned to training. Weeks later, she joined the American team in Paris for the World Cross Country championships, on March 9. She had high hopes after New Zealand; reality was different. She finished twenty-sixth, ninety seconds behind Waitz, who won. She'd felt sick to her stomach on the flight to France but brushed it off as jet lag. A few days after World XC, she tried to race again in Milan and couldn't even make it to the line. She cut her European trip short, flew home, tried to get her feet under her, then flew down to Florida for a ten-mile Shamrock Shuffle on March 22. She won easily, but very slowly, more than six minutes per mile, slower than marathon pace—a shuffle indeed. Worse, the Florida sun should've baked her, but she was shivering cold, still sick to her stomach, and had a searing pain in her abdominal muscles.

Again, she tried to avoid seeing a doctor, instead scheduling a massage the next day to work out what she figured was muscle tightness. She nearly leaped out of her skin when the masseuse touched her abdomen. Twenty-four hours later, she was undergoing an emergency appendectomy. Her surgeon advised her to take it easy for at least a week. The day he released her from the hospital, she went running. In fairness, she ran much less than usual—only a few miles. "Of course, there was some discomfort," she later confessed, "but I couldn't let my muscles go soft." To make up for lost running, she attacked her stationary bike with the zeal of a medieval flagellant. "I can't slow down because the part of the brain that drives me won't allow it," she wrote. Instead, it pushed her to train harder, to do more. "I can hover above sensations of pain if I think I'm doing my training some good," she said.

A week after the appendectomy, she finally had the hydroma removed; it was the size of an egg. She ran ten miles before checking into the hospital, just in case she was laid up for a few days. Three weeks after her two surgeries, on April 26, she ran a short race—a 3K at the Syracuse YMCA. The next day, she drove to New York and ran a ten-miler. She came in fourth, a reasonable finish considering that she'd just gotten her miles back over one hundred per week.

Though she still wanted to keep running for as long as she could, she also had a nagging voice in her head saying that running was trivial, wasn't a real career. That spring, she'd taken a job as a long-term substitute teacher at her old high school. She was thrilled to be back in Maine—it was the only place she felt truly comfortable. But she felt out of place among the faculty—her former teachers—and she barely looked any older than the students, some of whom were younger siblings of her old classmates. Teaching PE tired her out more than running did, but showing her students the value of exercise and health, and instilling in them the joy she found in moving her body—that felt worthy, exhaustion and all. Which was good, because her postcollegiate running career, pocked by inconsistency, seemed to be going nowhere.

On May 31, she drove back to New York for the L'Eggs Mini-Marathon in Central Park: fourth, more than three minutes behind Waitz.

June 8, she set a course record at an eleven-kilometer race in Litchfield, Connecticut.

June 29, she flew to Oregon for the Cascade Run Off 15K and finished fourth.

July 20, she drove down to Massachusetts for a half marathon: first, but very slow.

Two weeks later, she flew to London for the Avon International Marathon and finished fourth in an inexplicably slow 2:38.

"When in doubt, train harder," she'd always told herself. But she was beating herself into the ground. She was on a wheel, spinning her legs as fast as she could—running in the mornings, on her feet all day teaching, running again after school, collapsing at night. Losing races at shorter distances grated against her competitive sensibilities, but Benoit knew she didn't have the same reservoir of speed the others did—Waitz, for example, could nearly match Mary Decker in the mile—and relished fighting as the underdog, scrapping to overcome their advantage. But getting beaten in marathons, especially running so slowly—that stung.

Teaching offered validation. But running was everything to her, and she realized that she couldn't train the way she needed to and be a successful teacher at the same time. She decided not to go back to teaching in the fall of 1980. Even after the school year ended, her times in races remained only good enough in spots to keep hope alive—and bad enough, often enough, for doubts to grow. She was getting left behind, and not just by Waitz. Patti Lyons Catalano, a fellow American whom Benoit had beaten at Boston in 1979, had run 2:29.33 at New York—the first American woman under 2:30.

Catalano was a throwback to the prewar road racers. Born in 1953, oldest of nine, Patti Lyons grew up in the working-class Boston suburb of Quincy, and she'd grown up tough. Her father was a second generation Irish American who boxed in the U.S. Navy. Her mom, a member of the Mi'kmaq nation, had run away from her home in Canada at age 11, landed in Quincy, and lied about her age to get work as a nanny. Patti wasn't an immigrant, but she was an outsider: in elementary school, her teacher asked each student to talk about their parents' roots; Catalano identified as Mi'kmaq, and her classmates taunted her with Indian whoops and feather jokes the rest of the day. When she got home, her mother smacked her for being so stupid as to say she was an Indian.

Catalano's parents worked two, sometimes three jobs; she looked after her eight younger siblings, and after getting them off to school and getting through her own school day, she worked various jobs on the night shift (she, too, lied about her age). Her father died when she was 17; her mother threw her out of the house shortly after. By age 20, she was working full-time in a hospital, smoking two packs of cigarettes a day, drinking too much, and guessed she was about forty pounds overweight.[11] Late one night in 1976, after finishing her midnight shift, she sat in a bar, and faced reality: she needed a change. She didn't know where to begin, but she'd been making her way in the world since high school, and if she needed to change course, she was more than strong enough to do it. She got a copy of Kenneth Cooper's *Aerobics*. Jogging was good for weight loss, said Dr. Cooper. OK, she thought; one afternoon, she changed at the Quincy Y—sweatpants, sweatshirt, and clunky Earth Shoes with a leather upper and a thick rubber sole with a negative heel drop—and tentatively stepped out the door. She walked over to the Quincy cemetery—she figured it would be deserted, so no one would see her. Mid-run, a police officer stopped her to ask if she was all right, if she was being chased by someone. She was better than all right: after seven miles, she was exhausted, her feet blistered, and felt more alive than she had in a long time—maybe ever. She stood under the shower at the Y and wept.

She knew that she had to keep running, but she didn't know how to train, what to wear, or even where she could run. She felt exposed, out of place; she didn't know any other runners. She did notice, one day as she changed at the Y, a group of men would gather at the front door, then take off together on a run. The next day, she waited, more or less hiding, until they started out, then trailed behind them, keeping up as long as she could. She did it again the next day, and the day after that, always running a block or so behind them. Soon she could keep their pace easily. The men weren't blind to the fact that they'd picked up a shadow; the tagalong soon became a regular member of their running group.

Six months later, having cut her smoking down to one pack a day, she won the Ocean State Marathon in Providence, Rhode Island. In the summer of 1978, she was thirty seconds behind Benoit at the Falmouth Road Race; in April 1979, when Benoit broke the American record at Boston, Catalano was only three minutes back, also under the old course record. Running had become her drug, and she binged. In a seven-week stretch in late 1979 (by which point she'd kicked the smoking habit completely), she ran three marathons—New York (fourth, thirteen minutes behind Waitz), Providence (first, in 2:40), and Honolulu (another win, another 2:40)—with a win at the famous Manchester Thanksgiving Day race thrown in as well. In March 1980, she raced back-to-back days: the fifteen-kilometer Jacksonville Gate River run on a Saturday (second place), New Orleans's Crescent City Classic 10K on Sunday (first). In September 1980, she broke the American record, running 2:30.57; seven weeks later, she ran her 2:29 at New York. For good measure, she threw in two more marathons: Honolulu in December and Houston in January.

Catalano, with a slight frame, straight, brown hair, and a soft, gentle voice, appeared unassuming, but at her core was a toughness that helped her quit her nicotine addiction, beat back her struggles with overeating, and leave behind a dead-end job as a nurse's assistant to become a champion. She ran well over one hundred miles per week—sometimes 150. She'd do hill workouts up Heartbreak Hill on the Boston Marathon course—ten times up, each one as hard as she could make it. "If they're gonna beat you, make 'em bleed," she said. At shorter races, she'd tack on five miles after the finish, and sometimes she'd run five miles before the start, just to intimidate her opponents. She lifted weights three times a week for ninety minutes and became obsessive about nutrition, taking a daily regimen of a dozen or so different vitamins and supplements. She got regular massages in the rubdown suite of Jock Semple—someone with whom she had a lot more in common than she did with the post–running boom elites.

Even though she found a home in running, she still felt like an outsider, different from her competitors; the other girls always seemed to know each other from college meets, or at least shared a common background. "Those little blonde, blue-eyed, pony-tailed college girls," she called them, "they worried about everything," she said with a laugh. "I'd been on my own for so long." Catalano knew real worries, like stepping between her parents when they started fighting, making sure her little sister had a good meal and a clean outfit, paying rent and keeping the heat on. And if she ran more races than most elites, she trained so hard that marathons were, in a way, a break from her usual grind. If any American seemed like a threat to Waitz's supremacy, it was Catalano.

***

Benoit, meanwhile, was still trying to get herself back on track. Nike offered her a job at its research facility in New Hampshire, so she moved down to Exeter in November of 1980. It was a new experience, a different type of opportunity from what she'd ever planned, but this was a real job—real enough to quiet the voice of judgment and flexible enough to let her train the way she needed to or disappear on a Friday to travel to races. She could float from project to project, department to department in the Nike lab—learning what each group did, meeting different teams, helping out as she could. The Nike research team had a start-up feel, young guys, hyper-enthusiastic about the work, bubbling with new ideas, and with the freedom to try nearly anything. She loved their energy, loved the mad-scientist vibe of the research team, and at least part of her job description was to run fast and win races—Nike was happy to support that aspect of her career. Many days, she would run with guys in the lab—all accomplished runners themselves—and as usual, the competitive juices flowed. Paces would slowly escalate, but she wouldn't back down, and everyone would end up running faster than was sustainable. Occasionally, she left them behind—and in some cases reduced them to walking home.[12] She felt fitter than she had in some time, and her eyes were fixed firmly on the 1981 Boston Marathon.

Her buildup was better and her races were faster: a half-marathon best of 1:13 in January, followed up by a world-best half-marathon of 1:11.16 on March 7. A week later, she lost to Catalano at the Jacksonville Gate River Run. But Benoit doubled back the next day and won the Shamrock Shuffle again in Florida, this time five minutes faster (and one appendix lighter) than the previous year. Three weeks later, she lost to Catalano again at the New Orleans Crescent City Classic. But the losses at the shorter distances did nothing to dampen her confidence going into Boston. Her half-marathons predicted a marathon under 2:30—well under, given Benoit's tendency to grow stronger as the distance got longer.

The weather for Boston was perfect: 50 degrees, overcast, wind from the west pushing the runners all the way from Hopkinton to Boston. Local press hyped a duel between two hometown heroes (Bostonians will claim any successful New Englander as their own—and Benoit had crossed the finish in her Boston win wearing a Red Sox cap, so she was theirs). But the early pace was fast, and Benoit couldn't hold it. Instead, Catalano battled a previously unheralded New Zealander, Allison Roe, who was gifted with what one elite runner called "the most perfect stride" he'd ever seen.[13] Catalano took the lead at the ten-mile mark and held it, over the hills and into the heart of the city, until, around mile 24, Roe struck. Roe opened up an ever-widening gap and finished in a shocking 2:26.42. Out of nowhere, Roe was within a minute of Waitz's best. Catalano, though soundly beaten, ran 2:27.51—her third time lowering the American record.

Benoit finished in 2:30.16, five minutes faster than her winning time two years before, and her best marathon time ever—good but not good enough, and slower than expected. So far, 1981 seemed like a repeat of 1980: a few bright spots, but no consistent progress. In the two months after Boston, she won a fast 25K, lost to Catalano twice, got blasted at the L'Eggs Mini-Marathon (seventh place), and won the TAC National Championship 10K on the track. She'd gone from Boston to Michigan to West Virginia, New York, Connecticut, Sacramento, and not only was she not racing consistently well—at least, not up to her standard—but her heels were beginning to hurt again. Time off might have made sense; instead, she geared up to race Falmouth in August (which she won), then tried to prepare for two fall marathons: she ran 2:37 in Ottawa in September, then a miserable 2:39 marathon in Columbus in October.

She ran as if afraid to pause long enough for her doubts to catch up. After each race, she seemed to turn to the next one as soon as she could, looking for another challenge, a reason for renewed optimism. But not only was Waitz disappearing into the distance, other runners were shooting by her. She seemed intent on racing her way out of the doldrums; instead, she continued to spin her wheels.

CHAPTER 9

For Love and Money

Roe and Waitz, 1981

FRED LEBOW WATCHED THE 1981 BOSTON MARATHON IN THE COM-
pany of Kiyoshi Nakamura, coach of the men's champion Toshihiko
Seko. But, of course, his eyes couldn't help but stray to Roe. Quite possibly before she even crossed the line, Lebow was already scheming to
bring her to New York that fall, imagining "the most dramatic showdown
ever in the women's race."

The New York City Marathon was on a roll. The number of entrants
was over fourteen thousand, already the biggest marathon in the world,
and he turned away nearly that many each year as well. Perhaps only
Lebow himself had foreseen the possibility of such explosive growth.
Growth wasn't the only change: its essential character had transitioned
from race to fun run. For the masses of new marathoners, the race wasn't
so much about competition as participation—still an achievement, but
more about being a part of the event than racing it.

The average finishing time had slowed from 3:30 for men and 3:59
for women in 1976 to 3:42 and 4:11 in 1980.[1] For a race director such as
Jock Semple, the changing nature of the runners would have represented
the takeover of the weirdies; for Lebow, himself a slow guy, it was part of
what he wanted marathoning to be: he still wanted the best in the world
in his race, but for everyone else, it could be less serious and staid, less
a spiritual journey, more fun. Crazies and weirdies had a home in New
York—Lebow had more than a little crazy in him. Bigger was better,

and the marathon had something for everyone, could mean something different to everyone. Embracing everyone wasn't just a growth strategy; it was a core belief about the meaning and purpose of the New York City Marathon.

But he still needed greatness to headline it, because part of what made it fun for the average runner, in the masochistic way marathons are fun, was not just the five-borough, citywide party that the race had become. It was the fact that it offered a chance to be part of something monumental and history making: something where runners would be proud to say, I was there—I was in it. By 1981, Lebow needed a fresh angle—even the story of the great Grete Waitz lost a little shine on repeat—and he was thinking especially big, because he had just signed an unprecedented four-year contract with ABC television to broadcast the marathon live. It would be the first live nationwide broadcast of a non-Olympic marathon. And now he saw it: the greatest duel in the history of women's marathoning.

Roe was the perfect challenger. Lebow once said of Waitz that if you asked a computer to design a perfect marathoner, it would simply copy Waitz. If someone asked the ABC TV producers and corporate marketing executives to design a perfect marathoner, they might copy Roe. One reporter wrote that she "made Bo Derek look like an eight." At a press event, another reporter leered at her, leaned in close, and told her, "It's amazing what you can do with blonde hair, long legs and half a brain."[2] "The greatest ass in sports," one anonymous runner declared of Roe, adding that running behind her was "the best 15 minutes of my life."[3] Of her win at Boston, marathon historian Tom Derderian wrote that Roe looked like "an actress coming on stage to take a leading role." Even years later, she seemed fixed in longing male memories: Tom Grilk, former president of the BAA, recalled a vision of Roe at the party after her Boston win "in an extremely flattering dress, dancing up a storm."[4] It is part of her legacy. As journalist and historian Roger Robinson wrote, "no honest story on Roe can omit her impact on the hearts of thousands of American men, especially runners and race spectators, by her super-model or warrior-goddess combination of beauty and strength."

So much attention on her appearance embarrassed her, but she rolled with it, even though those who focused on her looks missed so much. Roe had talent—she was the youngest-ever winner of the New Zealand cross-country championships, taking first place as an 18-year-old in 1974. Her training wasn't marathon-specific—she typically topped out a little over seventy miles per week, but she'd done her distance runs along the trails and roads of New Zealand's legendary Waitakere Range, where Arthur Lydiard had his charges do their weekly distance runs. He'd produced Olympic medalists and record holders such as Murray Halberg, Peter Snell, and Barry Magee, and Roe now ran in their footsteps.

She was refreshingly engaging and brought a spontaneity to running. "It was quite by accident that I ever ran [my first marathon]," she told the press—in 1980 she jumped into the Auckland marathon just for a change of pace. "I thought after 12 or 15 miles . . . I'd give way," she confessed. "And I actually tried to at one stage, when I walked a bit. But the crowd was too persuasive." She finished second, twenty minutes behind Benoit.

Of Boston, she said, "I decided to run only two weeks before, after a good Sunday 20-miler . . . I felt so strong and everybody started talking me into going."[5] She faced the press after her Boston win in the Prudential Building parking garage, holding a dozen roses and a cigar. She called Boston's legendary Heartbreak Hill "actually overestimated"[6] (which, compared to the Waitakeres, it was) and described Catalano as going "a little bit wobbly" in the last miles[7]—but all in a way that caused no ruffle among the generally thin-skinned Boston media.

And she was shrewd. One wonders if she played up the carefree demeanor. Not that it wasn't part of her personality, but in amplifying it, she may have been deploying a psychological weapon against her opponents: you can take things as seriously as you want, she seemed to say—but I'm still going to beat you. Because while the shallower members of the running world focused on her looks, and the media basked in the glow of her engaging personality, they missed the ruthless competitor hidden within. She may have run less than most of her competitors, but she spent far more time than they did on mental training, honing a psychological edge. At Boston, she spent several miles before her decisive surge lurking about ten meters behind Catalano. "I wanted to let her feel the pressure of me behind her," she said. Catalano would feel stalked; Roe would feel like she was "relaxing and having a holiday," Roe said. She waited patiently, controlling the race, letting Catalano's mental state erode, letting Catalano fight to hold the lead, while Roe drifted serenely in her wake. Roe made it look easy, which only brought more attention to all the fighting her opponents had to do.

***

Lebow wasn't blind to Roe's telegenic qualities—"The statuesque, twenty-five-year-old blonde," he called her. When Roe committed to the 1981 New York City Marathon, "we expected fireworks," Lebow said. But the Roe-Waitz duel nearly fell apart that summer, when Roe embroiled herself in a controversy that threatened to bring the entire Olympic movement crashing down. Her crime? Openly accepting prize money at the Nike-sponsored Cascade Run Off in June of 1981.

Avery Brundage, president of the IOC from 1952 to 1972, was fond of pointing out that the root of the word amateur was love; it was the foundation on which the Olympics rested, and the Olympic code permitted only amateurs to compete in the Games. However, no one was quite sure what amateurism meant. "Madly contradictory," wrote Pierre de Coubertin of the varying definitions across sport and country. It was a high-minded soup of ideals, but the International Olympic Committee defended amateurism with a zealous devotion. "Amateurism," said Brundage, "is a sort of religion."[8]

More important, it was a "social marker"[9] that separated athletics from its rather more colorful past: professional—in that the contestants got paid—running, jumping, and ultra-endurance contests in the nineteenth century were among the most popular sporting events in the public sphere. Britain was the epicenter of pedestrianism, as the sport was known; it arose in the industrial cities. In the United States, pedestrian events became a fixture across the country, from big cities in the east to small cattle towns out west. They attracted thousands of spectators, and crowds tended toward raucous and drunk, and regularly turned violent. Races received extensive, sensationalist coverage in the papers. Barnum & Bailey's circus often billed races among professional sprinters as main attractions, and in 1891 it advertised, along with a race of "ponies ridden by monkeys," the ever-popular man versus horse race and "a ladies hurdle race."[10] And like professional sport today, pedestrianism was a golden ticket out of poverty for a fortunate, talented few.

Making a living as an athlete didn't necessarily involve winning: gambling fueled the rise of pedestrianism, and fixing matches was common, in fact often assumed. Sometimes established favorites would throw a race to a nobody; sometimes ringers would compete in disguises or under false names, with the sharps betting on a supposed nobody to defeat the established local favorites; sometimes, what seemed like the one was actually the other, with tragic consequences. In 1893, James "Cuckoo" Collins, one of the great American sprinters, saw his career nearly ended when he was beaten in a match race in New Jersey by a supposed "easy mark." A saloon keeper named Patrick Dolan set up the race (and presumably wagered a large sum on its outcome) and warned Collins not to throw the race or he'd shoot him. Collins lost; Dolan shot him. The easy mark? A ringer, a champion sprinter from Scotland racing under an assumed name. Collins, bullet lodged in his spine, recovered and continued to race. Dolan never faced a judge; he paid Collins $1,000, gave him a train ticket back home to Wisconsin, and charges were dropped.

Distance events were often very long distance—the forerunner of ultramarathons—and often, professional pedestrians didn't even need an opponent, only a bet. In 1864, Emma Sharpe, a 32-year-old Englishwoman, stood to make £500 if she completed a feat known as the Barclay: one mile every hour for one thousand hours. She laid out a 120-yard track near a pub, The Quarry Gap, in Bradford, England, and, wearing a red-and-black checked coat and matching "inexpressibles" (what newspapers called pants when a woman wore them), set off on September 17, 1964. Sharpe's attempt attracted thousands of spectators and heavy wagering, most of which came in against her. As it became clear that she would complete the Barclay with no trouble, bettors sought to tilt the odds. Some tried to trip her, others threw burning embers in her path. Rumors flew of efforts to drug her food or chloroform her. A smattering of plainclothes police, hopelessly outnumbered, tried ineffectually to keep Sharp's path clear. For the final two days, Sharpe engaged a friend to accompany her with a loaded rifle, and she traded in her walking stick for a pistol, which she fired occasionally over the heads of the crowd. She completed her thousand miles on October 29, in front of an estimated twenty-five thousand spectators—some cheering, many hostile—and a brass band.

Trying to move the Olympics beyond the sport's nineteenth-century pedigree was an understandable impulse, but almost immediately amateurism became an ideal ardently embraced and comfortably skirted. By the 1920s, the best athletes from certain countries found employment in the military or police forces—and coincidentally found themselves exempt from most work responsibilities. After World War II, when the Soviet Union and other Eastern Bloc countries rejoined the Olympic family, the United States and its allies accused them of running state-sponsored sports programs—especially after the Soviets topped the medal table for the first time in 1956. The Soviets, in turn, pointed out that the American collegiate scholarship system looked a lot like pay for play as well.

"The amateur," wrote John Underwood in *Sports Illustrated* in 1969, "is the balding accountant who runs laps at the Y and finishes 168th in the Boston Marathon. Nobody would pay to see him run." Which, from the athlete's perspective, was the problem: everyone else—especially meet promoters and the officials who ran amateur sport—was getting paid. TV only sloshed more money into the system: CBS paid the AAU a minimum of $440,000 to televise ten "amateur" track meets in 1969. Top athletes expected their cut—but didn't want to lose their Olympic eligibility. Shamateurism was born. On the European track circuit, meet promoters would offer "bets" to top athletes—as in, "I'll bet you can't jump over this duffle bag here—but if you can, you can keep what's in it." In 1972, a pro track league—the International Track Association—started up, seeking to end the sham. Dwight Stones, 1976 gold medalist in the high jump, said he didn't join the ITA because he'd have had to take a pay cut.

In addition, sporting goods companies had always used athletes to advertise their product; as television increased athletes' visibility, and athletic gear grew into a multibillion-dollar business, shoe companies started paying Olympic athletes to wear their shoes. Athletes, in turn, were willing to sell their feet to the highest bidder. In 1960, German sprinter Armin Hary wore Puma spikes en route to the 100-meter gold medal—but wore one Puma shoe and one Adidas shoe on the medal stand, as he had taken money from both brands. At the 1968 Olympics, one American official estimated that only five members of the track and field team had not taken money from either Adidas or Puma. Many had taken money from both; some switched shoes between the prelims and finals. Adidas tried to have athletes sign quasi-official contracts; athletes took copies of the contracts to Puma and negotiated for more. The shoe companies, outraged but with no legal recourse, demanded that the IOC do something.

The IOC did nothing—television rights to the 1968 games had topped $10 million worldwide. The lords in charge of the sport recognized that great performances drove the public's interest, and citius, altius, and fortius were mostly out of reach for athletes squeezing in training after a full workday. Money was flowing everywhere, and if athletes were looking for their share, it seemed fair. The system worked, but it was tawdry, tiresome, and a little insulting for athletes to be taking unmarked envelopes of cash instead of receiving public, financial acknowledgment of their worth as performers. "It's the hypocrisy that's killing us," said Bill Toomey, 1968 decathlon gold medalist, "not the money."

Female athletes, with very few exceptions, received much less, if anything, in the under-the-table market, on the theory that spectators weren't paying to see women. Open payments wouldn't necessarily mean equal payments, but they would likely level the playing field somewhat—the Cascade Run Off did offer equal prize money for men and women. Further, it would legitimize their work, validate their career choice—no more would Waitz's neighbors ask her how she made a living. Public recognition as pro athletes might make some of the doubts dissipate. And in the chase for the first Olympic marathon gold, they knew they would have to train and live like professionals; they might as well get paid like it, too.

"There are no longer true amateurs in track," acknowledged Adriaan Paulen, head of the IAAF. "We're searching for new solutions," he said. "Our duty is to control the situation and find an equitable solution."

Control was the key word. The IAAF controlled athletes' eligibility for the Olympics and other major championships. Of course, the Olympics still had its mystical allure—athletes would compete for the honor of being an Olympian—but in addition, performances at major championships—the Olympics as well as national championships, continental meets such as the Euros or Pan-Am Games, the World Cup, and World Championships—determined their earning power at all the other meets on the circuit. The IAAF's control rested on compliant athletes, who felt they had no other option but to play along. But its control was somewhat illusory—the IAAF, too, was playing along, pretending to enforce a code of amateurism in a professional sport. Paulen and others knew change was coming; they just wanted to control its course.

Road racing forced the issue. Sponsors forked over tens of thousands of dollars, and tens of thousands of runners forked over their own cash in entry fees; race directors had ready money and were more brazen than European track promoters—Lebow, after all, was their role model. The Road Runners Club of America's handbook for race directors suggested setting aside money to attract top athletes and warned that it could get expensive. Further, race directors had minimal ties to the largely European-based IAAF establishment, were less willing to maintain the fiction of amateurism for the sake of appearances, and understood that big prize purses would mean big publicity. A year before Cascade, at the July 1980 IAAF Executive Council Meetings, Ollan Cassell, president of The Athletics Council (TAC), warned his fellow council members that a nascent road racing union in the United States was preparing to offer prize money. It was "very strong and should not be underestimated." The issue merited "immediate attention," lest the IAAF lose control over road racing. If distance runners saw more value in competing on the road circuit for prize money than they did in competing in the Olympics—a viewpoint held more commonly after the United States and sixty-five other nations boycotted the 1980 summer Games—and if race promoters saw more value in attracting the top runners than they did in maintaining official IAAF (or TAC) sanction, the IAAF would either have to change its rules or cede authority over road racing. The council voted to table the issue until its next meeting.

On June 12, 1981, when the newly formed Association of Road Racing Athletes announced that the Cascade Run Off in two weeks' time would offer open prize money to the top finishers, the IAAF's search for new solutions was forced to accelerate. Frank Shorter, seeking a compromise, proposed setting up athlete trust accounts, to be overseen by the national governing bodies, into which prize money could be placed, out of which athletes could draw to cover expenses for travel and training. Cassell lobbied other federations on the trust idea, but the process ground along at the IAAF's usual, tortured, glacial pace.

Meanwhile, Roe's fellow New Zealander Anne Audain won the race and pocketed the $10,000. Roe finished second, and won $4,000. "I understood the consequences that I could receive a lifetime ban from the sport, but I just wanted to be a professional," Audain said. "I had travelled the European track circuit and seen all the under-the-table money the men were getting. My aim was to finish fifth or sixth, to earn enough money to stay in the States a bit longer, but I ended up winning the race and receiving $10,000."[11] She put hers in an escrow account—a trust, essentially. Cassel, told by the IAAF to enforce the rules as written, banned the prize-winning athletes from racing in TAC sanctioned events, which included the New York City Marathon.

Lebow's marathon had its own very public reputation for paying under-the-table appearance fees and prize money, as the *Washington Post* reported in April 1980. "I've heard the same rumors myself," said Lebow, the wink in his voice audible. Patricia Owens, longtime elite athlete coordinator for the Marathon, was often the bag lady, dropping off envelopes of cash in Bill Rodgers's hotel room to ensure that he would run. "The time has come to put this on the table," Lebow said. TAC appointed Aldo Scandurra, former president of the New York Road Runners, to investigate whether Lebow—current president of the New York Road Runners—had offered improper payments to runners. "If anything, Aldo will be tougher on us than anyone else," said Lebow. Jeff Darman, president of the RRCA—the group that advised race directors to set aside money for under-the-table payments—said, "I can't think of a better choice . . . than Aldo Scandurra if one was [sic] to guarantee that they'll come up empty-handed."

In August 1981, Roe's prospects of racing at New York still seemed in doubt, but the tide was turning in her favor. She hired a tenacious lawyer to contest the suspension. The New Zealand Amateur Athletics Association backed her and came out in favor of open prize money for athletes. Cassell, trying to garner support for the trust plan, didn't seem too enthusiastic about the suspensions. And keeping athletes out of a race that maintained only the thinnest veneer of amateurism seemed hypocritical at best, a losing gambit at worst. Other road races had welcomed other suspended athletes—such as Audain and Moller—with open arms, so it wasn't entirely certain that Lebow would keep Roe from racing in New York. In late August, the IAAF agreed that any athletes who put their money in trust accounts would remain eligible, and Roe was once again eligible.[12] The IAAF finally approved the trust proposal at the IAAF Congress in Athens in 1982, one year after the Cascade Run Off, and Audain's suspension was lifted in time for her to win gold in the 3,000 at the 1982 Commonwealth Games.

***

After a twisted journey that brought historic change to the sport, Roe was in New York, ready to battle Waitz. But Waitz had arrived in New York unsure of whether she could run at all. Throughout 1981, Stolba continued to work on speed and strength, prescribing shorter, faster intervals—and lots of them. One workout, she did 15 x 500m as fast as she could. She finished, doubled over, nearly crawling. "OK, now two more," Stolba said. She nearly cried. But she wouldn't back down. He added drills—hops, bounds, short sprints elongated strides—and boxing to her fitness routine. He made her stronger, with a goal of lengthening her stride.

But marathoners need light, quick foot strikes, right underneath the body; some of the best marathoners run more like penguins, but what looks awkward actually is compact and efficient. The longer the stride, the harder the landing, and the bigger the shock that zings up into the leg. And the impulse toward longer stride tends to lead to overstriding: the foot gets out in front of the body, and a foot out front acts like a brake on the body's motion and sends even more of a shockwave up the leg.

For a marathoner, even the slightest increase in the shock the legs must absorb is multiplied over thousands of steps per run—millions of steps in a training cycle. Whether it was Stolba's training or just the accumulated wear of years of hard training, Waitz's legs were paying the price. By October, what had been a nagging pain in her lower leg had become debilitating.

Waitz called Lebow to tell him a marathon was doubtful. Injured or not, he needed her—if not to race, at least for the hype. Her injury made for an even better story: the wounded lion against the new challenger. He convinced her to come to New York—he'd set her up with the best doctors the city had to offer, see if they could help her get ready to race. And if he needed her, she'd be there. She spent the week in New York getting treatment, tried an easy twenty-minute jog on Tuesday, and came back with minimal soreness. She tested it again a day later, and decided she could start. She wasn't sure she could finish, but Waitz was still Waitz—injured or not, she still inspired awe. Beating her, Roe had said after Boston, "seems sort of impossible."

Roe, wearing F2 (she'd forgotten her bib number at the hotel and was actually wearing F2000 with the trailing zeroes hastily cut out), started out content to attach herself to Waitz, to go "trundling along after her," she said after the race. Rarely, if ever, did runners dare to take the lead and push the pace against Waitz. "In past years," mused ABC broadcaster Marty Liquori, "Waitz could have walked the first miles and I'm convinced half the women would've sat right behind her." But one challenger, sensing blood in the water, took the race out. American Julie Brown hadn't completed a marathon since running 2:36 in 1978—she'd failed to finish the Nike OTC marathon just six weeks prior to New York—but she had been the world XC champion in 1975, and she'd made the U.S. Olympic team in the 800 and 1500 in 1980. She had speed to burn, impressive range, and a fearless approach to racing.

Brown hit three miles in seventeen minutes, and seven in 38:26—just under 2:24 pace. She looked smooth, flowing through male competitors in the field, even dodging spectators who leaped onto the street to get on camera (crowd control still being a developing science at major marathons). Behind her, Roe ran with Julie Shea and Ingrid Kristiansen, who had run 2:34 at New York in 1980, some nine minutes behind Waitz. Waitz tried to stick on the tail of this chase pack, while Brown continued to press the pace ahead, building a lead of two hundred meters.

***

Mid-race, ABC cut to an interview with Lebow in which Jim McKay asked about paying athletes. "We hear figures like ten, twenty thousand dollars," said McKay. "That's a lot of expenses."

There was just the hint of a smile under Lebow's beard. "But that's just a rumor."

"They say you give prize money . . ."

"Well, um, we treat the runners very well here," said Lebow, wearing a serious expression. "Anyone who wins here, or comes in second . . . the promotional benefit is staggering. A win in New York is equivalent to winning Wimbledon. And . . . that will obviously benefit the athletes."

"But you didn't really answer my question."

Lebow utterly failed to hold back a smile.

"I have a feeling the holes in your statement that you've left out may say something to us too."

Lebow: "Well, it's the hole in the doughnut."

You can't see it, but you know it's there.

ABC had also reached out to Cassell for comment on athletes receiving payments. He responded, "Right now, except for newspaper reports, no one has filed any charges of misconduct against the New York Road Runners Club in connection with the New York City Marathon. Until such time as we receive specific complaints or direction from the IAAF, our framework will not allow such investigations."

***

Back in the race, Roe had cut Brown's lead nearly in half, and Waitz stuck doggedly at Roe's shoulder. Together, the two pressed on, while Brown's stride started to look a little less liquid. By mile 16, Roe was within ten seconds, Waitz just barely hanging on. On the Queensboro Bridge, Roe struck, surging by Brown and leaving Waitz behind. A monstrous roar greeted Roe as she came off the ramp into Manhattan. Packed spectators leaned out over the bridge, and crowds hung off balconies and out of windows as she rolled down onto First Avenue and all but disappeared from Brown and Waitz. The strain on Waitz's face turned progressively into a hitch in her stride, and by 17 miles she had to drop out. Roe's lead grew to nearly three hundred meters, and now the race was her against the clock. Liquori noted that she had only a pack of male runners for company. "Well," said McKay, "she's a very attractive young woman—I'm sure she often has a pack of men around her."

Roe seemed to grow stronger, powering up the hills in Central Park, her stride smooth as ever as she neared the finish, which she crossed in 2:25.28—thirteen seconds faster than Waitz's record from the previous year.[13] Only minutes earlier, Alberto Salazar had shattered the men's world record. Lebow had two world records on the same day, both captured on the first live nationwide broadcast of a full marathon outside of the Olympics. He was giddy. "Now," he said, "there is nothing left to dream." It was nearly perfect day, with a Lebow-esque finish: his contracts with sponsors stipulated that the male winner would cross under a Perrier banner, the female winner under a Manufacturers Hanover banner. But Lebow had been so engrossed in Salazar's record, he forgot to switch the finish chute, and Roe crossed under Perrier as well.

Roe became an overnight hero back home. New Zealanders watched the broadcast on Monday morning—Labor Day in New Zealand, a holiday; home from work, the sports-mad citizens of the tiny nation sat glued to their TV sets as she dominated the field in the biggest marathon in the world. The next weekend, Judy McGregor, the first female editor in chief of a major New Zealand daily paper, ran a full-page color photo of Roe in mid-stride on page 3 of the *Sunday News*. The page three girl, a typical feature of Rupert Murdoch-owned tabloids, was usually a soft-porn pinup shot, a topless woman sunbathing on a beach somewhere. McGregor couldn't help herself. Roe was a different type of beauty icon—"statuesque," perhaps, but also powerful, athletic, tough, and competitive. The Sunday edition with Roe disappeared from newsstands as women and girls rushed out to buy it.[14]

The events of 1981 proved several things: For those dreaming of an Olympic medal, running would have to be their full-time job, and they would get paid like the professional athletes they were. Second, 2:30, a seemingly unattainable mark just three years earlier, wouldn't be fast enough to make the podium at the Olympics. And finally, Waitz, who for so long had seemed untouchable, was no longer out of reach.

INTERLUDE

SANTA MONICA, CALIFORNIA, AUGUST 5, 1984, 8:09 A.M.: *As the athletes exit the track onto the roads, Regonesi and Duerbroeck run even, about ten meters ahead of Masuda, who is fifty meters up on the rest of the field. Masuda and then Regonesi slow and soon fall back into the pack; Duerbroeck continues out front. Spectators are plentiful here, and the crowd remains mostly on the sidewalk along the course, though only a thin yellow rope strung between portable A-frame construction barriers separates them from the runners. There are sporadic chants of USA! USA! But flags of many nations are visible. A young girl sprints down the sidewalk, keeping pace with Duerbroeck for about one hundred meters before giving up.*

Duerbroeck has no illusions about her chances. She has raced many of the women here at the World Cross Country Championships; her best finish was fifty-second. She seems aware that she must look odd to be so far out front; she glances back once, mostly out of curiosity, wondering where the others are. It is easy to label Duerbroeck foolhardy to be leading her far more credentialed competitors, but she has plenty of experience and understands how to race. Once out on the roads, she is running about 2:37 pace for the marathon; she will finish in 2:38.01.

Waitz, Benoit, Mota, and Kristiansen have established positions near the front, but the pace is languid. Waitz, especially, seems to be the center of gravity for the pack. She is in the middle front, with Benoit to her left. Julie Brown of the United States takes the lead briefly, though she doesn't push the pace any. The third American, Julie Isphording, nudges her way to the front row but is content just to sit once there. Mota pushes up to a spot just behind and between Waitz and Kristiansen. Patience is a virtue, especially at the Olympics. Athletes tend to stay within themselves, give their bodies time to find a natural tempo. The racing can wait: there is a collective expectation that the sun will soon bear down on all of them. In their training and preparations, the athletes have been drilled by coaches, trainers, and doctors to be ready for the heat. But at least at the beginning, temps remain comfortable: a marine layer envelops Santa Monica in a light damp fog, bringing a blessed cool to the start of the race. In the crowd, some spectators wear lightweight jackets.

The pack passes the mile in about 6:00, Duerbroeck still out front. They have now run farther in competition than any other female athletes in Olympic history.

Front page of the *Boston Record-American* (now the *Boston Herald*) after Gibb ran the 1966 Boston Marathon. The center photo, of Gibb in a polka-dot dress making fudge, was staged. (Reprint by permission of the *Boston Herald*)

Young Bobbi Gibb—taken around the time of the marathon. (Photo from Gibb's personal collection)

Kathrine Switzer and Jock Semple get "a wee bit o' notoriety" at the start of the 1973 Boston Marathon. (Getty Images)

Joan Benoit running in her first Boston Marathon, in 1979, alongside George Hirsch, who would become publisher of *Runner's World*. (Photo from George Hirsch's personal collection)

Benoit Samuelson and Hirsch at the Boston Marathon forty years later. Her goal was to run 3:15, or within forty minutes of her 1979 time of 2:35; she ran 3:04. (Photo from George Hirsch's personal collection)

Grete Waitz and Patti Catalano run side by side at the 1981 L'Eggs Mini-Marathon. (Paul Sutton/Duomo/PCN Photography)

Benoit winning the 1984 Olympic marathon. In the background is Waitz, roughly one lap from the finish. (Paul Sutton/Duomo/PCN Photography)

Ingrid Kristiansen on the final lap of the Olympic marathon. (Paul Sutton/Duomo/PCN Photography)

Benoit, Waitz, and Mota on the medal stand at the 1984 Olympics. (Paul Sutton/
Duomo/PCN Photography)

Benoit Samuelson leads Kristiansen at 1985 Chicago Marathon. (Paul Sutton/
Duomo/PCN Photography)

Fred Lebow embraces Waitz after her victory at the 1988 New York City Marathon, the last of her nine victories in New York. (Paul Sutton/Duomo/PCN Photography)

Lebow and Waitz embrace after the 1992 New York City Marathon, which Lebow ran while battling terminal brain cancer. (Paul Sutton/Duomo/PCN Photography)

Benoit Samuelson and Waitz at the New York City Marathon in 2005. (Victah Sailer, Photorun. net)

Benoit Samuelson and Mota at Waitz's memorial service in 2011. (Kjell Vigestad, Kondis)

Benoit Samuelson at the home of Jack and Grete Waitz after the memorial service, holding Waitz's Olympic silver medal. (Toni Reavis)

A history of women's marathoning in one photo: Front row (l to r): Bobbi Gibb (1966 pioneer and three-time Boston champion), Sara Mae Berman (Boston champion 1969–1971), Jacqueline Hansen (1973 Boston champion), Nina Kuscsik (1972 Boston champion), and Cheri Blauwet (two-time Boston champion and member of the BAA Board of Governors); back row (l to r): Former BAA President Joann Flaminio (first female BAA president), Uta Pippig (three-time Boston champion), Catherine Ndereba (four-time Boston champion), Kathrine Switzer, Benoit Samuelson, and Gloria Ratti (a BAA official for more than fifty years, she worked to ensure women's running received its due). (BAA/Fay photo)

Gibb sculpting in her studio. (Photo © David Watts Jr.)

Gibb and 2016 Boston champion Atsede Bayisa. After the 2016 marathon, Bayisa gave her trophy to Gibb to honor Gibb's 1966 marathon. (BAA/Mary Kate Shea)

Gibb "officially" breaking the tape at the Boston Marathon in 2016, fifty years after her first unofficial marathon. (BAA/Fay photo)

CHAPTER 10

Out with the Old?

Benoit and Waitz, 1981–1982

IN THE SUMMER OF 1981, BENOIT GAVE HER NOTICE AT THE NIKE research lab in New Hampshire and accepted a job coaching the women's cross-country and track and field teams at Boston University—even as the amateur era was coming to an end, Benoit still wasn't ready to ignore the voice in her head saying that she had to do something besides just run. And she still wasn't sure her running career was heading in a sustainable direction. Coaching could be another outlet for her competitive fire, and she obviously had plenty of experience and knowledge to share. But she'd be working with mere mortals—young women who couldn't match her drive and didn't have her ability—and putting her athletes' needs ahead of her own was potentially detrimental to her running career. She'd have to fit her training around her athletes' practice and race schedule, and organize travel. She'd be on her feet all day on the weekends at meets. But having others depending on her could help pull Benoit out of her own head.

Even among distance runners, who tend to be an introverted and individualistic lot, Benoit was something of a lone wolf. She was admired and respected on the road-racing circuit, well-liked by those who got to know her, but at races she kept to herself. She couldn't sit down to dinner at night with runners she was going to try to grind into the asphalt the next morning. It sapped her energy—she'd be sizing them up across the table and simultaneously worrying that her own nervousness was showing through, that she'd betray some weakness they could use to their advantage in the race. She'd do the occasional training run with other women and counted runners such as Jackie Gareau and Judi St. Hilaire as good friends. But she'd learned that her natural competitiveness made training with other women an unhealthy exercise—especially if they wanted to remain friends.

She did have Scott Samuelson. They'd begun dating in college—he was a pole vaulter on the men's track and field team at Bowdoin—and had gotten very serious in the year after graduation. He didn't run with her regularly, not that she'd want him to anyway, and he wasn't one to step into a coaching or advisory role, the way Jack did for Grete. No, Scott's role was that of sounding board, pillar of support, and the person who kept her functional. As major races approached, her focus narrowed to the point where she'd lose track of the basic details of life, such as car keys, appointments—she even once forgot to bring her shoes to a race. Scott was goofy, gregarious, and would never match her intensity or competitiveness. But he understood it, didn't try to change it; they balanced each other—something Benoit desperately needed. He, along with her family and a small circle of (mostly) Mainers, helped her turn off that feverishly obsessive part of her mind that could suffocate the rest of her. They loved her and weren't overly impressed with running: her mother once sent her a photo of her mid-race, with a note attached: "if this is how running makes you feel, please stop!"

At BU, she started doing occasional easy runs with Bob Sevene, who helped coach the men's team. Sev, as everyone called him, had grown up just outside of Boston, in the formerly industrial town of Waltham—though the long, red-brick factory buildings on the banks of the Charles River were mostly abandoned by the time he was born. He'd taken up running in high school, and running took him to Alfred University in western New York—ninety minutes from both Buffalo and Rochester. He graduated in 1966 and enlisted, serving in Vietnam until 1970, when his helicopter crashed in the jungle, and he dragged his fellow crewmen to safety. He returned from the war with a Bronze Star, the Air Medal, and a Purple Heart, only to find that his service didn't rate much; in one job interview, he was told he'd wasted his time in the army. He was adrift.

He ran every day, some days two or more hours. He started helping his old Waltham High track coach just to keep himself occupied until he found a toehold on a career path.

Instead, he found his calling. Coaching made him whole. He went back to grad school, then hopped from school to school before landing at Boston University. The army had developed, or revealed, a leader; he was not a rah-rah, inspirational speech kind of coach, not a man overly exuberant or effusive in his praise. There was nothing fancy or flashy to Sev's training—he took a methodical approach, layering a steady progression of workouts on top of a strong foundation of strength and endurance. He was a keen observer—he read everything, spoke to everyone, listened and learned, and had an obsessive attention to detail. But the key to his success was simple: he just inspired trust. He was unfailingly loyal to his athletes—his runners could call him any time, from anywhere, and he'd be there for them. His care for them was boundless, and his love for the sport nearly palpable; he gave so much to his athletes and to the sport that he made his athletes feel not just stronger and faster but more worthy.

"I don't think anyone ever coached Joanie," Sev would say later. But if Benoit didn't need a coach, perhaps she needed someone like him: a kindred spirit, someone as intense, obsessive, and tough as she—perhaps more so. He was tall but seemed to stand taller, with hard-edged features: a hawk-like nose and sharp blue eyes that darted side to side constantly, as if he were potential prey for some larger animal. He had a gravelly voice that carried easily across the track and could cut through the din of a raucous crowd. Though only in his thirties, he had the demeanor of a gruff and grizzled track lifer twice his age. He had strong opinions on nearly every aspect of the sport, a firm sense of what was right, and said what he thought. He could be an intimidating presence.

Benoit would chart her own course, as she always had, would trust her body to tell her when to run hard and when to back off, when to race and when to rest. But it helped to have someone in her corner. He could give her frank advice—what Sev thought of her training and racing plan, he would say—and his passion, care, and loyalty, not to mention faith in her toughness and talent, were just what she needed whenever long-festering doubts began to creep to the surface. And Sev needed someone like her: someone just as fiercely loyal, who would run until her legs stopped working, and then try to run one more mile—someone who shared his sense of right and wrong in the sport, who had the same hard edge.

His first order of business as unofficial consultant to Benoit was to try to get her to see a doctor to treat her still-inflamed heels. Initially, he failed. But as much as she didn't like doctors, loath as she was to admit weakness, finally she had to admit that she wasn't making any progress. She scheduled an appointment with her old friend Dr. Leach. After a consult, he scheduled surgery for both feet, but blood tests revealed that her iron levels were so low as to make her essentially anemic; he postponed surgery until she got her iron levels back up. She celebrated the delay by flying down to Tampa, Florida, to race a half marathon in early December. She finished third, in 1:17. When at last she bowed to the inevitable, Dr. Leach found bone spurs in both heels, a partially torn right Achilles tendon, and two ruptured bursa sacs—fluid-filled sacs that lubricate joints, and in extreme cases of repetitive stress (such as running insane amounts), the blood vessels in the tissue can tear. Though the surgery was successful, Dr. Leach conspired with Sev on an added pre-caution: he put her in walking casts, which wasn't strictly necessary, but would keep her from running right away.

The return from surgery would be a long process—especially for someone as impatient as Benoit. She would need to take baby steps back, to bring her mileage and speed back up very gradually. Even then, she had no guarantees of a full recovery. But hitting bottom brought with it a strange lightness: the road ahead was straightforward—rehab and recovery entailed difficult but concrete steps. It was the kind of challenge that energized Benoit and brought out the best of her competitive spirit. She didn't have time or energy to worry about the future of her running career; she had to focus on more immediate tasks. Two days after surgery, she furiously pedaled a stationary bike in her walking casts, the first of many such workouts she'd attack with vengeance; three days after surgery, on New Year's Eve 1981, she and her casts danced the night away at a friend's apartment.

***

The end of 1981 brought change for Waitz as well. She parted ways with her coach, Stolba. "It was an experiment," she said, "but I did not want a coach for always. I am back to my old way of training now, and I am happier."[1] After recovering from her lower leg injury, she set her sights on winning the 1982 Boston Marathon.[2] In part, she had commercial considerations: her sponsor, Adidas, liked having her visible in the United States, and outside of New York, Boston was the biggest American race in terms of publicity.[3]

Don't start too fast at Boston, everyone warned. "If you're going to make a move early," said Boston Marathon winner Greg Meyer, "you'd better have the fitness to carry it out or the course will eat you alive. And so will the other people."[4] But a runner who runs even pace for Boston has started too slow. The course has a net elevation drop of about 450 feet, most of it in the first half. The trick is to let the downhills carry you with minimal effort on your part—stay relaxed, enjoy the ride, don't push the pace as the course levels out. Preparing to run Boston, so the common thinking goes, means preparing to run the hills around mile 20; the reality is, as Roe baldly stated, Heartbreak Hill is overestimated. Preparing to run Boston means preparing for the downhill sections, being able to run them smoothly and efficiently, especially after Heartbreak Hill, where the course curves down into Cleveland Circle and onto Beacon Street.

Race day broke a little warm, and Boston's adherence to the traditional noontime start ensured that runners would suffer through the hottest part; temperatures would peak in the 70s. Waitz started fast, and in Wellesley, a little past the halfway point, she felt her quads twinge a little as she came down an incline just past the town center. She crested Heartbreak Hill as if running on clouds. She held a massive lead, though how big wasn't exactly clear, as the Boston Marathon didn't track the women runners that closely. Germany's Charlotte Teske, who was in second place, would say afterward that she hadn't seen Waitz since the earliest miles. Waitz hit the Lake Street checkpoint, a little more than 21.5 miles, in 1:59.55, which put her around 2:23–2:24 pace. Coming down the hill into Cleveland Circle, she felt her quads twinge again, then bark insistently. She kept on, gingerly, but two miles from the finish, still on world record pace, she stopped to walk. She stretched a little, tried to loosen up, tried to jog again—and her quads locked up and she nearly toppled over.

Teske continued to plug along, not realizing that Waitz had dropped out. She turned onto Boylston and was met by a thunderous wave of cheers—quite sporting, she thought, for the runner-up. She crossed in 2:29.33, unaware that she was the Boston Marathon champion until a policeman told her after the finish.

Jack, meanwhile, had been waiting at the finish—expecting Grete around 2:23, getting worried as the clock ticked past 2:28, finally being told that she had dropped out. She had been whisked to the hospital to get checked out—"My first time in a, what do you call it, an ambulance?" she'd say later. It seemed like overkill to her; she left the hospital under her own power, caught a cab, and met Jack in front of their hotel. "I am not disappointed," she said hours after the race. "I was running very fast. I looked at my watch and I was on the time for a 2:23. If I had been going at a 2:30 pace, I would have been very unhappy to drop out, but, with this, I cannot be upset." If she harbored any doubts after failing to finish her last two marathons, they didn't show. In fact, she seemed more positive after dropping out than after breaking the world record. "I still think I can run a very fast marathon. I will try again in the European Championships."[5]

***

The European Athletics Championship barely registers in the United States, but outside of the Olympics it is the most significant international track and field meet on the calendar. Europe is the spiritual home of athletics: tens of thousands of rabid fans pack stadiums in Oslo, Monaco, Helsinki, Rome, or London. The oldest extant running race in the world, the Palio del Drappo Verde (Race of the Green Cloth, named for the prize given to the winner), was first contested outside of Verona since 1207 or 1208 (and took a two-century hiatus before being revived in 2008) over a roughly nine-kilometer course. It is referenced by Dante in the *Divine Comedy*, and incidentally, included a women's race starting in

1393. (The rules stated that it was open to "honest women, even if only one is to participate," and open to prostitutes if no honest women chose to run.)[6] And of course, the original Olympic footrace, the 197-meter stadion, had begun in Greece.

Athens hosted the European Championships of 1982. The most dominant national track and field programs in the world (with the exception of the United States) would face off: at the 1980 Olympics, which the Americans boycotted, European nations—the Soviet Union, East Germany, Great Britain and Italy (both competing under the Olympic flag in a nod to the boycott), and Poland occupied the top five spots on the athletics medal table. And the Euros would host the first official women's marathon at an IAAF-sanctioned continental championship. The women's marathon was, in a manner of speaking, being vetted after the IOC had approved it. A poor exhibition at Euros—mass dropouts, or a few exhausted women dropping to the track at the finish—probably wouldn't result in the IOC pulling the marathon from the Los Angeles Olympics. But it would increase the likelihood of 1984 being the first—and last—women's Olympic marathon. The sport needed a good show.

But the show would not include the sport's biggest star. Waitz, hobbled by yet another lower leg injury, could not run. In her absence, the race felt wide open. Germany's Teske, the 1982 Boston Marathon champion, Italy's Laura Fogli—fourth at New York, winner of the Rome Marathon—and Norway's Kristiansen, runner-up to Roe at New York, were the odds-on favorites. Though Kristiansen had been running competitively since 1976, she still seemed somewhat new to the sport. Only in 1980 did she commit fully to running: in 1978, she represented Norway at the world XC skiing championships. She loved the team aspect of skiing—traveling together on the national team, working with her teammates at the touring centers, bonding through the brutally long and difficult workouts. Running never fostered that same sort of camaraderie. But skiing took up so much time: she had to drive an hour to the nearest ski training center and spent hours (as skiers obsessively do) waxing and preparing her skis. Running seemed simpler. She entered the 1978 New York City Marathon but had to pull out at the last minute because she had a major university exam scheduled for the following week and couldn't afford to miss the study time. After graduation, she began working full-time as a medical engineer in a cancer research lab and found the time commitment to skiing untenable. She had some modest marathon results before her breakthrough second place to Roe at the 1981 New York City Marathon; the Euros seemed like a golden opportunity to establish herself as an Olympic threat.

Kristiansen and Fogli broke away with Portugal's Rosa Mota, who was running her first-ever marathon. In her career, she'd never finished higher than eighteenth at World Cross-Country, had never raced longer than a half marathon, and at that distance her best time was an undistinguished 1:16, which put her twenty-second on the world list in what was a sporadically contested event. Earlier that week in the Championships, she had raced the 3000, finishing twelfth—the Portuguese athletics administration hadn't wanted her to run the marathon and would enter her only on the condition that she ran the 3000 first. Nothing in her career to that point suggested she had the makings of an elite distance runner; even at the peak of her career, her times were slower than those of her rivals, especially at shorter distances. But she relished brutally hot and humid conditions, and she could run forever.

The three women raced neck and neck all the way into the final kilometer, a downhill stretch to the old Athens Olympic Stadium. Each had tried to surge, had tried to break the others; none had given an inch. And it was Mota, despite having the slowest times of the three, who broke away from the others, putting thirty seconds between herself and runner-up Fogli in the final three minutes. Kristiansen was only ten seconds behind Fogli. Their times were slow—2:36—but they had to be: the heat, humidity, hills, and smog of Athens all ensured that the race would be only against the competition, not against the clock. Some of the favorites wilted—Teske ran 2:45, more than sixteen minutes slower than her Boston time just months earlier, and finished twelfth; "I'm just not a heat runner" was all she could say. But only four women dropped out, and the medalists could all take heart that they'd proven themselves in conditions similar to what they'd face in 1984: Athens's "heat and smog-laden air" offered a good preview of what runners might expect in Los Angeles, suggested James Dunaway in the *New York Times*.

Mota seemed ideally suited to the heat and was suddenly an Olympic favorite, not to mention the first winner of an IAAF global medal in the women's marathon. Kristiansen, undaunted by her bronze medal, came out of Athens believing that she could be the best in the world. Others in Norway viewed her skeptically, but she had felt strong throughout, had handled the hills and heat just fine, and just didn't have the closing speed on the downhill section. She knew she could start faster and run harder. She made it her goal to win the first IAAF World Marathon Championship, which would be held the next summer in Helsinki—a crown that only weeks before had seemed destined to go to Kristiansen's own countrywoman—Waitz.

"The Grete Waitz Era Is Over," proclaimed newspapers in Norway. She had lost the world record, failed to finish her last two marathons, and hadn't even made it to the line for Euros. A new generation had gravitated to the sport, lured by the promise of Olympic gold and the potential for sizable paydays in the big races. Waitz had paved the way for them, had elevated marathoning; the field, now crowded with talented and tough competitors, seemed to have caught up, if not surpassed her. But if Waitz mourned the supposed passing of her so-called era, she didn't show it; in fact, she was right where she wanted to be, and she had, at last, what she'd always said she wanted in the marathon: rivals worthy of the name.

CHAPTER 11

Don't Call It a Comeback

Benoit and Waitz, 1982–1983

ON THE SAME DAY AS THE EUROPEAN CHAMPIONSHIPS, HALF A WORLD away, Benoit made her post-surgery return at the Nike OTC marathon in Eugene, Oregon. Unlike Athens, Eugene offered ideal marathoning conditions: temps in the 50s, a light breeze, overcast skies, and a fast course. The Nike OTC Marathon had been the site of numerous records: Jackie Hansen became the first woman under 2:40 when she ran 2:38 in 1975, Liane Winter set a new world record of 2:37.57 in 1977, and Julie Brown broke Hansen's American record with a 2:36 in 1978. The course was fast, the weather perfect; minutes before the start, Benoit threw her watch at Sev and said, "If I don't break 2:30 I'm retiring." It was a joke, probably; she and Sev had a deadpan sense of humor, often with an edge. But even if Benoit targeted 2:30, if that were the time that would give her validation that she was back on track, she knew that focusing on her pace would only get in the way; she'd either get discouraged if she was too slow or scared if she was too fast. She needed to just run hard and trust her fitness.

The casts had come off in February, and she began doing easy runs, often with Sev. But soon—too soon, according to any rational post-surgery recovery plan—the runs got faster. Subconsciously, perhaps, she'd speed up just a little, and when Sev matched her, she'd ratchet down the pace again. Soon he'd be just hanging on with all the tempo he could muster—she'd have him in his best shape since the army. In early May, she ran a 25K tune-up race in Michigan and came away feeling like she was ready to test herself against the best.

Lebow's Mini-Marathon, now sponsored by L'Eggs, had come a long way—from sixty-four runners (give or take a few Playboy bunnies) in 1972 to more than six thousand entrants a decade later. He no longer needed to chat up women in singles bars to try to get them to the race—by 1982 the top athletes in the world flocked to Central Park for what amounted to the women's 10K world championship road race. Waitz had won it three times in a row, rarely pushed. In 1982, on a warm day in which the slight drizzle only made the heat more suffocating, Waitz, Teske, and Benoit took the early lead. They stayed together through half-way, at which point Waitz, driving a relentless pace, dropped the other two. Benoit ran 32:36 and beat Teske; more important, she didn't let Waitz disappear, losing by only thirty-six seconds. "Last year," she said, "I lost sight of her early." Publicly, she acknowledged Waitz's greatness: "I knew there was no catching her, unless she had an appendicitis attack and I got a sudden burst of energy."[1] Privately, she told Sev, "I can beat her."

But the short races were mere tune-ups. At the OTC marathon, Benoit went through five kilometers in 16:20—same as her pace at the Mini and 2:17 pace for the marathon. Around ten miles, she noticed that there was only a strung-out pack of male runners up in the distance. She caught one guy, asked him if he felt like surging up to catch the next pack in front; somewhat breathlessly, he told her that pack was running well under 2:20. She went under the American 20K record en route (1:07.44) and hit halfway in 1:11.30. She backed off considerably until the final miles, then surged again, hitting the tape in 2:26.12—smashing Catalano's American record by one minute, forty seconds.[2] And she felt like she could've kept going, cranking out miles at that pace for as long as she wanted. She leaped into Sev's arms and nearly toppled him over.

For the time being, retirement plans could be shelved.

***

After watching the European Championship, Waitz cautiously rebuilt her fitness, and targeted the 1982 New York City Marathon for her return. It was a windy, blustery day—she felt like she nearly came to a standstill going across the Verrazano-Narrows Bridge at the start, and the top women bunched together through a relatively easy ten miles. Waitz surged, and the field let her go; soon her lead was more than a minute. She let herself cruise into the finish in 2:27.14, feeling more relief than excitement—a "safe" run, she said. Not until she crossed the Queensboro Bridge into Manhattan, around sixteen miles, was she confident that she could finish. "I'm just glad to get through it," she said of her first full marathon in two years.[3]

She was now fully invested in the marathon and planning her road to the Olympics. Though Los Angeles was still two years away, going easy in New York was part of the plan. She got a victory, a stepping-stone on the way to the next major race: the Helsinki World Championships. Her injury-plagued year made her wary of overdoing it at Worlds: "If I go 100 percent for 1983, there will be nothing left for 1984," she said.[4] Her build would be gradual, she would stay within herself. She had a new coach, Johan Kaggestad, and she valued his input. But she would train on her own terms, trusting herself more, doing what she felt she needed to do rather than acquiescing to his demands.

If she planned to keep her training and racing low key in 1983, it was the kind of low key that would be the envy of any other runner. She won her fifth world cross-country title in March, then turned her sights to the first major marathon of the spring season: the London Marathon. Though London was only in its third year, it had already established itself as one of the majors. Race director Chris Brasher had copied Lebow's blueprint successfully: the race toured much of the city and hit all the major landmarks. Hundreds of thousands of spectators came out to watch, and in 1983, London even surpassed New York in the number of runners. More important, London's course was flat and fast. London and Boston were the same weekend in April; Benoit and Roe headlined the Boston field, but Waitz had sworn she'd never run Boston again after her painful experience on the downhills.

The media expected a world-record attempt; Waitz as usual said nothing on the subject, but her splits in the early going suggested that she knew exactly how fast she had to run. Conditions were amenable: cool temperatures, and the pelting rain at the start gradually lessened. The gentle downhill start had her slightly ahead of Roe's pace through the first half. But at mile 22, she was nearly exactly even, and with a mile and a half to go, she'd drifted thirty seconds behind record pace. Spectators thronged the last miles, the cheers for Waitz louder than they'd been for the men's winner, Englishman Mike Gratton. Black-coated bobbies lined the route as she drove straight up the Mall toward Buckingham Palace, weaving through the male runners strung out before her; she reached the foot of Westminster Bridge, just one hundred meters or so from the finish. Up toward the crest of the bridge, she drove toward the finish, her final kick a dead sprint, honed by years on the track. She angled toward the far right of the finishing chute; course marshals frantically waved her back left; they'd set up a special chute for her. The clock above the chute ticked the last seconds toward 2:25.29. She broke the tape somewhere between 2:25.28 and 29.

Unofficially, 2:25.28; more precisely, 2:25.28.66. Waitz patiently submitted to an interview for the live broadcast ("Grete, many congratulations—that's your fastest time." Sympathetic smile from Grete, and an awkward pause while she waited for an actual question. "Yes, it is," she said finally.) Meanwhile, almost immediately after her finish, word went out that Waitz had broken Roe's record by one second. But marathon times were, in 1983, rounded up to the nearest second, so officially, Waitz had tied Roe. By the time an official correction got out of the gate, word had already reached Roe in Boston that Waitz was now the record holder.[5] Grete, as usual, was none too impressed with her time. She found Jack, and they made their way to their accommodations. That night, they made a friendly wager on how much faster Benoit would run in Boston than Waitz had just run in London.

***

Benoit's preparation for Boston had been good—better than good. Her workouts were fast, and recent races had been, by her standards, blazing: a 4:36 mile in February took nine seconds off her previous best. When asked if a marathon world record was a possibility, Benoit allowed, "If the weather is good." She always tried her best to reveal nothing to the press, lest she inadvertently tip her hand to her competitors; for her to say the record was a possibility was a flat-out boast. She'd run more than 120 miles just two weeks before the marathon—a habit she had of kicking up the mileage when she got nervous and excited. Sev could only shake his head—two weeks before a major race was a time to ease off. "The problem," he said, of working with athletes like Benoit, "is trying to keep [her] down . . . Jeez, they train so hard."[6] "There's really no rhyme or reason to my training," she said. "I like to be able to run a marathon with three or four weeks' notice."[7] She'd only committed to Boston in March, after the World Cross-Country Championships. The day before World XC, she'd gone on a long run with Kenny Moore, who had finished fourth at the 1972 Olympic marathon. She kept escalating the pace; by the end, Moore was hanging on for dear life. That run, and the subsequent fourth-place finish the next day, convinced her that she was ready for a fast marathon. And if Sev thought she was overtraining since then, he kept that to himself going into the race; he knew that physically she was ready to do something special. The last thing he wanted to do was sow any doubts in her mind before Boston.

As confident as Benoit felt, she'd let Roe play the role of favorite, let her feel that pressure. Since Roe's record-setting run in New York in 1981, her life had been a whirlwind. She signed multiple sponsorship deals, became a spokesperson for the New Zealand Board of Tourism, and appeared on countless magazine covers. She traveled the globe for photo shoots, sponsor appearances, and races. Her first win at Boston, in 1981, seemed long ago—a different world and a different Roe: back then, Roe said, "I felt I had nothing to lose. There was absolutely no pressure."

Now it seemed, there was nothing but pressure. She'd been fighting injuries for the better part of a year: She tore a calf muscle in May 1982, came back too quickly, injured her Achilles, and couldn't get right for the rest of the year. Her buildup had been gradual, making sure she didn't reinjure herself, and the fitness started to come around. She was doing her long runs on her favorite hilly Waitakere route faster than she had in 1981. She'd run workouts, repeat 3000-meter intervals, in under five minute per mile pace. She was fitter than she'd ever been. "The hardest thing," she said, "will be the racing. I'm down on racing. I'm working on my mind, teaching myself to concentrate." She'd lost just a little bit of belief in herself. In 1981, she'd stalked Catalano, struck with authority, and left Catalano near tears; in 1983, looking back at that race, she confessed she'd wanted to drop out mid-race. "I thought to myself at the finish, I was very lucky to win."[8]

She knew Waitz would go after the world record in London, expected her to break it. Boston would be her chance to get it back. "I lay awake for hours just thinking about it," she said. Roe called Benoit as soon as she heard about Waitz's London run. She knew that they were both going after the record and suggested that they work together in the early going to set the pace. Benoit was having none of it—she politely declined, saying she only wanted to run her best race. But in her hotel room before the race, Benoit plotted out the splits to run 2:25, then immediately tried to forget about them. "It blew my mind," she said. "There's no way I can run that fast."[9]

Most successful marathon world record attempts follow a similar pacing strategy: nearly even splits, if anything slightly slower over the first half, with a very fast finish. Benoit's first mile was 4:47 (2:05 pace), and she hit 5K near her personal best of 15:40, which worked out to 2:12 pace. "Watch it, lady!" some male runners cautioned as she screamed past. She claimed later that she was just doing what she always did in a marathon—running the way she felt. On this day, she felt like burying Roe early on, giving her no chance to hang around and surge for the win as she'd done before. Benoit tried to ignore the splits completely, but she did hear one: she hit ten miles in 51:38, 5:09 per mile—ninety seconds faster than the ten-mile American record she'd set in 1982, and on 2:15 pace. "[That] scared me a bit," she said after the race.

Mid-race, worry creased her brow. She saw Sev along the course and told him she felt blisters bubbling up on her feet. "Just move your feet around a bit in your shoes," he advised. "Does that work?" an onlooker asked. "I don't know," he said, "but what else am I gonna tell her?" It probably wasn't about the blisters, he thought. She'd just come back down to earth a bit—the emotion had worn off, the rational part of the brain kicked back on, and she had a long way to go. If he could give her even a bit of confidence, a way to take the focus off whatever negative thoughts were trying to worm their way into her consciousness, that would be the best thing he could do.

Benoit hit halfway in 1:08.23. At seventeen miles, in the hills, she felt a side stitch. By this point, the blisters had shredded her feet; moving them around a bit in her shoes could only do so much. If there was a time for the race to come apart, this was it. She had slowed dramatically—how could she not?—and her last ten miles had been 2:29 marathon pace. In Cleveland Circle, her Boston University athletes had climbed on top of the T station and were cheering madly. She let her concentration break, let out a huge smile, and gathered herself for the final push. The race was hers; the only question was the final time.

Benoit flew through the remaining miles and leaped across the finish line, arms raised. Her time astounded even her: 2:22.43, a full seven minutes ahead of second place, thirteen minutes faster than her winning time in 1979. Deep down, buried beneath the rational part of her that had looked at 2:25 and thought it was too fast, she'd been expecting something in the 2:24s, hoping for 2:23. Sev wasn't surprised at all. "You knew that was coming," he said. "She's just an animal." Her training had been more astounding to him than the race. Tommy Leonard, by this time known to the Boston press not only as the barkeep at the Eliot but as the unofficial Boston Marathon greeter and "running guru," said of Benoit, "If she was a running back, instead of running around people, she'd run right through them . . . she's Maine tough . . . a Maine lobsterman in the middle of February. She's a female Paul Bunyan."[10]

The temperature had been in the mid-50s, with overcast skies and a light westerly wind blowing Benoit toward Boston. And she'd had company for part of it—she hadn't wanted company, but a local TV station had paid a sub-2:20 Boston-area marathoner, Kevin Green, to run alongside the women's leader and provide occasional commentary. He caught up with Benoit in the middle of the race and ran next to her. Some in the running press argued that Benoit had been paced, that she'd had an unfair advantage. In a way, she had: at the start, she saw Green line up next to Roe—in effect, his prediction that she'd be the winner. If Benoit had needed any extra motivation, this unintended slight provided it.

From the gun, Roe had been left in a state of shock. She tried to match the pace early on but felt her calf nearly cramping. "Joan's pace was so fast," she said, almost wistfully. "I should have paid more attention to the time." Instead of recognizing that Benoit's pace was unsustainable, she felt the race slipping away from her. Around seventeen miles, she slowed to a jog—she was hurting, could feel her calf more than she wanted. Jack Fultz, 1976 Boston winner, himself slowed by injuries, pulled up beside her and tried to get her to refocus on just running the rest of the way in—maybe hoping for Roe's sake Joanie would come back to them. Roe tried to get herself going again, but when Canada's Jackie Gareau passed her, she sat down and cried. She and Fultz walked a mile or so to a house belonging to a friend of Fultz's, where a marathon watch party was in progress. Roe took a shower, borrowed some clean clothes, and watched the finish on TV. She graciously stayed at the party, playing the role of guest of honor, chatting with everyone, hiding her disappointment. Hours later, Fultz drove her back to the house where she'd been staying.

Sometime after midnight, Benoit was still dancing the night away at the Eliot when Lebow walked up to her. "Don't you have to be up for the morning TV show?" he asked. "I don't plan on going to sleep at all," she said.[11] She danced through the night, blisters forgotten, aching muscles ignored. In the morning, after her TV appearance, she'd soak her feet, take care of her body, plan out the week's practices for her BU team. And she'd have to face a tidal wave of media attention unlike anything she'd seen since her first Boston win in 1979. This time, at least, she knew it was coming; she'd still feel swamped and suffocated, but she could gird herself for it.

The Olympic year loomed ahead, and after Boston, Benoit was finished with marathons until the Olympic Trials. Hard as it was to miss out, she'd skip the World Championships; she'd need to rest and recover for the rest of the year. The qualifying race for Worlds was June 2, and even assuming she could get herself ready to race again in six short weeks, and assuming she made the U.S. team, the World Championships were in August. Three hard marathons in five months was too much of a grind, mentally and physically. Further, the Trials, which were in May of 1984, was a win or go home race: if she didn't finish in the top three, she'd be watching the Olympics in Maine. On time, she was minutes ahead of any of her fellow Americans, but so many things could go wrong in a marathon; you were only partly in control of your fate. The Trials was the one race where you wanted complete control—it was the one race where nothing could go wrong. Then, if she did qualify for the Olympics, the turnaround was too short—only twelve weeks to recover, recharge, and prepare for the most important marathon in the history of women's running. And she'd just established herself as the unquestioned favorite, the American hope for gold in a historic race on American soil—with all the pressure, expectations, and unwanted attention that came with representing not just her country but all women everywhere. If she let herself think about what lay ahead, she'd probably want to curl up in a ball in her bedroom in Maine. It could all wait for daylight. The rest of the night, or at this point, the rest of the hours before dawn, were for celebrating.

Roe flew to Italy to try to redeem herself in the Rome marathon the very next weekend. Food poisoning kept from making it to the starting line.

***

After London, Waitz turned her focus to the World Championships in Helsinki. No qualifying races for her—the Norwegian Athletics Association, Norges Friidrettsforbund, had different rules than the United States for choosing its team for Worlds; they simply named Waitz to the marathon team. Her buildup had been nearly perfect. She'd kept her mileage lower: for all of 1983, she had only eleven weeks in which she topped 140 kilometers (88 miles); fewer miles at a faster pace seemed to suit her. And she did her long runs very fast—under six minutes per mile. In the buildup to Helsinki, she did long runs occasionally with the men's world record holder, New Zealander Rob de Castella. Mile repeats close to 5:00 felt easy; she ran a hilly five-mile interval in the middle of a ten-mile run at 5:20 pace, cruising easily; during one workout, she ran a 5K interval in 15:23–4:55 per mile, and fifteen seconds faster than Benoit's best time in a 5K race. She took the line in Helsinki supremely confident.

The race began at 3:05 local time on the first day of the first-ever IAAF World Championships. Temperatures crested in the 80s, but organizers wanted the women's marathon to start as a sort of prelude to the Championships, with its finish in the stadium at the conclusion of the opening ceremonies. "It's a warm day . . . very humid, too," warned the race announcer. "It's going to need a great deal of discipline." The course was deceptively hilly—no major hills, but they were constant: only 20 percent of the course was flat, level running. Grete and Jack had looked at the weather forecasts, studied the course, and had come up with a plan to stay as conservative as possible until 30K—nearly three-fourths of the way through the race. Waiting so long into the race would set Grete on edge—she liked to make her move earlier, make the others react to her. But she could keep herself under control and stick to the plan. Starting on the track, in front of a packed stadium, Japan's Rumiko Kaneko led early, going through the first lap in an exuberant eighty-some seconds. She led the field out the gates to the roads in 2:29 pace; she'd finish in 2:58. Waitz and the other contenders hung back. By 10K, Jackie Gareau of Canada, the 1980 Boston Marathon champion, held the lead with Ireland's Carey May. The pace had slowed to a leisurely 36:10, nearly 2:32 marathon pace. Nonetheless, Waitz stayed in the middle of the main chase pack—though they were hardly chasing—about ten seconds behind.

Ireland's Regina Joyce took over the lead by 20K and hit halfway still just a little under 2:32 pace. Waitz waited, running in a pack of ten others, thirty seconds back, and getting edgy. And at 30K, precisely according to plan, she brought down the pace. The pack dwindled to four: Waitz, Soviets Raisa Smekhnova and Lutsia Belyayeva, and American Marianne Dickerson. Joyce was glancing back regularly, and soon the chase pack swallowed her up. Waitz applied more pressure; the pack fell off—first Belyayeva, then Joyce, then Dickerson, and finally Smekhnova. Waitz ran the ten kilometers from 30–40K (roughly, miles 18–24) in 33:13—2:19 pace. The final kilometers, 40–42, were significantly faster, and the final lap, around the track at Helsinki stadium, was well under five-minute pace—ten seconds faster than Kaneko had led the field out. Waitz finished in 2:28.09; she had run the second half four minutes and twenty seconds faster than the first. At the finish, she told Jack, "If you asked me to go out and run another 5K like that, I could have done it easily."

More than two minutes after Waitz finished, Smekhnova, who'd been second to Waitz at the World XC championships in March, sprinted into the stadium, chased by Dickerson. Four hundred meters from the finish of the first-ever world championships, Dickerson had only ten meters to gain to earn a silver medal. Down the backstretch, Smekhnova clung to her lead as her body inexorably tightened, while Dickerson found a final gear. She overtook Smekhnova and put ten meters between them by the finish. Smekhnova crossed, dejected, but immediately went to shake Dickerson's hand. Waitz found them both, and together, arm in arm, the first three women's world championship marathon medalists stood to greet the other finishers as they came across.

Dickerson, a 22-year-old graduate student, had run only two marathons previously: a 2:43 in 1982 and 2:33 at the U.S. championships. She'd been a surprise even making the U.S. team. At worlds, she had run 2:31 and could barely contain herself. "Oh, there's lots left," she said after the race. "I know there is."[12]

In the year after the Grete era had supposedly ended, Waitz had broken (or tied, depending on your perspective) the world marathon record, won the World XC title for the fifth time, and been crowned world marathon champion. It had been a long, difficult climb back, but she'd achieved all she'd set out to do and more in the marathon. In the closing stages of the World Championship, her margin having ballooned to three minutes, she ran, all alone, oblivious to the roaring crowd and Jack's exhortations, and her mind turned to the runner who wasn't there: Benoit.

After the medal ceremony, Jack and Grete left the stadium, Grete feeling, she said later, "as hollow and empty as the tunnel we walked through." They got back to the hotel and shared a long moment of silence. "Well," she asked, "what now?"

INTERLUDE

SANTA MONICA, CALIFORNIA, AUGUST 5, 1984, 8:17 A.M.: *Duerbroeck's lead lasts twelve minutes; a pack of thirty runners absorb her at about two miles. They have picked up the pace, but only slightly, and most of the thirty are still well within their comfort zone as they approach the first water station. Runners veer sharply left—like New York cabbies cutting across multiple lanes of traffic—to grab sponges soaked in ice water. Others surge ahead, stutter-stepping to pick up a sponge, then ducking back out away from the tables. One volunteer gets caught in the middle of the runners, backpedaling, juggling cups of water and sponges, trying to hand them out while not falling over or crashing into any runners. He very nearly causes a catastrophic pileup less than three miles into the race.*

Waitz stays in the middle of the street, clear of the whole mess. Her stride is always crisp and efficient; today, in the early going, it looks almost too crisp, robotic even—as if she is thinking about each step. At 5 foot 7, she is tall for an elite marathoner, which only enhances the sense that she floats just above the hurly-burly of the pack. If her eyes betrayed some anxiety before the race, now they focus solely on the patch of road ten feet in front of her. Most runners sneak an occasional glance at the others around them, and when they do, their eyes are drawn to Waitz—with good reason: not one of them has ever beaten her in a marathon she finished. Nor, for that matter, have they ever beaten her in the only other major international distance competition for women, the World Cross Country Championships. Though Benoit holds the world marathon record, Waitz is the runner the others hold in awe.

At the aid station, Benoit, too, stays out of the fray; Julie Brown has ducked in to grab two sponges and hands one to Benoit. Benoit wipes the back of her neck, then turns to her right and offers it to Waitz, who declines. Benoit makes as if to toss the sponge over the heads of the other runners to the sidewalk, but then she turns to her left and offers it to Mota, who takes it and hands it back to Laura Fogli. At this stage of the race, they are all in it together.

After the brief disruption of the water station, the pack settles back into the easy rhythm of the early stages of a championship marathon. At the front, Isphording stumbles, her leg perhaps clipped by someone behind her. It is a sign of their lack of urgency that the pack spills across most of the road, even threatening to swamp the sidewalk; a group of runners in full flight assumes the shape of an arrow, or a comet—one runner, or perhaps several, at the point, with a long trail of runners stretching out behind. Waitz seems content to not dictate the pace yet. Kristiansen sits on Waitz's shoulder. Mota's strategy seems to be to let the heat take its toll on the others before she makes a move.

Of the runners in the field, Benoit's disposition suggests that she will take out the race. Tactically, she knows that she lacks the pure speed of Waitz and Kristiansen; if the race comes down to a duel in the last miles—and Benoit expects that six or so of them will still be running together at mile 18—she knows they can outkick her unless she burns the kick out of them with a hard early pace. And her competitors are well aware of how fast Benoit took it out when she set the world record in Boston. Some still have their doubts about Benoit's record: Boston is a net downhill course, and she'd had a favorable wind that day. Maybe, they think, she had been paced. They aren't convinced that she could run 2:22 at New York or London. And conditions in LA are different: the course is less forgiving, the heat will punish early aggression, and if Benoit goes out hard, she'll have the very best in the world chasing her down.

"If she's gonna win it," says Johan Kaggestad, who coached both Kristiansen and Waitz, "she's gonna have to take it out hard. But if she's gonna take it out as hard as everyone says she is, well god bless her."

PART III

CHAPTER 12

Groundwork

Olympia and the World, 1983–1984

ON A LATE SUMMER DAY IN OLYMPIA, WASHINGTON, IN 1982, LAUREL James, the owner of Super Jock 'n Jill—likely the first female-owned specialty running store in the nation—hosted a postrace debriefing with her fellow members of the organizing committee for the First Annual Capital City Marathon. The race had been a smashing success; they were basking in the glow of a near-flawless event—and probably dreaming of a return to normalcy. They were wrung out after weeks of little sleep, of late-night meetings, of chasing down every last detail, of waking in the dark hours. So James's final item on the agenda caught them by surprise: she looked around the room and said, "Folks, I've got one more task for us." She then outlined a truly audacious plan: to put together a bid for Olympia, population thirty thousand, to host the first-ever U.S. Olympic Trials for the women's marathon.

In some countries, the athletics governing body selects participants for the Olympics, evaluating each athlete's work over an extended period; Waitz, for example, was assured of a spot on the Norwegian team so long as she could run. The United States uses a single race. The top three finishers at the Olympic Trials make the team; everyone else waits another four years. It is one of the most compelling races in the world: the best runners in the country all peak for one race, and the pressure is often greater than the Olympics themselves. One bad day, and the Olympic dream is over—or at least postponed. Even more than the majors like

Boston and New York, the Olympic Marathon Trials brings the attention of the entire American running community to one place, one town, one race.

Bids were due in a few short months, and site selection would take place in early December at the TAC convention in Philadelphia. Olympia was a longshot at best. Lebow and the New York Road Runners were preparing a bid and had a strong case: he had encouraged women's marathoning even before the AAU approved it, had organized the protest in 1972 to allow women to start with men, had made Crazylegs into the greatest women's-only 10K in the world. And New York was where Grete changed women's marathoning forever—she would have set world records no matter where she ran, but she'd chosen New York, and had made women's marathoning a major story in the biggest media market in the world. On its history alone, perhaps New York deserved the Trials. Los Angeles was also readying a bid, and because it was the host city of the Games, it would be logical to give the U.S. athletes a preview of the Olympic course. But James wanted this historic event for her corner of the Pacific northwest. Most members of the TAC selection committee couldn't even find Olympia on a map, but James made ready to steal the Trials away nonetheless.

Laurel James had a Lebow-esque flair to her marketing approach, relentless drive, loads of charisma, and . . . experience, in a lot of things. She'd been married to an air force pilot, moved herself and her five kids to Seattle when he shipped out to Vietnam. They divorced in the early 1970s, and she needed a job. She tried selling real estate—"that wasn't great"—moved on to selling insurance—"that didn't really work either"—and met a bunch of coworkers who were runners. One week in 1975, she had an idea for a running store. "The Jock Shop," she thought jokingly on Monday. Then, "Super Jock," she thought—there was a popular children's toy by that name in the 1970s—by Wednesday. By Friday, it was Super Jock 'n Jill. She rented an old gas station, cleaned it up, and was in business. By 1977, she was looking for a bigger location; in 1978 she moved into an old Masonic temple.

She joined the TAC regional committee, was soon on the national women's Long Distance Running Committee and became a race director.

She'd been involved with site selection for national events, so she had experience with the process; she knew Olympia would have to make a splash—to out-splash New York, and Los Angeles. Her son Brent, a shoe designer at the time, leaned on friends from Nike's marketing team to put together their slideshow for the pitch. They touted Olympia's weather—average temps in the mid-50s—and a fast, flat, scenic course. And they promised big. "Mom was . . . mom," said Brent, who became head of the Women's Olympic Trials Committee. Laurel would propose crazy ideas; Brent and a host of others would have to figure out how to make them happen. Olympia pitched a weeklong event, with every qualifier flown to Olympia and lodged in a mini-Olympic village, chefs to prepare meals for the runners, entertainment, tours, running clinics, top-flight medical care throughout the week. Their presentation was only half of the pitch: in Philadelphia, Olympia put together an ostentatious hospitality tent: cases of Washington apples, fresh oysters, smoked salmon—even a Douglas fir tree. And beer. Lots of Olympia Beer. And as a topper, they flew in Washington's Senator Slade Gorton to lobby the TAC committee.

Lebow made his pitch for New York in his usual attire—running shoes and a track suit. The final vote: Olympia, 22; New York, 15; Kansas City, 5; Los Angeles, 1. Turned out, that was the easy part for Olympia. They had overpromised; "Grandiose," scoffed the director of the men's marathon trials, John Chew, of Olympia's pitch. Now they had seventeen months to deliver—above all, to raise the $1 million they'd told TAC they would budget for the Trials. Even Lebow, who knew something about overpromising, thought that an outlandish number.

The James gang had counted on Olympia Beer as a major sponsor, but TAC rejected that idea because two of Oly's primary competitors, Budweiser and Miller Lite, were major sponsors of the Los Angeles Olympics. American Express had, yes, expressed interest—but withdrew. Avon offered to sponsor the Trials, but demanded exclusive marketing rights, which was a nonstarter: James wanted a wide base of local sponsors involved. (And the locals were eager to get involved. Local swimmers staged a swimathon around Mercer's Island—twenty-two miles round trip—to raise money. Weisfield Jewelers ("since 1917") offered to donate $10 to the Trials committee for every pair of diamond earrings sold.

Volunteers staged a phone-a-thon and sold coupon books. Collectively, though, the locals were short of $1 million by several orders of magnitude.) There was talk among those on the long-distance committee of looking for an alternate site; Avon again offered to sponsor the Trials—if they could move it to Los Angeles. Finally, in October 1983, Dole, the pineapple company, came aboard as an anchor sponsor, and soon American Airlines offered to fly athletes to Olympia.

For the organizers in Olympia, the Trials wasn't a race but a season. St. Martin's, a local Benedictine college, started its academic year early and shortened some school breaks so that the school would let out in time for the dormitories to be used as the Olympic-style village for the athletes. Trials organizers sent letters to each qualifier, asking, among other things, what they liked to eat—chef-cooked meals would be available in the cafeteria, and organizers hoped to accommodate most athletes' preferences—and what attractions they might like to visit during their stay in Olympia.

On college breaks, the Trials organizing committee hosted "work parties" to repaint the St. Martin's cafeteria and lounge areas, repaint and refurbish the dorm rooms. Kay Walters, who directed Olympia preparations for the committee, stated that "each room will be given a homey atmosphere with items donated locally such as posters, pictures, magazines, and flowers"; the draperies would be cleaned or replaced as needed, and beds would have new bedspreads, Walters said. Local schoolchildren made the posters—"Go for the Gold!" one encouraged—and the local J. C. Penney store donated five hundred pillowcases, which volunteers then embroidered with the Olympic Trials logo. The Olympia Junior Women's Club invited "those interested to submit an 8-inch-by-8-inch quilt piece to be incorporated into one large quilt which will be displayed at the trial events and housed as a permanent remembrance in an area museum after the trials."

On April 11, local Brownie Troop 94—comprised mostly of first graders from Garfield Elementary in Olympia—planted rhododendrons in Marathon Park, a greenspace on the shores of Capital Lake that was renamed in April 1983 to honor the coming Olympic Trials. The Douglas fir that had been in the hospitality tent in Philadelphia was planted in the park to commemorate the event. Wes Gisse, a local field rep for the natural gas utility, spent the spring designing and testing a twelve-foot-high Olympic-style pillar with a cauldron for an Olympic flame. On April 21, an Olympic torch relay traversed the course; Governor John Spellman took the torch and lit the flame at a ceremony featuring local bands and entertainment. All through the celebrations, work continued to prepare Olympia for the Trials: a final request went out to the community on April 26 to join a weekend painting party to finish painting the dorm rooms; a final, final request was posted in *The Olympian* on May 3 for help "from today until next Tuesday" to complete the job.

***

TAC's long-distance running committee set the qualifying time at 2:51.16—the one-hundredth fastest time by an American woman in 1982. By the cutoff date for qualifying, April 16, 1984—not coincidentally, the date of the Boston Marathon—268 women had run under the standard. Among them was Cathy Schiro, born in 1967, three months after Jock Semple had attacked Switzer at the Boston Marathon. Schiro, from Dover, New Hampshire, won her first high-school state championship in 1980 while still an eighth grader. She held multiple national high-school records by her sophomore year, and as a junior in the fall of 1983, won the Avon International Half Marathon in New York City. Her coaches, Tom and Marcia Dowling, gave her an interesting alternative for her junior spring: rather than preparing for the track season, she could train for the Olympic marathon Trials. They laid out the splits she'd have to run; it didn't seem too hard for her—she'd gone faster on training runs, and besides, if her coaches thought she could do it, she knew she could do it. In February 1984, she ran a local marathon in Hampton, New Hampshire, and won easily in 2:45. She was going to the Trials as a 16-year-old.

The year Schiro was born, Sister Marion Irvine had been a member of the Order of Dominican Sisters for twenty years. She was a teacher and an elementary school principal, and a two-pack-a-day smoker. In 1978, at age 48, her niece, who was trying to lose weight, asked Sister Marion to run with her. "I'd see these people out there sweating, and it didn't look like much fun," Irvine recalled. But her niece asked, so on Memorial Day, they went out together for a short jog. "From the first day," she said, "I wanted to do it again." In September she gave up smoking for good; two years later, she ran her first marathon—and finished in just over three hours. By 1983, she was running more than one hundred miles per week. "I didn't think I had the capacity to be a good runner. I didn't think I was that gifted," she said. In December 1983, at the California International Marathon, she ran 2:51.01—the first woman over 50 years old to break three hours. Sister Marion, "The Running Nun," would be running at the Trials as a 54-year-old.

Patti Catalano's last marathon had been in 1981. Since then, she'd been injured, sometimes from overtraining, sometimes from random accidents, like breaking her tailbone while bodysurfing in Hawaii. Her second marriage, to her coach, Joe Catalano, was starting to fall apart. And she had more or less checked out of competitive running: she raced three times in 1982, and midway through 1983, hadn't yet raced at all. She reckoned she was forty pounds over her racing weight.

Even so, the Trials called to her. She wasn't sure why—she'd never dreamed of being an Olympian, never truly felt a part of the women's running community. Running for history? That, she thought, was for the college girls. But she'd always loved running, since that first day in the Quincy cemetery. It had given her direction, had been part of her identity. Professional running had been a living—she'd fought alongside the others to bring prize money into the sport, and she'd signed marketing deals with Nike and others. She'd earned everything she got, and what she'd got, no one could take away from her: she'd proven that she was faster than most of the other runners, and if she wasn't faster, she could be tougher. But she had thought she was retired.

She started training again in the fall of 1983 and ran a few shorter races, but she hurt her hip. Thanksgiving rolled around, and she had to decide. She still wasn't sure why it mattered to her, but she decided to give herself a shot at making the Trials. Her hip still hadn't healed, so she couldn't do hard, fast workouts, couldn't do the hill repeats on Heartbreak she'd loved so much. But she could run long, and she could discipline herself to drop the weight. "I had to learn to run with fatigue again, to develop the feeling of being able to push through it." She knew she wasn't nearly as fast as she'd been but thought she'd at least regained the toughness that had been her greatest asset. She set her sights on the Houston Marathon in January.

"It knocked my socks off," she said. She qualified, by the skin of her teeth: 2:50.35. It came at a price—she'd gone deep into her reserves, perhaps deeper than she'd gone in any of her American record runs. "It took me a while to recover physically and emotionally." Putting herself through so much just to run 2:50—that stung; she still had memories of the days when she'd do easy runs at that pace. But she could call it a victory: she'd come back from nowhere, had given everything she had, and she'd achieved her goal. Maybe that was enough. She asked herself, "Do I really want to run the Trials? Do I care about how I do?" She wasn't sure. But she booked her trip to Olympia—if she went, she'd be going to the Trials as someone who used to be the most feared runner in America and now was a nearly forgotten 31-year-old with one of the slowest qualifying times in the field.

***

Around the world, the other medal contenders, if they didn't need to worry about a qualifying race like the Trials, focused almost entirely on preparing for the Games. Often their thoughts drifted to concerns over heat and smog. Waitz, after winning Worlds, maintained her form through the 1983 New York City Marathon—her third marathon in six months. She ran mostly out of loyalty to Lebow, but she ran conservatively and won easily, in 2:27. That winter, she and Jack stayed in Bermuda—a wealthy Norwegian owned a hotel there and let them stay for free. They traveled less (in the winter of 1982, they'd gone to Australia and New Zealand to race) and raced less; Waitz ran longer, as focused and intense as always, and hoped the warm Bermuda winter would help prepare her for the Olympics. Even though she won the world championship in sauna-like conditions in Helsinki, she feared the heat and expected that its toll would really come due in the last six miles in Los Angeles.

Mota, the European Champion, spent the winter in Portugal, racing sparingly. She'd finished fourth at Worlds—a disappointment, perhaps, but she'd run a new best time of 2:31.50. At Chicago in the fall of 1983, she won, and lowered her best to 2:31.12. In the heat of Portugal, she trained mostly by herself and considered the best tactics for Los Angeles. The top marathoners, the ones who had run 2:25 or better, were—on time—more than a mile ahead of Mota. And the runners with good track backgrounds, such as Waitz, had more top-end speed. If the pace was slow, Waitz and the others would leave her behind in the last miles. But if the pace was too fast from the start, she probably couldn't keep up. She'd have to walk a fine line between not overextending herself early on and finding a way to burn the kick out of the faster runners before the closing stages. If she couldn't outrun the competition, she'd have to outthink them.

Kristiansen was just returning to form in the winter of 1984. Back in 1982, she'd come out of the European Championships with aspirations of claiming the World title in 1983; instead, her life took an unexpected but not entirely unwelcome detour. In January 1983, she won the Houston Marathon in 2:33, and she went into the World Cross Country Championships in March 1983 expecting to place highly—perhaps even to challenge Waitz. She finished thirty-fifth. She felt sluggish, ill. When she went to the doctor, she learned she'd run World XC while four months pregnant. Her son Gaute was born August 13, 1983. Like any working mother, Kristiansen found herself juggling Gaute's needs, her professional responsibilities, and the need for rest. Gaute was up twice a night for feeding; after the 5 a.m. feed, Ingrid could squeeze in an hour run before her husband, Arve, left for work. Then she'd get in another workout when he returned.

In January 1984, five-month-old Gaute in tow, she returned to Houston and won again—this time in 2:27. In her first race in ten months, she lowered her marathon best by more than two minutes. She returned to Norway to resume training through the cold, dark winter months. Much of Kristiansen's training was on a treadmill—she stayed in Norway, preferring friends and the familiarity of home over decamping to a warmer locale for training. And the treadmill suited her training style—"I need to run fast," she said. "I have to be used to high speed." Even in spring and summer, she was on the treadmill two or three times per week. "This is my work," she would say to herself. She would not listen to music or watch TV while on the treadmill. Instead, she watched her competition. "I had pictures of my main competitors in front of me—Joan Benoit, Grete Waitz, Rosa Mota . . . and that is who I would look at. I would tell myself, 'I will beat you.' You can't listen to other things when you are training hard. You must concentrate."

She practiced visualization when she wasn't running. "I would see myself doing the toughest part of the race"—often 25–30K—"I would go through that part in my head." This mental preparation was often only five minutes a day, but it demanded her full focus in ways that running never did. "You have to concentrate or you won't do it well; you have to be there. If you can't concentrate you should put it away for a few days."

***

At the end of the 1983 school year, Benoit requested a leave of absence from Boston University and moved back to Maine. Much had changed in Benoit's life since she left. Maine, thankfully, was much the same as always: locals respected her privacy and insisted that out-of-towners did, too. She was still bombarded by requests for interviews and appearances, and cars still honked and waved when they drove by while she ran (no longer did she pretend to stop to pick flowers), but here she was at least on the periphery of the running community, slightly less reachable than in Boston. And she had Scott and a strong support network of nonrunning friends and family.

After the world record, her training took on a new ferocity, as if to stave off complacency, or to prove that 2:22 was no fluke. For the most part, she trained by herself all winter, through freezing rain, snow, and subzero temperatures. In races, though she often claimed to have no strategy, she often ran as though trying to run the entire field into the ground. In training that winter, she appeared to be trying to do the same, trying to grind all her past successes—her record above all—into dust. Generally, said Toni Reavis, she trained "at a pace that didn't include others." That winter, she seemed to be trying to outrun even herself. Her main workout was a twenty-mile loop she'd been doing for years; likely it was longer, because she always undercounted and always stayed wide around curves to add on a few feet. Over the winter she kept pushing herself faster and faster over the loop. On a small, gloomy indoor track at a local college, she'd crank out hard speed workouts in the dusty air— repeat miles and 400s around the tight turns. Her fitness in the spring of 1983, when she'd broken the world record, had been near-superhuman. She aimed to surpass that before the Olympics.

But first came the Trials on May 12. Benoit knew that most observers considered the Trials a formality for her, but she couldn't afford to think that way. A race was a race. "I can't go to a race and run easy," she said. "I can't just jog through . . . if I don't run hard, I'm apt to get beaten, and beaten badly."[1] Even assuming the Trials went well, her work was only beginning. After a major marathon, she would feel empty, listless, and restless, and she needed time to recover mentally. Physically, she thought her body needed about one day for each mile of racing to recover enough so that she could start training hard again—about four weeks after a marathon. With only twelve weeks between the Trials and the Olympics, she wouldn't have the luxury of an extended mental or physical recovery.

So, she trained relentlessly, honing her body, she hoped, for the races to come. And on March 16, seventeen miles into one of her hard twenty-milers, Benoit felt a tightening in her knee. She tried to loosen it up, but the knee got worse, and the pain kept growing. Benoit, who'd limped around the track in high school, trying to run on a broken leg that hadn't yet fully healed, who'd gone running the day she was released from the hospital after appendix surgery, who'd trained for six months with a partially torn Achilles and two ruptured bursae, was forced to stop and walk. The Trials were in fifty-seven days.

Chapter 13

The Trials before the Trials

Benoit, Spring 1984

Benoit grew more and more panicked on the long walk home. She'd been dreaming of the Olympics since she'd been a child—more than twenty years now. She fought through injury, surgery, fears, doubts, anxiety; she'd stacked hundred-mile week on hundred-mile week through rain, snow, subzero days, icy blinding storms—all of it, for years, in pursuit of that dream. She couldn't allow herself to succumb to a setback now. And the setback—this was different, she could feel it. It wasn't the pain. Pain was simply a matter of self-control. This time, her leg just wouldn't move, just got tighter and tighter.

Fortunately, the house was empty when she got back; she could collect herself in solitude. Her first call was to Sev, who did what coaches do: he tried to reassure her without downplaying her fears. Take it easy for a few days, he counseled; she was plenty fit—a few days wouldn't hurt her. And he suggested calling Dr. Leach, who'd operated on her heels. She calmed down enough that she thought—hoped, perhaps—that maybe she was overreacting. Usually, like Sev suggested, a few easy days was all it took to get things right and get back on track. She didn't want to be alarmist, didn't want to waste Dr. Leach's time, didn't want to make trouble for anyone else, and couldn't yet give in to the idea that the knee problem wasn't an obstacle she could overcome on her own. Today was Friday; she'd wait the weekend. She'd probably be better by Monday; if not, she'd call Dr. Leach then. She took Saturday completely off—nearly unheard of for her. On Sunday she did what was for her just a short run, eleven miles. The knee was tight and sore but OK. Monday morning, she ran six easy miles—again, fine. But that afternoon she went out to do the same six-mile loop and couldn't even make a mile. She called Dr. Leach and set an appointment for the next day.

Dr. Leach examined the knee slowly, methodically, trying to rule things out as much as to determine the cause of her pain and tightness. The knee was inflamed, certainly, but he couldn't pinpoint a cause. His best guess, similar to what Sev had told her, was that the inflammation was fairly minor and could be brought down with plenty of time for her to be ready for the Trials. He recommended a cortisone shot and a few more easy days—a conservative approach but one that made sense; if he jumped right to surgery, she'd miss weeks of training, not days. So, in the absence of something more definitive than what he could detect, he felt it best to wait and see.

Benoit trusted Dr. Leach completely, but she knew it wasn't a minor injury or simple overuse. After all her years of running, all the times she put up with nagging injuries, she understood her body on a level no doctor ever could—her entire training philosophy was based on running the way she felt, according to what her body told her, and she'd learned to listen closely. She knew his recommendation made sense, and knew it was wrong, but she couldn't explain all this to Dr. Leach, couldn't push back against his diagnosis. On the roads or in a race, nothing intimidated Benoit, but in Dr. Leach's office, she shrank from the moment, didn't want to seem like she was challenging his expertise. So, she promised to ease off for a few more days, took the cortisone shot, and hoped for the best. It was March 20—fifty-three days to the Trials.

***

While Benoit rested, her rivals arrived in New Jersey for the World Cross Country championships, staged in the Meadowlands on March 25. Although the Olympics were only months away, the race still attracted many of the world's best and offered a good early test of fitness. Waitz finished third—at first glance a disappointment, but it worried her not a bit: the Meadowlands course was flat and fast, not a true cross-country challenge. It didn't play to her strengths, and she'd lost only to two 3000m specialists from the Eastern Bloc: Romania's Maricica Puica and the Soviet Union's Galina Zakharova. The two had a massive speed advantage over Waitz, yet she'd finished within seconds of both.[1] A week later, she turned the tables on Puica on a hilly, difficult course in Italy. She felt fitter and faster than expected at this point in her buildup for Los Angeles.

Benoit, after her week off, resumed running and quickly built her training back up to normal levels; the cortisone shot seemed to have worked. She ran easy for four or five days, then reestablished her routine: 15–20 miles per day, one fast twenty-miler per week, two or three hard weight-lifting sessions per week, and a fast track session to keep her sharp, all with no trouble from her knee. On April 10, she did a long run near her house in Maine in the morning, then drove down to Boston for an evening track workout: 3 x one mile at sub-5:00 pace. She felt smooth, easy through each one. Minutes into her cooldown jog, she felt her knee tightening again; she finished nonetheless, somewhat in denial. The next morning, April 11, she tried to run ten miles but could barely get through three. She called Dr. Leach, almost apologetic that his recommended treatment hadn't worked. They set an appointment for the next day. She had thirty-two days to the Olympic Trials.

That same week, Mota ran 32:47 at the 10K Boston Milk Run—her fastest road 10K to date. A week earlier, she'd won the Cherry Blossom ten-miler in D.C., one of the biggest and fastest road races in the country. She seemed to be in the best shape of her life.

On Tuesday, April 12, before her appointment with Dr. Leach, Benoit tried an easy twelve-miler—a test, in hopes that her knee would be fine and she could call Dr. Leach's office and say, false alarm, sorry to have bothered you. She barely finished, running a stiff-legged penguin shuffle the last three miles on a knee that would hardly bend. Again, Dr. Leach examined her carefully, but without cutting into the knee, he couldn't see much. Now a month before trials, he felt it was almost too late for surgery; he recommended another cortisone shot, and four days off completely from running. Benoit knew what her body was telling her, knew that the days off wouldn't change anything; again, bowing to his expertise, she swallowed her tongue.

That weekend, she flew to Tucson, Arizona, for a promotional event for Dole, with whom she'd recently signed an endorsement contract. The second cortisone shot notwithstanding, she could hardly walk down hills, let alone run. She had a speaking gig on Monday April 16, then an easy fun run with Dole executives on Tuesday. She barely got through it—she gritted her teeth, smiled, and made small talk while they jogged, trying not to limp. Near tears, she called Sev from Tucson. He told her to book a flight to Eugene; he'd meet her there for another consult.

***

While Benoit was in Tucson, it was marathon weekend in Boston. With the Trials in four weeks, most Americans stayed away, but a few hopefuls came to Boston for their last chance at qualifying, among them Jackie Hansen. The former world record holder had no illusions about being able to contend for anything, though some reporters asked her if she would go for the win on Patriot's Day. Her only goal was to qualify for the Trials. She'd worked most of her adult life to make the Olympic marathon a reality. She'd made peace with the fact that her running prime had come and gone without the opportunity to race for a medal; now, her Olympic gold would be just standing on the starting line in Olympia with the new generation of contenders. But she was running out of time.

In November 1983, she'd had surgery on her hamstring—she suffered from chronic compartment syndrome, a very painful buildup of swelling and pressure in a muscle group, typically occurring in the lower leg. It was fairly rare to see it in the large hamstring muscles of the upper back of the leg, and because the hamstrings undergo major contractions to move the leg through the running motion, they usually require longer recovery time after surgery. Hansen was running within a week. She took her first shot at a Trials qualifier in February 1984 at the LA Marathon; her hamstrings cramped, and she finished in 3:04. Three weeks later, she tried again at Los Alamos: 2:53. Boston was her last chance.

Marathon morning, she woke up to heavy, wet snow smacking the darkened window of her hotel. Hansen nearly cried. At the start of the race, the temperature was 39 degrees. The snow had switched over to rain, mixed occasionally with hail. Briefly, she felt herself let go of her goal. But the day was going to be miserable whether she ran 2:51 or not; running slower only meant she'd be miserable for longer. She started out on pace and progressively got faster. Her legs were numb to the pain—an advantage, perhaps. The miles clicked off through the dark day, and she crested Heartbreak Hill on 2:44 pace; all downhill from there. The final miles passed in a blur. She lost track of pace but still felt fast—to the extent that she could feel anything. She drove on toward the finish, through the last mile . . .

And woke up in the medical tent. She had no memory of the finish.

The doctor standing over her wore a mix of concern and relief: she was awake, but her body temperature had gotten dangerously low; she'd finished the marathon in a hypothermic state. She didn't care; she just needed to know her time. She insisted and grew agitated. The doctor, bemused at this point, perhaps resigned to the reality of ministering to runners at the finish of the Boston Marathon, dispatched a nurse to find the results. Moments later, Hansen could rest happily: 2:47.48. She was going to Olympia; it would be her fourth marathon in four months.

Allison Roe also returned to Boston, needing to convince the New Zealand Athletics selection committee that she was worthy of an Olympic spot. Since dropping out of Boston in 1983, injuries had derailed her training. She'd only managed a 2:38 at the Osaka International Women's marathon in January. Her countrywoman, Lorraine Moller, was also in the race; the two friends were in the awkward position of each needing to catch the eye of the selection committee—likely at the expense of the other. Occasionally they ran together in training and helped each other set the pace in races; today each was on her own.

Roe took off at the gun and held the lead through five miles in 27:40—5:32 per mile, just under 2:25 marathon pace. Moller stayed back, out of the top ten, well over a minute behind. But by mile 10, she was in third; second at mile 15, and closing fast. Up ahead, Roe's stride had grown ragged. She was hanging on as best she could, but doubts about her fitness, about the injuries, crept in. Around mile 20, on Heartbreak Hill, Moller swept by her friend and went on to win by four minutes.

Her time, 2:29, in miserable conditions, cemented her spot on the New Zealand Olympic Team and established Moller as a medal contender. Sweden's Midde Hamrin passed Roe for second place around mile 23—"which didn't surprise me," Hamrin said, "since I had heard she wasn't in all that great shape." Roe was nearly walking at that point. She teetered when Hamrin went by, held on for a few hundred meters, and, somewhere around mile 24, dropped out. Her hamstring, she said, had been bothering her throughout the race; it was the same problem, she said, that caused her to drop out in 1983.

***

Two days after Boston, April 18, Benoit was in the office of Dr. Stan James in Eugene, Oregon. She felt a little as though she was betraying Dr. Leach, but she and Sev both felt that she was best off staying out west rather than shuttling back and forth across the country before the Trials. James worked with many of the Nike-sponsored athletes; Benoit, who was sponsored by Nike, wasn't a regular patient of his, but they knew each other. However, he wasn't entirely comfortable usurping Leach's role: not until the two doctors consulted extensively by phone, and not until James felt he understood completely Benoit's history and Leach's diagnoses did he feel ready to treat Benoit. James examined her carefully, but like Leach, concluded he couldn't determine the cause of inflammation without going into the knee. James recommended waiting, resting for five days. At this point, unspoken in the room, was the reality that surgery meant that running the Trials was almost certainly impossible; from that perspective, it didn't matter whether she had surgery that day or in a week—if she went under the knife, her only hope of making the Olympic team was to recover fully in time for the track trials in June and try for a spot in the 3000m. But that was a longshot. Her best time ranked her fifth in the United States, and the athletes ahead of her all possessed a finishing kick that could leave Benoit in the dust at the end of a championship 3000.

Benoit knew that surgery was the only option. She'd been patient, had tried less invasive remedies, had rested and waited, and now felt she had no other recourse. Waiting at this point wasn't a medical prescription;

it was just hoping. But again, Benoit found herself unable to challenge her doctor. She said nothing in his office, just nodded. Back in Sev's car, beyond hope, frustrated and powerless, she bit back tears, beat her fists against the dash. Three days into her mandated five-day resting period, Benoit tried to go for an easy run. She couldn't even make three miles. She had twenty-one days until the Trials.

On April 24, she met again with James. Again, he had a long consult with Leach. James broached the idea of flying Benoit back to Boston so Leach could perform the surgery, but if she had any hope for a miracle recovery, flying back and forth would only lessen the odds. The doctors agreed it best if James performed the surgery. The next day, James inserted an arthroscopic device—essentially, a tiny camera mounted on a tube that had a diameter about half the width of the fingernail on her pinkie finger—through a very small puncture-like incision into Benoit's knee. Scoping was the least invasive surgical option, but the camera view was fuzzy—like video of the moon landing, only much smaller and less clear. James probed carefully, looking for the source of her pain. After several passes, he still could find nothing, but then he spotted a thin fold of tissue—a plica, barely visible with the scope.

Plicae are fairly common: they are left over from the embryonic development of the knee joint, and they remain in about 50 percent of the population. Though they typically cause no harm, in some cases they can cause inflammation and tightness in the knee joint. James didn't think Benoit's joint looked inflamed around the plica; was this tiny band enough to prevent the knee from getting through its normal range of motion smoothly, enough to cause such discomfort for an athlete with a nearly inexhaustible tolerance for pain? He couldn't be sure, but very carefully and meticulously, he shaved the plica down with a cutting instrument inserted through another tiny puncture in Benoit's knee. He pulled his instruments out and closed the puncture holes; the surgery went as well as it possibly could have, though James had no idea whether he'd resolved the problem. None of them would know for sure until she started running again.

Benoit came out of anaesthesia an hour after he finished. She called Sev's assistant, Mary Angelico, and told her to come pick her up at the hospital so she could go running. James, having consulted with Dr. Leach, insisted on keeping Benoit overnight—ostensibly to keep her under observation, mostly to keep her from doing exactly that. Sev came to see her that night; she asked him if he'd take her running tomorrow. James insisted on one week of rest. Maybe some swimming or light, slow biking, but nothing else until they met again on April 30. Sev got a hand bike so that she could at least pedal with her arms and get her heart rate up. She had seventeen days until the Trials.

By the time news broke of Benoit's surgery, members of the women's long-distance running committee had been having delicate conversations about whether, hypothetically speaking, if a world record holder were injured and unable to run at the Trials, the LDRC could grant a waiver and name such an athlete to the Olympic team. The point of the American qualification system, ruthless as it was, was to keep politics out of choosing the team. Runners made it on their merits, and the committee didn't want to cross that line. But surely, a world record counted as merits? Lebow, though he was not on the committee, made the issue public, stating to the press that Joanie should be on the team, no questions. He declared that he would formally petition the LDRC—though what a formal petition meant, no one on the committee knew. Others speculated on whether Benoit could somehow make it to the line. "Let's assume she doesn't have any problems with the surgery," said Steve Bramwell, team physician for the University of Washington athletics department. "Conceivably, she could be jogging within a week to 10 days. It wouldn't surprise me if she showed up. . . . Realistically, it's a long shot that she could recover in time for the Trials, but this is a once-in-four-years type of thing, and athletes do funny things."

On April 29, four days after surgery, Benoit insisted on going for an easy run with Sev, maybe two or three miles. A mile in, Sev said they should turn around and head back. "I don't have time to turn around," Benoit snapped. They ended up running six slow, painful miles.

That same day, Waitz and Kristiansen squared off at the Norwegian cross-country championships. Waitz hadn't lost a race in Norway for years until Kristiansen beat her that day by sixteen seconds over the six-kilometer course. A week later, Kristiansen again beat Waitz in a 10K on the roads. As with her third place at World XC, Waitz considered these losses to be no big deal. She'd all but ignored track speed in her buildup to the Olympics while Kristiansen thrived on faster workouts. Waitz knew she had the endurance to last the marathon; she felt she'd need to be in sub-2:20 shape to win in LA—not that anyone would run nearly that fast in the heat and smog, but that would be the level of fitness required. She was there, she felt—and losing to a greyhound such as Kristiansen at shorter distances was a minor disappointment compared to her belief in her own fitness.

For Kristiansen, beating Waitz was a very big deal. Aspiring to be the best in the world was difficult if she was only second in her own country. She'd been working with a sports psychologist who felt she had a near-perfect makeup to be a champion, with one, large, Waitz-shaped mental block. Even in her visualizations, she'd had a hard time envisioning herself beating Waitz. Kristiansen knew she'd gotten faster—results in workouts and on the treadmill told her. Beating Waitz told her she was getting stronger mentally, too; perhaps, finally, she was ready to supersede Waitz on the world stage. With Benoit recovering from surgery, Waitz became the firm favorite for marathon gold, but Kristiansen was establishing herself as 1a.

On April 30, ten days before the Trials, Benoit had her follow-up with James, who—somewhat unnecessarily, as Benoit had already started running—gave her the green light to begin training. But slowly, he said, and prescribed a great deal of physical therapy and cross-training. She threw herself into it. Running hurt, not just because of surgery, but because she felt unsteady, stiff, and uncertain of her foot strike. So, she attacked the stationary bike with special ferocity, swam an hour a day, added in weightlifting sessions, and spent as long as eight hours doing physical therapy.

On May 2, her knee felt fairly stable. She decided, ready or not, she was back. She started running twice per day, lengthened the distance, and did as she always had—cranked the pace lower and lower the longer she ran. On May 4, her left hamstring hurt so bad she could hardly run. This was fairly common for athletes in recovery: whatever was injured may feel fine, but other parts of the body have been compensating for the injured part and need to be babied back up to speed. Benoit was never one to baby her body. The hamstring strain was now a bigger, more debilitating problem than the knee. She told her brothers not to bother coming out to Olympia—there was no point, she said; even if she could run, she had no chance of making the team. The trials were eight days away.

Through members of Athletics West, Nike's elite team based in Oregon, Benoit heard of a device called the Myopulse Electro Accuscope. According to the technology's acolytes, the machine could identify damaged tissue areas by analyzing the difference between the electrical conductivity of healthy versus damaged tissue, analyze the appropriate electrical current to help stimulate the damaged tissue, and promote the body's own healing. Jack Scott, the biggest evangelist for the (still) unproven technology, explained, "the acuscope [*sic*] sends electronical charges into injured areas" to get the body's electrical charge working properly again.[2] Scott, whose PhD was in sports psychology, was actually much better known for his role in helping Patty Hearst and the leaders of the Symbionese Liberation Army, Emily and Willman Harris, escape from California: he had helped them elude the authorities, and drove them to a secluded farmhouse in the Poconos, where they stayed for several months. Nevertheless, Dick Brown, who coached Mary Decker, America's great hope for gold in the 1500m and 3000m, swore by Jack Scott. "Each cell has a charge that it loses when it's hurt or tired out. Recharging seems to decrease healing time," he explained.

Benoit figured she had nothing to lose and added sessions with Scott to her already crowded schedule. After putting in eighteen-hour days of rehab, cross-training, light running, and myopulsing, Benoit decided she needed to know. On May 9, three days before the Trials, she set out on a sixteen-mile run. It was a risk: in Benoit's condition, running that long might take two hours or more and might very well overload her precarious muscles. But she needed to test herself. The whole run felt awful, like running across very thin ice—she'd lost her stride, couldn't run naturally, couldn't do much but try to cushion her right knee and her left hamstring. With each step, she expected something to tighten up. But she made it, and nothing had gotten worse over the course of the run.

The day after her sixteen-miler, she did something she rarely did: she ran with her now-fiancé, Scott Samuelson. It was easy, short, and carefree.

She had two days to the Trials; she'd had surgery just fifteen days before. She wasn't pain free, couldn't be sure the knee wouldn't tighten up again as it had before, knew the hamstring could still go at any time, still hadn't tried to run at race pace, and had no idea how her body would respond to the rigors of competition. But if nothing else, she'd make it to the starting line. She shoved all her doubts down as deep as she could, quieted all the worries and what-ifs that crowded her mind, and prepared to race.

CHAPTER 14

The Trials

America's Best, May 12, 1984

ONE WEEK BEFORE THE TRIALS, ATHLETES MOVED INTO THE DORMS IN Olympia. Locals offered tours (the Olympia Brewery was a popular choice), the Ford dealership donated vans to ferry athletes around, and boat owners offered to pilot cruises around the lakes. There were lectures on the history of women in sport, including a "historical women's sportswear fashion show." Nightly and on race day, two downtown parks—Capitol and Sylvester—offered various entertainments, including performances by Miss Thurston County (and candidates), The Olympia Nordic Dancers, The Olympia Jazz all-stars, The Puget Sounders, The Olympia Highlanders Bagpipe Band, The Olympia Gymnastics Team, Tumwater Drill Team, Olympia Square Dancers, The Capital High School Band, and The Mud Bay Cloggers. The night before the race, the Women Can-Do Committee hosted a "spaghetti feed" in conjunction with a running clinic and a scientific congress on running. The morning of, there would be dueling pancake breakfasts, one hosted by the Zonta Club in the Olympia high school gymnasium, the other by the Kiwanis at the Olympia Community Center—these in addition to the buffet brunch for the local senior citizens who would serve as flag bearers at the start of the race.

More than thirty volunteer licensed massage therapists worked in shifts at the dorms all week on the 268 qualifiers; even runners who were injured and unable to run were flown in and lodged to be a part of the celebration. If Laurel James and the bid committee had over-promised, the organizing committee and the local community over-delivered: Olympia had turned out. It was (and remains) the smallest town ever to host an Olympic Trials marathon, but never before had a community invested so much of itself in a national championship race; never before had female athletes been treated so well at a U.S. championship. It was a historic race, and Olympia accorded the athletes a status that the occasion deserved.

***

For race morning, Tommy Leonard took out an ad in *The Olympian*: "WE LOVE YOU Joan Benoit and the rest of the greater Boston Runners. BEST OF LUCK IN THE TRIALS!! Friends and customers of the Eliot Lounge, Boston, Mass." Back in Boston, the Eliot Lounge would be open for business and packed with marathon fans.

Benoit spent race morning trying to tune out the world. Music blasting from her headphones preceded her well down the hallways of her hotel; true to her nature, she had decided not to stay among the other runners in the dorms. Against the odds, she'd made it; she would be part of history, one way or another. She was mostly confident she could finish the race, though she knew a slow sixteen-mile run on Wednesday was nothing compared to twenty-six miles of racing. Her fitness was far from ideal, and she wasn't sure she could hold onto a top-three position, even if she was able to keep up with the leaders at the start. In a strange way, her circumstances played to her strength: the issue wasn't whether she was good enough but whether she was tough enough, whether her body could handle what she would ask of it. Toughness had never been a problem.

In the early hours of race morning, 1,283 volunteers took their positions—one at each intersection, alleyway, or driveway "to keep cars, dogs, people, and bicycles off that course." Race-day weather was nearly perfect: temps hovered in the mid-50s, though showers had been predicted. ("Well, we never promised you 90-degree sunshine," opined the morning edition of *The Olympian*. "That you can contend with this summer in Los Angeles, along with its many other dubious attributes.")[1] The showers held off, but cloudy skies prevailed. An ABC TV crew would broadcast the race live, essentially doing a dress rehearsal for how they'd cover the Olympics. They had helicopters (which would have to be grounded if the rains came), a fleet of electric motorcycles, and a crew of nearly one hundred, including Kathrine Switzer, who would be doing race commentary.

Olympia had banned open burning for May 12 and strongly discouraged it during the previous week; air quality was as pristine as one could possibly hope—the kind of day that, under different circumstances, would have been ideal for a record attempt. Instead, Benoit tried to remind herself she didn't need to win, only make the team. A healthy Benoit would have imposed order on the race, would have set a hard pace from the beginning. Another favorite to make the team, Julie Brown, also had a history of pushing the pace, but she had made it plain she planned on running as easy as possible while still making the team. From the start, Benoit tried to relax and run easy, and none of the others tried to test her. Instead, they all seemed to be waiting for someone else to do something.

Although the pace was slow, easy felt anything but. Benoit's hamstring twinged with every stride. Switzer thought she saw her leg buckle in the first mile. Benoit fought back—not against the pain but against her mind. Her biggest enemy now wasn't another runner, wasn't even her leg, but letting her worries get loose and snowball into panic over whether she could finish. She worked consciously to disassociate: Running through Olympia reminded her a little of home; the inlets that stretched all the way to the Pacific were similar enough to the coast of Maine that she could imagine herself back home on a training run. Certainly, she'd hammered the back roads around Freeport faster than she was running now.

Around mile 4, the waiting ended. Betty Jo Springs made a move and established a slight lead. Benoit soon joined her, and the two headed a small pack of six. Springs added another slight surge, and only Benoit stuck to her. Springs and Benoit were alone, running as a pair, at 2:28 pace. Getting out of the pack and finding a slightly faster tempo seemed to help Benoit. For Springs, the pace was a venture into the unknown; her best time was 2:37. Shortly after twelve miles, Benoit felt the need to pick up again, to "run her own race," as she said afterward. The 5:40

miles had slowed slightly, and Benoit wanted separation, wanted to avoid needing to kick at the end.

Again, faster felt better—she could almost relax. Sev, however, worried over every tight corner, every dip in the course, every downhill, any misstep that might tweak the hamstring and end Benoit's race. Benoit, however, seemed to have found her rhythm. Her expression, which betrayed some anxiety in the early going, resolved itself into its usual unreadable mask as she steadily added to her lead over Springs: eight seconds at halfway, twenty-three seconds at mile 15, fifty-four at mile 16. Springs dropped out at mile 17, and Benoit's lead over the rest of the field was nearly four hundred meters. Sev still worried, and he couldn't hide it.

At seventeen miles, Benoit rolled past him and said, "Sev, I'm fine." Famous last words for any marathoner at mile 17, and starting around mile 20, gradually, inexorably, her stride began to lose power, each step seemingly shorter. Aerobically, she did feel fine; mentally, she was still strong. Her legs were giving her all they had and felt stable—but everything she had might not be enough; her pace slowed to six minutes per mile. Her legs simply didn't have the strength to go any faster. All she could do was keep her tempo as high as she could, focus on keeping a quick rhythm, on getting to the finish line. If the pack caught her, she'd try to go with them, but she knew she had no other gear, no possible way to win a sprint finish. If they caught her, they'd leave her for dead.

They never did. Julie Brown, by then running in second place, never tried; she finished thirty-seven seconds back, 2:31.41 to Benoit's 2:31.04. Behind Brown, Julie Isphording, buried in the pack through the first half, made a furious charge in the last miles. With three to go, she was still fifty-eight seconds behind Lisa Larsen for the last spot, though they were headed in opposite directions. Larsen began to falter; Isphording dropped her pace to 5:20 per mile. When she caught Larsen, she flew by with an extra surge to discourage any lingering hopes Larsen might have. Isphording finished forty-four seconds ahead; Larsen would later say that she was an Olympian for twenty-four miles.

At the finish, Benoit broke down. She hid her face in her hands, then buried it in Sev's shoulder. She stayed wrapped in Sev's bear hug for several long moments, trying to compose herself before she faced the cameras. Then, she limped off to talk to the press. "I don't deserve this," she said. As much as the spectators, media, and even U.S. athletics officials were rooting for her, so were her fellow athletes. "I can't say how much the support of the women and the camaraderie helped me."

Over the eight weeks since her injury, she'd gone through waves of doubt, impatience, frustration with her own reticence in pushing her doctors. On multiple occasions she'd come close to giving in and going home. Throughout the month before the Trials, Benoit had done all she could to keep focused on the race and maintain belief that she could make it to the line; during the race, only her mental strength and agility could keep the moment from growing too big and her worries from over-whelming her. She often said she only ran on feel; truthfully, she relied as much on her brains. But now, she could let her emotions off the leash. "Somehow, with all the people who helped, all the people who love me, I made it. I can't believe it." She could say it now—making the team had seemed a longshot.

Brown told reporters that she'd wanted to run easy—"the slower the better," she said—and save as much as she could for LA. The Trials was just another day at work, and she'd executed her race plan professionally, almost coldly. "I didn't see any sense in trying to catch Joan," Brown said after the race, but added, "I won't be holding back in the Olympics." Isphording was beyond ecstatic; she, too, had executed her race plan (start slow, chase people down) to perfection—but even so, a spot on the team had seemed like a pipe dream. Lisa Larsen, asked by race announcers how she felt about finishing fourth, gave a one-word answer: "Fuck!" she said, after which she and the mildly surprised—and mostly amused—crowd shared a laugh and a moment of sympathetic solidarity.

In ninth place was Schiro. She'd briefly challenged Larsen in the lat-ter stages, before Isphording shot by them both. But she'd be back—she'd make the Olympic teams in 1988 and 1992.

In sixteenth was Catalano. She'd come to the Trials alone, almost for-gotten by the new generation. From the runners who did recognize her, Catalano felt the stares, the whispers, the pointed fingers of those who were surprised to discover that she was still running. She spent much of the weekend in the dorms, by herself, wearing headphones to tune out the world. But she'd made it, stood on the line, and again, given every-thing she had in the race. She'd run 2:36, a spectacular improvement from Houston, but nearly ten minutes off her best. She hurt. "I didn't finish very high. It's done. Good. It's over." She went back to Boston, filed for divorce, and moved to Vermont. "The fight was gone," she said. She ran a few races, and told herself, "If I really want to do this, I'll do it." But mostly, she discovered that no, she didn't want to anymore.

Leatrice Hayer finished last, in 3:21. But spectators had come back out of their houses to cheer for her, and she earned a massive ovation at the finish line. Hayer was six months pregnant. She'd held seven-minute per mile pace through eighteen miles, and then, the contractions hit. Nothing to worry about, she said—it happened all the time on long runs. But contractions did make it hard to breathe, and she had to slow. She even walked for a spell around mile 24, but that only made her feel worse. So, she jogged it in and finished with a slow shuffle, to the delight of the waiting crowd. She waved, rested a bit, got some water, and the contractions, as they always had before, stopped.

Postrace entertainment included an air show over Capital Lake, featuring The Northern Knights and Air Circus. Local Girl Scout troops picked up trash along the course. Benoit sported a rainbow beanie cap with a propeller on top, the Olympic rings stitched on front. Julie Brown walked by; they made plans to meet up later that afternoon. "A beer?" Brown suggested. "How about two?" replied Benoit. By that time, Sev had already left for Eugene; he had athletes running in an all-comers meet, and he wouldn't miss their races for anything.

"The greatest damn athlete in the world!" Sev had shouted several times after the finish of the Trials, to everyone in hearing range and to no one in particular. Later, in a quiet moment, he began to worry that she'd run too hard, that she could have taken it easier and still qualified. "Shit," he said of her victory. "She didn't have to do that. I hope she's OK."

**

One day after Benoit won the Trials, Kristiansen toed the line for the London Marathon. Unlike her rivals, she kept up a full racing schedule throughout 1984; she felt she had energy to burn and liked to use races to keep herself sharp. London indicated that she was very sharp: she ran 2:24.26—a minute faster than Waitz's best and the second-fastest time in the world behind Benoit's 2:22 at Boston the year before. To those who felt Benoit had been aided, either by the tailwind, Boston's net downhill, or by the alleged pacer, Kristiansen was now the world record holder. And given Benoit's injury problems, Kristiansen was now at least cofavorite for gold, along with Waitz.

That same Sunday, Benoit drove to Portland, Oregon with Scott. She limped around the zoo with him and just tried to relax. Tuesday they flew home; Wednesday they celebrated her twenty-seventh birthday; Thursday she went for an easy run with an old friend in Freeport. For the next ten days, Benoit's main goal was recovery: a lot of swimming and physical therapy, and almost no running. Her body was still sore in odd places, the other muscles having worked overtime to protect the knee and hamstring. Her knee felt mostly fine—the tiny incisions through which the camera and cutting instrument had been inserted would take a while to heal fully, but they were essentially like tiny bruises now. The hamstring required a little more caution. Her body was still trying to repair itself, but was out of time. What had been a twelve-week turnaround to the Olympics was ten by the time she got back to regular training.

Her running felt sluggish for most of June. She traveled sparingly. It was an unseasonably hot, muggy summer in Maine—perfect, in a way, to steel Benoit to what awaited in LA. Since the 1968 Olympics in Mexico City, elevation seven thousand feet, many runners had turned to high-altitude training camps to improve their body's ability to carry oxygen in the bloodstream to working muscles. Sev called humidity a poor man's altitude training: humidity makes it harder for the body to cool itself, and training through it has the effect of increasing blood plasma volume and improving oxygen delivery, similar to the effect of running at altitude. Given the weather, the state of her body, and her overall recovery process, Benoit stuck to her bread and butter in training, her security blanket: long runs, high mileage. As always, her pace on her daily runs began to inch faster and faster: "If people are right in saying you're running too hard if you can't carry on a conversation," a common bit of folk-running wisdom for judging the appropriate training pace, "then I'm running too hard 90 percent of the time," she said.

She did make one short trip down to New York for the L'Eggs Mini-Marathon in June. Though she wasn't racing, she was in town to do an Olympic promo appearance with Waitz, who won the Mini in 31:53, nearly two minutes ahead of second place. Benoit and Waitz filmed a short TV spot, then had breakfast together afterward. For two rivals who had circled each other warily for years, it was an enjoyable time. Though each was careful not to reveal too much about training or racing—regarding her knee and hamstring, Benoit would never say much more to anyone than "they're fine"—they talked summer plans, excitement for the Olympics, the media circus they both endured.

Benoit's only race after the Trials was a 10,000m exhibition race at the Olympic Track and Field Trials, held June 17 in Los Angeles. Jackie Hansen and the International Runners Committee had continued to press for equity in the Olympics; the race was to call attention to the fact that the Olympic marathon was only a first step in that direction. Benoit, though not one to march in protests or give speeches, was a firm supporter of the cause and felt a responsibility to do her part. Racing was her demonstration; she ran 32:07 (5:10 per mile) in the heat, her best by nearly thirty seconds. Her hamstring felt fine, and her stride looked great. Watching trackside, Sev could barely contain himself: if she could do that with no fast workouts, no mile repeats to prepare herself to run that pace, she was, he thought to himself, "ready to rumble."

Ten days later, at the Bislett Games in Oslo, Kristiansen ran 14:58.89 for the 5000m on the track—the first woman to run under 15:00, ten seconds faster than Mary Decker's world record. Lost in the excitement of Kristiansen's run was Mota's 15:30 in the same race—for Mota, a startling improvement. That summer, she'd also run her fastest 3000m—8:52. Benoit's best times were 15:40 and 8:53. Kristiansen's incredible range of performances marked her as the fastest distance runner in the world going into LA. Mota, however, relied on strength and endurance rather than raw speed; her track times, though not in Kristiansen's league, suggested that she was even fitter and faster than she'd been that spring.

On May 7, five days before the Benoit's miraculous victory at the Trials, eleven women, representing priestesses at the ancient Temple of Hera, gathered in the other Olympia, the site of the original Greek Olympics, for a sacred ritual. Using a parabolic mirror to focus the rays of the sun, they ignited the wick of the Olympic torch, which was then used to light three safety lamps, which were then flown by U.S. government plane across the Atlantic. On the morning of May 8, starting at the United Nations Headquarters in New York, the reconstituted Olympic torch began its 9,000-mile, 82-day journey through 33 states to Los Angeles in time for the Opening Ceremonies on July 28.

History awaited.

CHAPTER 15

The Games

Los Angeles, 1984

THROUGHOUT THE SPRING, THE LOS ANGELES OLYMPIC ORGANIZING
Committee worked to make ready the Olympic venues: Dodger Stadium, the Rose Bowl, Santa Anita racetrack, the dormitories at USC
and UCLA that would house the athletes, the numerous college facilities
at nearly a dozen different campuses, and the Los Angeles Coliseum.
Venues stretched over hundreds of miles, from the rowing and canoeing
venue on Lake Casitas northwest of Los Angeles, to shooting events at
Prado Recreation Area to the east, to the modern pentathlon venue at
Coto de Caza, south of the City.

Starting in June, the Olympic colors were everywhere. Originally,
organizers had planned on a red, white, and blue theme, but one of the
designers on the committee, Deborah Sussman, suggested they step back
from such an overtly jingoistic scheme to something with a more festive,
southwestern flair: magenta, aqua, vermilion, and lavender. The Executive
Committee wasn't altogether ready to let go of their all-American colors,
but Sussman and her partner convinced them that the Games weren't just
about the U.S. of A., but about the world: the new color scheme would
set a welcoming, California tone. By mid-June, 20,000 street banners,
20,000 signs, 35 miles of decorative fabric, and 11 miles of glitter strips
blanketed the region. The organizers had done a makeover on southern
California.

Benoit arrived in LA on July 23, five days before the Olympics began. She stayed away from the village, not only because of her aversion to interacting with fellow competitors: she was afraid she'd get so hyped up being so close to the action at other venues, that she'd be emotionally exhausted a week before the marathon. She stayed in Santa Monica, nearer to the marathon start, in a guesthouse that Jackie Hansen had arranged for her. She spent as little time as possible on the actual course, which would only get her more keyed up. The hay was in the barn, as the saying goes; all she needed to do to be ready on race day was relax and run easy for two weeks.

She tried to stick to her routine, tried to be good and just run easy. Instead, she found she couldn't get out for a run without attracting at least a few well-wishers—some of whom wanted to run a few miles with her. And she couldn't run with someone without escalating the pace, After a few days of going hard on nearly every run, she was ready to pack her bags immediately. She had to get out of LA.

She stayed through the Opening Ceremonies on July 28, wanting to feel at least that part of the communal Olympic experience. Opening ceremonies are typically a propaganda exercise for the home country; for LA, organizers chose to downplay the story of American wealth and power in favor of entertainment: Hollywood glitz and American music. Just before 4pm, church bells tolled across Los Angeles, and on the stage under the Coliseum peristyle, 150 trumpeters blasted out the Olympic fanfare. One thousand performers holding massive, five-foot-wide balloons filled the infield—gold balloons forming the Olympic rings, white balloons making a border circling the field. William Suitor, aka "rocketman," wearing a white suit with a jetpack strapped to his back, launched off the top of the stage, piloted around the Coliseum, and touched down right on target in lane 4 of the track. The gold ballooners shifted formation to spell out welcome, while the thousand-voice Olympic choir, all in white, sang a Marvin Hamlisch-composed tune called "Welcome." Some 165 young women in frilly summer dresses and wide sun hats strolled through the stands handing out flowers to the audience. Performers released their balloons, each with a banner saying welcome in the different languages of the 140 different Olympic delegations.

An eight-hundred-person marching band filled the stage, the aisles of the lower bowl, and much of the infield, playing Aaron Copeland's "Fanfare for the Common Man," followed by "Rodeo," during which three hundred members of the Olympic dance corps—men in cowboy attire, women in bonnets and pioneer dresses—settled the "West," built a frontier town, and danced a hoedown. The band, joined by a drill team, then formed a Mississippi steamship on the infield, accompanied by Dixieland and gospel music. Next, eighty-four grand pianos—sets of two, stacked three high—rose on platforms in each of the fourteen archways of the peristyle. The pianists—all men, each "representing George Gershwin," organizers suggested when the rather remarkable gender imbalance was pointed out—played "Rhapsody in Blue," accompanied by the orchestra.

As the pianos crescendoed through the last notes, men in silver ties. top hats, and white tails, accompanied by women in diaphanous white gowns—"representing Fred Astaire and Ginger Rogers"—danced to a medley of Hollywood musical numbers while other members of the cast held up rectangles of what looked like patches peeled off a disco ball to catch the afternoon sun and sparkle the audience. The band then cycled through Glenn Miller, Count Basie, and Duke Ellington standards while flag-snapping drill teams performed alongside hundreds of dancers on the floor. The band pivoted to "One Singular Sensation" from *A Chorus Line*, followed by "Fame," then Michael Jackson's "Beat It," then back to "One Singular Sensation."

In a building annex adjacent to the Coliseum, some seven thousand of the eight thousand athletes participating in the Games sat and waited. Organizers required them to arrive two hours before the Ceremonies, four hours before they were to parade onto the track. There was supposed to be a live feed of the ceremonies on movie screens around the annex, but the feed fizzled out in the first few minutes, leaving the athletes bored and hot in the airless, overcrowded room. Although they were supposed to stay with their delegations, soon athletes were hopping from country to country, taking pictures, chatting with rivals, friends, and people they'd just met.

Per tradition, Greece led the parade of Olympic delegations, after which teams filed in alphabetically. Two white-skirted escorts, holding a white banner with the country name, led in each team. Most marched in formation around the track, and stayed in formation when they took their place on the infield. The host nation traditionally marches in last—and the U.S. team, the largest delegation, strode into the stadium to a thunderous roar. Six hundred strong, the Americans marched in what could only be called casual-friendly formation: teammates walked arm in arm; one athlete carried a frisbee. Most had cameras and stopped to take pictures or pose for others. All wore red, white, and blue sweatsuits and held small American flags, which they waved to the crowd. There was much fist pumping in the audience and on the track. Chants of USA! USA! rang throughout the Coliseum, and the American team joined the patchwork of color on the infield.

But not for long. Gina Hemphill, granddaughter of Jesse Owens, ran into the stadium with the torch, and by the time she made it around the track to where the American delegation was positioned, her way was blocked. American athletes spilled out across the lanes of the track to take pictures of Hemphill. She slowed to a walk-jog and took it all in with a brilliant, insuppressible smile. An Olympic official threaded through the crowd of athletes to carve a narrow path for her, and slowly she made her way through the rest of her circuit. The crowd erupted once more as she handed the torch to 1960 decathlon gold medalist Rafer Johnson, who completed his own lap through the throngs of athletes before climbing the hundred steps to the top of the peristyle to light the torch.

The final act of the Ceremonies involved representatives of "all the ethnic groups of the Los Angeles community" marching into the Coliseum "in traditional costume." A local performer, Nikki McClure, then sang "Reach Out and Touch Somebody's Hand," and encouraged the crowd to do exactly that. Spontaneous dance circles broke out as athletes and performers mingled, and the ceremonies concluded.

More than 9,000 performers took part in a spectacle witnessed by nearly 90,000 people in the stands, and an estimated 2 billion people across the globe. The budget for the opening ceremonies was more than $5 million; intentionally or not, American wealth and power were on display. Before the Games, Peter Ueberroth, the president of the LAOOC, said he knew that "the world would stand still and judge this country and judge the games by what was going to take place on the field during those opening ceremonies." David Wolper, the director, said he was going for an "emotional, twenty-goosebump experience." Steven Spielberg, sitting in the stands, cast a professional eye on the production. "I think David's redefined the word 'epic.' It's like Cecil B. DeMille and Busby Berkeley all rolled into one," he said, a tinge of envy in his voice.

***

The day after the Opening Ceremonies, Benoit flew up to Eugene. Mary Angelico, Sev's assistant, offered to let Benoit stay with her for a few days before flying back to LA. Benoit was restless, distracted—and had very little to do besides an easy run twice a day. Though seldom remarked on, the boredom of the long-distance runner is a reality in the buildup to big races: athletes who have ordered their lives around intense physical activity are suddenly asked to do comparatively little of it. Instead, they are supposed to simply rest, which is harder than it sounds; teammates of one elite runner once spoke admiringly of her ability to lie on the couch and stare into space for hours. Benoit was particularly bad at doing nothing. In Eugene, she stalked around the house, while Angelico tried to distract her with games, movies, books—anything. In such a state, Benoit tended to overtrain: without realizing it, she'd put in huge mileage weeks and run even faster than her usual blistering pace. It was her body's way of coping with stress. On the phone, Sev reminded her constantly not to run too much; he probably would have put her back in walking casts if he could.

Sleep was nearly impossible for Benoit; she'd lie on her bed staring at nothing, nervous energy fizzing through her body. She couldn't keep her mind anywhere else—always, her thoughts came back to the marathon. The rest of the world, the rest of her life, faded to background noise. Basic details of living escaped her attention, and Scott, the functional half of their partnership at such times, hadn't come up to Eugene with her. One afternoon in Eugene, Benoit, starved for activity and missing her Maine blueberries, went raspberry picking. Back at Angelico's house, she set about making jam—mashing the berries, putting them on to boil—then promptly forgot about them and went out for her run. For the hour she was gone, the berries boiled, and boiled—and splattered all over Angelico's kitchen by the time Benoit returned.

On August 3, two days before the marathon, Benoit flew back down to LA. In the week she'd been gone, American enthusiasm for the Games had exploded, beyond the highest hopes of organizers. The weather cooperated: temperatures, which had been stuck in the 90s two weeks before the Games, turned comfortable and mild. Smog levels, which had been dangerously high, dissipated in time for the Opening Ceremonies. The Soviet boycott, retaliation for the American-led boycott of the 1980 Moscow Olympics, had largely fallen flat: only thirteen other nations joined the Soviets. If anything, the boycott only galvanized an American determination to make the Games a success in the eyes of the world, the kind of party that those who stayed away would regret missing. Los Angelenos were almost aggressively welcoming and helpful to foreign visitors, and American fans supported all the Olympians—though they were especially vociferous in cheering for Team U.S.A.

American athletes, buoyed by the home crowds (and, it must be said, benefiting from the absence of the high-powered Soviet and East German teams), exceeded expectations: In the first week, Americans won twenty-one gold medals in the twenty-nine swimming events; the next best team, Canada, won only four. The women's gymnastics team recorded its highest-ever finish—silver, behind the Romanians; since 1952, the Soviets had swept every team gold. American Mary Lou Retton won the first-ever American individual all-around title, with stunning perfect 10s in her final two events to overtake Romania's Ecaterina Szabo. The importance of the Games to the hundreds of thousands of Americans who gathered in LA and the tens of millions who watched on TV dwarfed anything else happening at the time; the Olympics had struck an unexpected chord, had tapped into a deeply hidden collective need, and mattered for reasons that went beyond mere sport: the success of the Games represented the resurgence of American esteem and optimism, and American athletes represented the highest aspirational ideals of the country.

When her plane began its descent into LAX, Benoit's stomach began to hurt.

**

Waitz also stayed out in Santa Monica, in an apartment she borrowed from an acquaintance who left town for the Games. Unlike Benoit, she did not attend the Opening Ceremonies, ostensibly to rest, but at least in part because of her aversion to crowds. She spent her time in the apartment with Jack and her brother and ran different sections of the course to familiarize herself with it. For Waitz, seeing the course helped settle her—to the extent that she could settle herself before a race. Her stomach was a mess; she'd hardly eat unless Jack reminded her. Between runs, she tried to distract herself: crosswords helped because they occupied her mind, but if she tried to watch TV or a movie, she'd forget whatever she was watching, and her thoughts would drift back to the race. She had to have lunch with Jack the day before a big race—just the two of them. She would spill her fears; she'd question why she was still running at all; question whether she could ever succeed, ever withstand the pressure she felt.

On August 4, one day before the marathon, Waitz woke up and could barely move. Overnight, something in her back had seized up. In tears, she hobbled out of bed to find Jack; together they called her coach. He brought over a masseuse who worked on her back, and gave Waitz some muscle relaxants, all to little avail. They drove to the warmup track, and Waitz tried jogging easily. She willed herself to run with a normal gait— no matter how painful running was, she couldn't betray any vulnerability in a place where other runners or coaches might see. She masked the pain as well as she could, but she knew that in her current condition, running a marathon was impossible. She spent the rest of the morning in treatment—more massage, more muscle relaxants—and hoped for a miracle.

After 1976, Waitz had given up on the Olympics. In 1978, she had retired from running. The marathon had brought her back, given her a second career. This Olympics was the opportunity she thought she'd never get: the chance to measure herself against the very best, on a level playing field, on athletics' biggest stage. Since her teenage years, she'd devoted her life to this moment, to finding out how she stacked up in an honest race. Years of training so fast and so hard that most other athletes shied away from running with her; years of steeling herself for the worst possible training conditions Norway could throw at her; years of struggling with her own doubts and fears, of dealing with near-crippling anxiety before races, of exposing herself to the judgment of others—her fourteen-year international career was meant to bring her to this one race. She just needed to make it to the line.

None of the treatments helped, and as the afternoon wore on, her situation seemed hopeless. Finally, a team doctor, well versed in what the Norwegians call *wis kvinne*, or "wise woman ways"—what English speakers might call folk medicine—told Waitz to fill up a backpack with heavy objects and walk around. Waitz had nothing to lose; she began walking. Gradually, the pain lessened. She didn't feel cured, but she felt like she could run. She'd had no time or energy to go over last-minute tactical considerations such as details of weather, course conditions, or other athletes. And she had had no lunch with Jack. No matter—self-pity wasn't a productive option; ready or not, she was racing in the morning. That night, she slept fitfully—normal the night before a race. In the dark morning hours of race day, she woke up pain free. Her body felt stiff, muscles tight all over; she was exhausted and wrung out. But she could run. Perhaps her back would seize up again, but at least she could start the race. That would have to be enough.

Like Waitz, Benoit woke up in the dark. As usual, she'd hardly slept, just laid in bed with her headphones on, listening to the theme from *Chariots of Fire* over and over and over. She'd hardly eaten the day before. She was restless, sleepless, and her stomach was in knots.

The race, at last, was here.

CHAPTER 16

The Race

Los Angeles, August 5, 1984

CHAMPIONSHIP MARATHONS HAVE A DIFFERENT RHYTHM FROM THE big city majors. Races like Boston, New York, London are often run for time, and they are common enough that taking a risk has relatively minor consequences; the next opportunity is, at most, six months away. The Olympic marathon, however, is a once-in-a-career moment for most athletes, and they tend to take fewer risks. The start tends to be conservative, as runners take stock of themselves—no matter how well (or poorly) their preparation has gone, no matter how good (or bad) they feel before the race, they can never be sure how they'll feel once the gun goes off. Athletes use the early miles to check their legs, their breathing, their energy levels, and each other; in the early going, the main contenders size up each other as if it were a fifteen-round title fight—and at three minutes per round in boxing, a marathon works out to forty-eight rounds or more. Given the historic stakes of the first women's Olympic marathon, and concerns about the heat, the slow starting pace is not surprising.

But just shy of fourteen minutes in, a slight ripple disturbs the easy rhythm of the pack, like a skip in the recording. Benoit is suddenly a meter in front. Almost unconsciously, like she's on Sunday morning run with a friend, Benoit has one-stepped the field. She glances to her right, at Waitz. Surely, just like a companion on a Sunday run, her competitors will match her. But no: she looks to her left, and to her right again, and finds herself all alone, now two meters ahead. Mota takes the spot at the head of the pack that Benoit just vacated, but makes no move to close the gap. Brown lines up directly behind Benoit and makes as if to move up to Benoit's shoulder, but then veers off to her right; the course is about to turn onto Wilshire Boulevard, and the pack crowds into the right-hand lane—except for Benoit, who stays out where she is, on the other side of the street. She looks as if she's about to make a wrong turn—make a left when the rest go right—but then she cuts a hard diagonal across the corner. It is an act of willful separation: She's not trying to break away, but she's not encouraging company either.

They are just past the four-kilometer mark, on a gradual uphill, running about 2:32 pace for the marathon. Benoit isn't trying to blow open the race, but she is running just under 2:31 pace, and she has increased her lead. She looks behind her, and a minute later sneaks another look back—then cranes her head all the way around for three full strides, as if she can't believe what she's seeing. The most important marathon in history, and they are letting her go.

In the pack, Brown looks again over at Waitz and Mota. Mota glances over at Waitz, as does Kristiansen, who is running just behind and between Mota and Brown.

For a moment, Benoit worries she's making a major blunder: you're going to look real stupid, she says to herself, if you take the lead now, then die and get passed later on. But she tunes out that thought and refocuses: she's still running comfortably, even if her stride has acquired a new sense of purpose. At this pace, she has no risk of falling apart. There's now enough room for two press vehicles—a pickup truck and a motorcycle with a sidecar—to slide between her and the rest of the field. It makes the break seem more real, bigger than it is; Benoit leads by only seven seconds. She sneaks one more look back. So, now what?

In a strange, somewhat inexplicable quirk of course setup, the next water station is on the right-hand side of Wilshire Boulevard—a wide, seven-lane street—just before the course takes a left-hand turn onto Bundy Drive. Benoit skips the water station, a clear sign that she's not interested in letting the pack close the gap. The other runners slow and stutter as they crowd to the right to get water, then turn sharply left back across the street to turn the corner onto Bundy. There is a sense of a scramble in the pack—the pace is still leisurely, but the runners seem to feel a bit of urgency to get water and get back to racing. Brown, who seems most reluctant to let Benoit go, also skips the water station and appears again to consider chasing after Benoit. But like the rest of the pack, her pace shows no real commitment to catching up. Benoit rounds the corner onto Bundy, still looking like she's on a training run—though now it is training run with intent: she's determined to run at a pace that does not include others.

Bundy Drive is a winding road through a shaded neighborhood, with tall palm trees bending over the sidewalks. None of the athletes run sharp tangents through the curves, instead loosely following the yellow line in the center of the street. Brown appears to be setting the pace for the pack. Her stride betrays some of her roots as an 800m and 1500m runner: her heels trace a longer arc behind her, she has a bit more forward lean, a bit more roll in her shoulders. It is less compact than a true marathon stride, but it looks easy and fluid, like a miler at a moderate gallop. The chase pack, still twenty-five strong, has accelerated to keep pace with Brown, but they are still spread out over the width of the road, and the gap between them and Benoit is still growing.

They are not yet one-fifth of the way through the race. The pack's pace has dipped under 2:30 for the first time, and the hangers-on are now probably running faster than they can realistically maintain; hope and ambition are over-ruling judgment and experience.

The top contenders are still running well within themselves, as they should be so early in the race. But mentally, some of them seem out of sorts. Often, coaches and commentators will talk about the emotional difficulty of leading a marathon: the pressure, the sense of being hunted, the focus required to set the pace all alone rather than just latching onto a group and disengaging mentally for a spell. Benoit, however, always seems happier out front, and her lead on this day appears to have bred uncertainty among the others: Mota and Kristiansen both glance over at Waitz once more, as if to ask, are we OK with this?

Waitz runs, eyes still down, studiously indifferent to the others. Her back is giving her no issue—a small blessing. If doubts gnaw at the others, Waitz feels fine, in complete control. She is certain that the heat will come for Benoit, and that Benoit's injuries over the spring and summer have left her fitness just lacking enough that she can't hold on for the full twenty-six miles. Waitz trusts her vision of how the last miles will play out, and for now, she holds onto her water bottle for a few extra minutes coming out of the water station, taking sips every few strides.

Just past eight kilometers, there is another near-disaster at a water station: Finland's Tuija Toivonen grabs a sponge off the table, but it slips from her fingers. Instinctively, she turns back to pick it up, and knocks into Canada's Sylvia Ruegger, who tumbles to the ground. Thankfully, Ruegger pops up, unharmed, and rejoins the pack. Brown accelerates out of the water station, perhaps just to get out of trouble. New Zealand's Anne Audain joins her, and the two give every impression of wanting to chase down Benoit in earnest. But again, they step off the gas, unwilling to test themselves so early, and the pack accelerates to rejoin them. Benoit's lead is ten seconds.

Up ahead, Benoit sneaks a look back, then snaps her head back around. She grimaces, then she shakes her head in irritation, as if chastising herself for giving into temptation. To this point, twenty-eight minutes into the race, fourteen minutes since she eased away from the pack, she seems to have been questioning more than racing: were they really letting her go? When would they really start chasing? The questions are wasteful—a drain on her precious mental energy. They were either coming for her or not; it didn't matter which. She looks up and to her right, where the sun would be if it were out, then fixes her gaze resolutely ahead—there will be no more backward glances. In the next three minutes, she doubles her lead, and reaches the 10K mark twenty-two seconds ahead.

Just past 10K, Brown surges again and opens up a slight lead over the rest of the pack. Waitz and Mota answer, bringing the others with them. Brown's head dips every few strides and brow is furrowed. She's now stuck in running purgatory: she hasn't dropped the pack, and she isn't any closer to Benoit. They turn left onto Ocean Boulevard, which runs parallel to the beach. A slight breeze plays at their backs, and the sky above is still hazy; it's not exactly cool, but the day still stubbornly refuses to warm up. The chase pack closes on Brown, though she remains at the front of the pack, unwilling to let the pace drop. Waitz matches her stride for stride.

Kristiansen is a front-runner like Benoit, most confident and happiest in the lead. She knows they started slowly today: at London, when she ran 2:24, she'd hit the 10-kilometer mark more than a minute faster. She looks around constantly: she knows that the others around her (save, perhaps, for Waitz and Mota) are all much slower than she; if the pack is running with her, she is not where she is supposed to be. Her thoughts teeter on the verge of a downward spiral: What is wrong? Why is she still with these others, who have no hope of winning? And why are they running so slow? She checks her watch twice in the space of thirty seconds, as if the watch has answers.

They are past the high point of the course, and running a long gradual decline—hardly noticeable, a drop of just one hundred meters over the next eight kilometers, or slightly more than 1 percent. And they have had a slight tailwind as they run along the water. The pack is down under twenty, its tail starting to stretch out behind Waitz, Mota, Brown, and Kristiansen. They appear still to be running comfortably—Waitz especially so—and it is hard to notice just how much they have accelerated. Despite Kristiansen's fears, they are no longer running slowly at all: they cover the distance from 10 to 15 kilometers in 16:46, or 2:21 pace—faster than Benoit's world record.

Benoit, however, is running 2:17 pace, and at the 15K mark, she leads by fifty seconds. Kristiansen turns to look at Waitz and says something. For the first time all race, Waitz breaks her focus and turns to look at Kristiansen. She says a word or two back. Again, Kristiansen turns to her and says something. This time, Waitz simply stares straight ahead. After the race, Kristiansen insists that she asked Waitz whether they should chase down Benoit, and that Waitz told her to wait, that Benoit would wilt; Waitz is equally insistent that she said no such thing.

The question is not who said what—memories are fallible in stressful situations—but why Kristiansen asks Waitz in the first place. Every part of the competitive racer in Kristiansen is telling her to surge, but something makes her hesitate. For months, coaches and trainers have drilled into her head to be wary of the heat; for years, she has looked up to

Waitz. Again, Kristiansen turns to say something to Waitz. Waitz shakes her head vigorously, annoyed. Kristiansen remains in the pack, on edge and full of doubt.

Around 16 kilometers, Mota surges, opening a small lead. Waitz, still holding her water bottle from the last station, leads the pack's chase, and within two minutes, they catch back up to Mota. The pack is down to fifteen, with two others desperately hanging just a few meters off the back. The course continues southward, parallel to the ocean, past Santa Monica pier, past Venice Beach. Again, Kristiansen says something to Waitz; this time Waitz gives her no response. She refuses to waste mental energy questioning her tactics, firmly believes in her ability to chase down Benoit in the last third of the race. Until she makes her final move, she will simply match anyone else's surge. On both Mota's and Brown's moves, Waitz leads the charge and closes them down in short order. Brown, meanwhile, is now barely holding onto the pack.

Around 19 kilometers, the course runs southbound on Via Marina, along the ocean side of Marina del Rey, then makes a hairpin turn and runs northbound up the other side of Via Marina: Benoit and the pack pass each other going opposite directions. Waitz is driving the pace now, Mota on one shoulder and Kristiansen on the other. The pack is thirteen; the tail of the comet is growing longer, but Benoit's lead has grown to just over a minute. Kristiansen checks her watch, twice. Benoit puts on another charge: in the minutes after the hairpin, her lead grows to ninety seconds.

The course then loops around Marina del Rey to the inland side: they have reached halfway and are approaching the most desolate part of the course, the Marina Freeway overpass—a roughly two-mile stretch of a six-lane freeway that rises over the concrete-lined Ballona Creek channel, over I-405, then back down into Culver City. The Los Angeles Police Department has decreed that no spectators will be allowed on the freeway during the marathon—security concerns, they say. The runners will be alone, as much as the leaders of a major marathon can be alone: press motorcycles shoot by them or keep pace while a cameraman zooms in for closeup shots; pickups and flatbed trucks packed with photographers keep a steady pace just in front of them; helicopters whup overhead.

Scrubby bushes and brown grass dot the sloping hillside off the freeway shoulder. Benoit feels isolated, comfortingly so, as if she's back in Maine in the near-dark hours of the morning. Behind her, the pack is down to twelve as they begin to climb onto the overpass. Waitz and Mota push the pace; Brown has finally lost contact. At the water stations, runners grab several sponges each to cool off. For the first time all day, their shadows appear distinct against the gray concrete. Benoit pops down the brim of her hat to protect against the glare. Twenty-five kilometers into the race, the heat has come for them. But if Benoit is to be caught, her competitors will have to do so in the hottest part of the morning.

***

Mota surges again, and in the brief moments it takes Waitz to reconnect, the pack is whittled down to six: Mota, Waitz, Kristiansen, Canada's Ruegger, Finland's Toivonen, and Italy's Fogli. In short order, Toivonen falls away, and the pack is down to five. But they are still losing ground; ninety minutes into the race, the gap is 1:50. In the ninety-fifth minute, Mota surges again, and again splits the pack. Ruegger drops, and Kristiansen can barely hang on. Waitz gradually works her way back toward Mota, and Fogli clings to Waitz's shoulder. Here, on the overpass, Mota's strategy becomes clear: her periodic surges seem intended to soften up the others; when she accelerates, her rivals accelerate even harder to catch up. If she can continue surging without depleting her own strength, she may be able to break the others or at least burn off their speed. Mota looks back, as if sizing up the others, looking for signs of weakness. Fogli is in uncharted waters, having pushed herself well beyond her capabilities. Kristiansen is grimacing, and her shoulders are beginning to hunch more than usual. But she seems less antsy; the all-out effort to keep up has had a calming effect on her mind. Kristiansen glances at Fogli, as if surprised she's still here, then edges up to Waitz's shoulder. Fogli appears lost, dropping back, but then fights her way back up to the others once more.

Ahead of them, Benoit is nearing the end of the freeway. From overhead, all alone, she looks impossibly small; against the six lanes of concrete, her white hat and gray uniform wash out to become mere splotches on the vast expanse of gray. Her progress seems slowed on the long descent back down to street level, as if she's beating against the tide. But up close, she appears unrelenting, her eyes fixed ahead, her face a mask. She closes in on eighteen miles, or twenty-nine kilometers—nearly an hour and forty minutes into the race. Here, she expected to be preparing to make a decisive, winning move to shed Waitz and the others in the last miles of the race. Instead, she's all alone. If she cared to look back, the others would be out of sight.

Benoit's task is straightforward: keep up her tempo but stay relaxed and don't overdo it. Since her breakaway, she's been under 2:20 pace, even as she turned inland, away from the cool and the breeze, even ascending the overpass, even as the sun burned away the cloud cover. Back on street level, back into the crowds, her head begins to dip slightly on occasion, and her right wrist goes limp for a few strides, as if she's a bird with a broken, floppy wing. These are the first signs of wear in Benoit's stride: A runner's arms must keep time with her legs, and in most runners, the legs tire unevenly. The wrist flops to pause the arm for a beat, to compensate for the fatigued leg—the flop keeps the arms in time with the new, slightly wobbly rhythm of the legs. In Benoit, it is not a sign of imminent collapse—she corrects the floppy wrist after a few strides. She's made it 18 miles, and looks strong and in control. But she has eight miles to go, or 2 miles longer than the next longest race in the Olympics.

Behind her, the chase pack comes off the freeway, and Mota surges again. This one appears decisive: she's nearly ten meters ahead of Waitz, who has a slight lead over Fogli. Kristiansen has fallen back. But Mota cannot break Waitz, and as Waitz regains her shoulder, Mota steps off the gas again, and Fogli and Kristiansen take advantage of the lull to crawl into contact. Mota glances back, again sizing up the others. Kristiansen and Fogli are hurting, clearly, but in Waitz, there's no sign of weakness to be found.

Just past 29 kilometers, Mota tries one more surge, but this time Waitz shoulders to the lead and soon opens a gap—only a few meters at first, but it causes Mota to tighten up. Fogli, at last, cracks—her race, marked by bravery, now becomes a bid to survive the last eight miles. Kristiansen, who has battled the course, the conditions, her rivals—and above all herself—looks ragged, barely hanging on to each surge. Waitz's move nearly breaks her, but she finds some final reserve of strength, edges ahead of Mota, and makes a last, desperate effort to tie herself to Waitz.

Waitz has forty minutes to catch Benoit. In the next five minutes, she takes ten seconds out of Benoit's lead—a start, but Waitz needs to close faster to give herself a chance. She glances back once to find that Kristiansen somehow has caught back up—surprise and annoyance flash across Waitz's face before she refocuses. Kristiansen has given everything to catch up; staying latched onto Waitz's shoulder is another matter entirely. Waitz is relentless—her stride somehow smoother than it was in the first miles of the race—and she picks up her tempo once more. Kristiansen can't hold on. The course has grown desolate again—long stretches of empty parking lots, brown grass, warehouses, chain-link fencing, with scattered oases of a dozen or so spectators cheering as the athletes pass by. The sun has become merciless; for the final miles, a long straight drive to the Coliseum, it is directly in their faces.

With thirty minutes left in the race, Waitz has closed the gap to under ninety seconds. Her eyes still aim downward at the ten feet in front of her, but now she glances up the road occasionally, searching for Benoit, for the press vehicles that mark the position of the leader. They are barely visible in the distance. Kristiansen has cracked; for Waitz, the race is down to an all-out chase and the slim hope of catching Benoit. She can't win unless Benoit falters, but if she can just get close enough to make her look back, maybe a bit of doubt will worm its way into Benoit's mind, maybe she'll tighten up a little—perhaps victory is still possible.

Two hours into the race now, and the lead is down to 1:20. It seems like not enough time, with only twenty-five minutes to go. But twenty-five minutes is eight kilometers—a little less than five miles, plenty of time for anything to happen. At the 1983 Chicago Marathon, Anne Audain had been comfortably running 2:27 pace, well in front—until 24 miles, when she faded badly, finished in 2:32, and Mota slipped by her to win in 2:31. At the 1983 World Championships, Regina Joyce led Waitz through 18 miles; Joyce hit the wall, and finished five minutes behind Waitz. But neither Audain nor Joyce is Benoit.

Benoit passes 37 kilometers in 2:06.36; since 32 kilometers, she has slowed considerably. She is hurting, but she is also saving herself—her focus is now on control, on staying within herself. She's weighing the odds: if she continues to push the pace, the worst-case scenario is that she redlines, falls apart, and struggles home desperately hoping that Waitz is too far back to run her down. If she steps off the gas now, the worst-case scenario is that she lets Waitz catch her and has to win it with an all-out battle down the stretch—but by keeping something in reserve for that possibility, she'll have another gear left if she needs it, while Waitz will have used everything she has just to catch up. Benoit chooses the latter; it gives her more control over her fate.

She crosses La Cienega, La Brea, and then Crenshaw Boulevard—ever closer to the Coliseum—and the crowds grow bigger, louder, more vibrant. The area outside the Carl's Jr. on La Cienega looks like an amphitheater, with rows and rows of spectators standing on the berm that borders the parking lot. The noise is the loudest since the start. Past Crenshaw, people spill off the sidewalks, waving flags, or towels if they don't have flags. Elderly women are dressed as if they're going to church, holding umbrellas against the sun. Dads hold up babies. People are dancing. Crowd control seems to be nonexistent—someone rides a ten-speed down the street right behind Benoit for a full block, then turns a corner and goes on his way. Benoit, who hasn't looked behind her since the early stages of the race, doesn't notice.

Just past the 39-kilometer mark, a large man holding a small flag crosses from the far side of the street, pauses right next to Benoit, and waves his flag very nearly in her face. He then tries to slide between Benoit and the two police motorcycles riding just behind her. One bumps into him, then brushes past; the other stops, has a few pointed words with the man, and waves him back onto the sidewalk. Benoit doesn't break stride, doesn't flinch, doesn't even appear to blink.

Behind her, Waitz is still in pursuit, and behind Waitz, Kristiansen desperately battles to hold on to the bronze medal. The pain and wear of the day are all over her face. Her stride looks like it takes extreme focus, like she has to explicitly order her legs to take each step. She chances a look behind her; Mota is ten seconds back, and her stride also looks kludgy. But Mota's face is calm, intent; she's hunting, and her prey is clearly wounded. Two hours and ten minutes into the race, scarcely fifteen minutes from the finish, Mota catches Kristiansen. For a minute or so, they run together, Kristiansen pumping her arms as if she's in a dead sprint, as if her arms can somehow carry her legs. Both look like the force of gravity has doubled, like they have to fight just to keep running. But Mota pulls away, slowly. She's not surging—neither has the strength for that—but the tiny gap between them grows gradually bigger. In the next four minutes of maximal effort, Mota gains four seconds over Kristiansen, but she might as well be a mile ahead.

Waitz is forty seconds ahead of Mota and Kristiansen, and she has taken more than thirty seconds out of Benoit's lead. But she's out of time. Two hours and seventeen minutes into the race, three kilometers from the finish line, she acknowledges defeat. She waves to Jack, whom she has spotted on the sidewalk, then eases her pace and acknowledges the crowd; they cheer in response. She could continue her all-out pursuit, but Benoit is not coming back, not on this day. She keeps her tempo high enough to ensure that neither Mota nor Kristiansen catches her, but the real racing is over.

Ahead of her, Benoit takes on water one more time. She's minutes away from the Coliseum and running slower than she has since the first kilometers of the race. But she's no less intent: only a catastrophe—a massive spell of cramping, or her hamstring suddenly seizing—could change the outcome; keeping herself in control and staying as relaxed as possible is of paramount importance. The crowd stands ten deep on the side of the road and five deep on the median in the middle it—she's running through a tunnel of noise. She turns off Exposition Boulevard and onto Menlo, a long, 800m stretch lined on both sides of the road by an eight-foot-high chain-link fence shrouded in the Olympic pastel color scheme, and suddenly she's alone again.

If she broke her concentration for a moment, she could hear the stadium announcer heralding her arrival. The massive bowl of the Coliseum sits submerged in the earth; only its upper levels are above ground, and Benoit makes a U-turn off Menlo to descend into the tunnel that takes her underneath the stadium to floor level. Cool and dark, the tunnel curves for nearly one hundred meters before emptying onto the track; briefly Benoit considers stopping there, not coming back out: she knows that just like after her first Boston win, and after her world record, her life will not truly be her own again for some time, if ever.

In the television studio, Al Michaels mouths to Liquori and Switzer, let the crowd take it, and when Benoit emerges back into the light, she is met by the deafening roar of more than sixty thousand spectators standing and cheering for her.

Switzer is struggling to stick to the job, to keep her emotions in check. Jackie Hansen is in the stadium with her son. Together, they rush down to the front row, Hansen in tears—she can't believe she's witnessing the gold-medal winner of the women's Olympic marathon circle the track, and she can't believe it took so long to get a women's marathon into the Olympics. She's struck by the thought that millions—maybe billions—of girls around the world are watching. On the other side of the country, at her home in Connecticut, Julia Chase, who first broke the AAU's prohibition on women running sanctioned road races, is sobbing in front of her television. Bobbi Gibb, also home, also watches in tears. Sev is outside the stadium, listening to the roar. At the L.L.Bean flagship store in Benoit's hometown of Freeport, a voice over the storewide public address system announces her imminent victory, and staff and shoppers alike cheer wildly.

Benoit has five hundred meters to go: one hundred meters down the home straightaway to the finish line, then one more circuit of the track. On the backstretch, she takes off her hat and waves madly to the crowd; at last, she can let go. She doesn't run through the finish as much as leap, arms outstretched. Her last lap of the race—four hundred meters—took her just over eighty seconds; her victory lap, slapping hands with the crowd, pumping a large American flag, is very nearly as fast.

Waitz completes her last lap waving to the crowd, both arms fully outstretched—an uncharacteristically emotive gesture for her. The crowd responds, staying on their feet. She crosses the line, and for the first time since she appeared on the track in Santa Monica—perhaps for the first time in days—her face relaxes and opens into a broad smile of gratitude and relief. She and Benoit share a hug, their faces close together. "No one was beating you today," Waitz says.

Less than a minute after Waitz, Mota crosses in third place, looking as if she has won: she raises her arms overhead, smiling and crying at the same time, then covers her eyes, then looks to the heavens, then covers her face again. She shakes her head, nearly overcome.

Kristiansen is rounding the track in fourth; with two hundred meters to go, she checks her watch twice. She finishes with arms out, palms up, dejection and confusion on her face, a shrug of disbelief. Waitz waits for her at the finish and puts an arm around her, whispers in her ear, and hands her a cup of water. The two countrywomen, teammates and rivals, walk away together.

Almost immediately after winning, Benoit is corralled into an interview with ABC's Jim Lampley. She makes a point of thanking the generation of runners who came before her, who paved the way for her historic moment. "If it hadn't been for the work of countless women pioneers in the sport, we wouldn't be here today," she says. "And let's hope that in 1988 we can also run a five and ten K, because we showed today that women can be very competitive over this distance."

Fogli finishes ninth. That she straggled in, helpless as others passed her, is beside the point. She gave herself every shot at a medal, went toe-to-toe with the world's best, and hung on beyond the limits of her body. She is rewarded with a new national record and best time of 2:29.28, her first sub-2:30 marathon.

Nearly twenty minutes after Fogli, Julie Brown struggles home in thirty-sixth. Her time, 2:47, is more than twenty minutes slower than her best. She came into the Olympics with the fastest-ever time in a women's-only race, 2:26.26. Had she run that same time today, she would have beaten Mota for bronze. She gets water, then walks back toward the tunnel, all but invisible, the trace of a limp in her walk. Her eyes are down, hands on her head.

Benoit, still giving interviews when she spots Brown, runs over to shake her hand and pat her on the back. Brown grabs the proffered hand, but never looks up and keeps walking to the exit—until it registers in her mind who it was. Her head pops up, and she walks stiffly over to Benoit. The two share a long hug. Benoit, several inches shorter than Brown, even tries to lift her off the ground. It's a hug that says more than any words

Benoit could offer. There's nothing to say really. In the marathon, success comes from determination, talent, indifference to pain, and focus. It is the product of hours of work stacked up week after week. And sometimes, the decisive factor is still luck: Brown had little of it at the Olympics, while on the day that mattered, Benoit was at her best. And at her best, Benoit was unbeatable.

INTERLUDE

Los Angeles, California, August 5, 1984, 10:52 a.m.: *On the downhill slope into the Coliseum tunnel, a runner, an Olympian, staggers across the road, then veers back to recenter herself. She is glassy-eyed and slack-jawed, and her head lolls around as if she can no longer fully support it. In her right hand she clutches her white cycling cap in a death grip, as if it is a lifeline; her right arm seems to be the only part of her body over which she has certain control. The ambulance that has been trailing her on the course pauses at the mouth of the tunnel. Briefly, the runner rests her hands on her knees, then pops up and jogs ten more steps with a loose, unhinged gait, still bent over at the waist: a slack marionette in motion. Her body lists to the left. Once in the tunnel, she stops to walk again. Four officials surround her, then two of them run out of the tunnel ahead of her to alert the medical personnel at the finish. One of the remaining officials has a megaphone: "Do not touch the runner! Do not touch the runner!" he commands.*

The cameras pick her up, and the crowd in the stadium see her image on the big screen.

She emerges from the tunnel onto the track, and in the glare of the sun, she puts her hat back on, with both hands. The crowd rises as one in a sustained ovation. On the straightaways, she struggles to hold her line, still staggering to the left; the curves seem nearly impossible for her to navigate: she veers first one way, then the other, punch-drunk, desperately trying to make her legs respond to her mind's instructions. Around the final lap, two medical officials walk next to her on the infield. A crowd of cameramen dart in and out.

Her body is cramping, and she continues to weave back and forth on her journey to the finish. The pain is intense, beyond anything she's ever felt in a marathon before, and she looks like she is on the verge of death, or at least critical system failure. But she is lucid—she can hear the crowd, like nothing she's ever heard before. An official walks onto the track toward her, and she turns to look at him, as if to say, stay away—this is the Olympics. She weaves around the final turn; it is almost a cruel joke that her body, which she's pushed so far beyond what it should have to bear, is unable to hold the direct, shortest path around the track.

In the broadcast booth, anger and fear creep into Liquori's voice; he is insistent that she should be carried off before she suffers permanent damage. Likely he speaks for many in the television audience. Switzer is just as adamant that she's earned the right to finish the race. The crowd, still standing, wills her to make it to the line.

As she crosses, two medical personnel take ahold of her before she can collapse. It has taken her seven minutes to make it through the tunnel onto the track and around to the finish. Gaby Andersen-Schiess, running for Switzerland, finishes thirty-seventh in the Olympic marathon with a time of 2:48.42. Moments later, she receives one more standing ovation as she leaves the Coliseum on a stretcher.

The pain is nearly unbearable for an hour or so after she finishes. Two hours later, she feels mostly fine.

It was "just a little bit of dehydration," she says to a fellow competitor the next day.

PART IV

CHAPTER 17

The Day After

THE MEDAL CEREMONY TOOK PLACE THAT EVENING. WAITZ LOOKED happy and unburdened. She turned to wave in all directions around the stadium and gave a little curtsy after receiving her silver. Mota beamed and waved excitedly with both hands when she was called up to receive her bronze. As the anthems played, Benoit resolved not to cry, but she blinked awfully hard. Waitz did succumb to tears as the flags rose in the night sky—tears of joy, she said; twenty-four hours earlier, she didn't think she would be able to run. Mota, standing on the medal podium, said to herself, "I have four years to be ready to win gold."

The next morning, Joan Benoit, gold medalist and newly minted American hero, woke up and went for a run with a few friends: Jackie Hansen, George Hirsch, publisher of *Runner's World*, and a few others joined her for what was meant to a be an easy shake-out, a fun way to relax and celebrate. Two things happened: First, Benoit began to one-step the group; soon her friends were barely hanging on as Benoit dropped the pace down into six-minute per mile range. Second, Benoit's entourage became a mob as more and more people joined in, then dropped out as the pace got too fast, and others tried to jump in. Overnight (if one ignores the years of training and racing that led up to it), Benoit had become a celebrity. Her near-solo race to victory meant that her face had occupied television screens for most of the live telecast; she was now one of the most recognizable athletes in Los Angeles. The next day, she found herself mobbed again. It was time to go home. Benoit and Scott caught the next available flight back to Maine, skipping the closing ceremonies.

In Norway, the morning-after newspapers excoriated Waitz for her performance. "Why did you let her go, Grete?" asked one. Even now, that is a common question. It is an unfair one: Benoit's winning time was 2:24.52; Waitz's best time to that point in her career was 2:25.28. Her best ever, at the London Marathon in 1986, was 2:24.54—still slower than what Benoit ran at the Olympics. Had Waitz's back not flared up the day before the marathon, she might have tried to go with Benoit. But Waitz never used her injury as an excuse, always stating that her tactics were based on her expectations of the heat and her belief that Benoit would falter. In the end, it is doubtful that different tactical choices could have changed the outcome. At the Olympics, Benoit was at the peak of her powers. All evidence suggests that Waitz's postrace assessment was correct: no one could beat Benoit that day.

Kristiansen might beg to differ. After the race, she was furious. "I ran someone else's race," she said. Often, her anger is assumed to have been directed at Waitz, but that was never the case. "The doctors and trainers had started telling us months before how warm it would be, about pollution; they told us don't push too hard, don't push too early, stay in the group," she said. Before and during the race, they were in her head. "I usually wake up on the morning of the race, say to myself, 'this is the weather today, this is the race,' and I try not to worry about it," she said. "I am a front-runner—I like to push the pace from the beginning. At the Olympics, I started to look around me, at the girls around me, and I think, 'these girls are five or six minutes slower than me—why am I here?' I was still new in the running community; the coach and others were being careful. But I think, if I had gone after Joan, or gone with her, maybe . . . " she trailed off. "I don't know if I could have beaten her.

"It is hard to know why I did it, but I did it. One of the stupid things I did," she said, laughing. "That's the game." Despite her disappointment, it did not take Kristiansen long to let go of the Olympic marathon. "Always look forward," she said. And when she got back to the hotel, her son, Gaute, just a week shy of his first birthday, was waiting for her, a big smile on his face. "There are always downs in your career," said Arve, her husband. "You have a child who needs you nearby. Life is much easier."

Ingrid would always be a runner, and more than that, a competitor. But Gaute changed her perspective. "My biggest goal was my son," she said.

The day after the marathon, Gaby Andersen-Schiess was up, walking around, sore and tired but otherwise OK. "I was kind of embarrassed that I didn't do well, and I didn't deserve all this attention," she said. "I would have traded anything for the tenth or fifteenth place instead of all that spectacle." However, over time, her perspective has changed. Perhaps more than Benoit's victory, Andersen-Schiess's struggle was the sign that the public fully accepted that the women's marathon belonged in the Olympics. Unlike 1928, when vastly exaggerated reports of women falling at the end of the 800m were enough to curtail women's opportunities for a generation, in 1984, Andersen-Schiess became hero, a true symbol of Olympic will, endurance, and fortitude.

***

The fall 1984 marathon season was, for obvious reasons, anticlimactic. Waitz, ever loyal, returned to New York and won over a lackluster field. Mota won Chicago in 2:26; Kristiansen was third in 2:30. In the brave new world of appearance fees and prize money, they all collected handsome paydays, but in neither race was there much evidence of burning competitive drive.

Benoit was, if not in hiding, at least trying to shelter herself. Mostly she'd been managing a deluge of obligations: a banquet for *Sports Illustrated*'s Sportsperson of the Year; a champagne brunch at Studio 54 for *Ms.* magazine's Women of the Year—initially she'd said no, until it turned out she was the only one of the dozen honorees who wouldn't be attending. An invitation to President Reagan's second inauguration awaited a response; it was affixed to her refrigerator with a Mondale-Ferraro magnet. There was a ceremony for her induction into the Maine Sports Hall of Fame; Joan Benoit day in Freeport; a parade in Portland. Charities came calling again; she had her favorites—the MS Society, the Special Olympics, Big Sisters—and tried not to let guilt consume her when she turned down others.

When she'd been in the tunnel under the Coliseum, when she'd briefly considered not coming out, her mind had drifted to her other life-changing races: Boston in 1979 and her world record in 1983. On those occasions, the public attention had been nearly unbearable. In that tunnel, she'd thought to herself, this isn't going to be a world record, but on the other hand, it will be the Olympic gold medal. In terms of the amount of added public attention she'd receive, she decided, one couldn't be any worse than the other. The aftermath of her first Boston win, in 1979, caught her unaware; "I really fell apart after that," she said. Post-Olympics, she was better prepared for what lay ahead, better able to say no, more accustomed to it. And she had a business manager. Still, she found herself wrung out again.

And she had a wedding to plan. She and Scott got married on a date and at a location that she guarded closely for fear the media would descend. It took place at the end of September, on the water, and ended with Joan and Scott sailing away in a boat that Scott had made for her. A three-day honeymoon in Bermuda followed, and somewhere in all of that she finally put to rest any thoughts of racing a fall marathon. She'd already told both New York and Chicago that the answer was likely no; both pursued her nonetheless, and her competitive streak meant that she surely couldn't help at least consider another race against Waitz in New York, or Mota and Kristiansen in Chicago. Bob Bright, the Chicago race director, kept escalating his offer. Rumor was, he went as high as $250,000; Bright insisted that he "only" went to $50,000—though it is possible another sponsor, such as Beatrice Foods, which sponsored both the Chicago marathon and Benoit, would have sweetened the pot. (For comparison's sake, Waitz got a $30,000 appearance fee for New York, whereas the top men got only $10,000.) But when it came to deciding on whether to race, Benoit navigated by a simple rule: "If I'm not ready, I won't race."

She was neither physically nor mentally ready that fall. She had been running steadily but not optimally: she'd yet to hit one hundred miles per week, the threshold that, when she hit it consistently, gave her the confidence to attack a marathon. Emotionally, she was exhausted—in very good ways; a history-making gold medal and a wedding made for a full year. At the top of her game as an athlete, embarking on a new journey together with Scott, Joan Benoit Samuelson began to contemplate marathoning mortality. Multiple surgeries and lost seasons gave Benoit a deep appreciation for how fleeting a running career could be, and she knew that few marathoners could count on more than a few years of true greatness. If she had a limited number of great races left, she wanted to make the most of them.

She figured she'd only run one marathon in 1985, and she was determined to make it count.

CHAPTER 18

Twilight

ANY OLYMPIC RACE, SIGNIFICANT AS IT MAY BE, IS ONLY A MOMENT IN time—contested and done with. The world does not stop, and after LA, neither did Benoit, Waitz, Mota, and Kristiansen. The first women's Olympic marathon might be seen as career defining, and surely, such a history-making race had the power to confer immortality on its contestants. But athletes also define the race: by their accomplishments both before and after the 1984 Olympics, the four athletes who led the field conferred upon the Olympic marathon the stature not just of a historic race but a truly transcendent one.

In 1985, marathoners awoke as if from a long winter's nap—refreshed and ready to battle once more. At the first major spring marathon, London, Kristiansen demonstrated unequivocally that her aim to be the best distance runner on the planet was not misplaced. Though her characteristic upright stride was unmistakable, she looked like a different runner from the Olympics. She ran tall, light on her feet, face expressionless except for her ever-present squint. She appeared to be perpetually surging through the field, constantly challenging the male runners who sought to keep pace with her. She hit the halfway mark in 1:10.10 and dropped the pace from there. Through twenty miles, she was on sub-2:20 pace, still looking confident and indomitable. Gradually, however, the pace took its toll. A hitch developed in her stride; her left wrist began to flop, and her head began to bob in the last two miles. Twice she checked her watch, as if she were desperate to know how much longer she had. Her face contorted into a grimace, and although she lost considerable time in the final stretch, she crossed the line in 2:21.06, smashing Benoit's world record of 2:22.43.

Waitz and Benoit had both talked about breaking the 2:20 barrier; Kristiansen's stunning breakthrough made clear that she was perhaps likeliest to do it. Her performance also set up a potential heavyweight battle for the fall. Waitz chose New York, as she always would. Mota, the defending Chicago champion, returned to Chicago. Kristiansen swore she'd never do New York—she felt they'd always favored Grete, and ignored her, until she broke the world record, and she too chose Chicago.[1] Benoit chose Chicago for its course, which was flatter and faster than New York. And Chicago paid handsomely. Altogether, Bright, the shelled out $370,000 in appearance fees—likely at least $50,000 each to Kristiansen, Mota, and Benoit—while New York's total budget for appearance fees was $70,000, much of which went to Waitz. In addition, Beatrice Foods added a $150,000 payment to Benoit to run Chicago. Although former world record holder Steve Jones and world champion Rob de Castella were in the men's field, Kristiansen, Benoit, and Mota were the headliners.

Kristiansen announced that she was going for sub-2:20. Mota said, simply and honestly, "that pace is too fast for me"; she could only run her race and hope that the others blew up. Benoit demurred: "I'd just like to be competitive . . . I'm looking forward to the marathon. I haven't run one since the Olympics. It's time I did." For Kristiansen, Chicago was a chance to put into practice what she'd learned at the Olympics. "Before the race, I said to myself, 'Don't think of Joanie. This is your race.'" She wanted to run on her terms and planned simply to string together thirty-three-minute 10Ks, which would result in a time of 2:19.15. Benoit said, "If she's going after it, I'm going to try to hang on and go with her."

"Ingrid went into Chicago to break 2:20," said Toni Reavis. "Joanie went into it to break Ingrid." Certainly, it appeared that way: at the gun, Benoit took off. Her first mile was 5:09—31:30 10K pace, 2:14 for a marathon. Kristiansen felt she had no choice but to try to hang on. "She was the boss," said Kristiansen. "In the first miles, I said, 'It is OK, fast is better for me than for Joanie, because my 10,000 time is much faster than hers." Kristiansen sat on her shoulder through the early miles. Benoit stared dead ahead, as if she were all alone, pointedly ignoring the current world record holder sitting on her shoulder. Kristiansen held on, through halfway, through sixteen miles, the two still under 2:20 pace. Benoit remained expressionless, but inside she was having doubts. "If Ingrid had kicked away just then, I'd have settled for second," she said. But just after seventeen miles, Benoit opened the slightest of leads, maybe five meters. Kristiansen, grimacing, closed it back up. If Benoit noticed—if she noticed anything at all—there wasn't a tell. Again, Benoit opened a slight lead, again Kristiansen fought back—but her head was bobbing, her wrist flapping just a little, and her grimace became more pronounced.

Twenty miles in, Benoit broke away for good. It is hard to say whether she surged; rather, it appeared that Kristiansen could no longer hold on to the metronomic Benoit. Slowly but inexorably, the gap widened: 5m, then 15m; soon Benoit led by over a minute. Inside, her wheels were turning. She let the pace slack a little. "I intentionally left something in the tank with the thought that Ingrid or Rosa might come up on me at the end," Benoit said. Afterward, she she said, "I thought, *Man,* I should've gone for a sub-2:20 marathon."

After crossing the line, Benoit looked back to see where Ingrid was—as if surprised to discover that Kristiansen was nowhere in sight. Her finishing time, 2:21.21, didn't quite beat Kristiansen's London time, but somehow it felt superior. It would stand as the American record until 2003. Kristiansen held onto second, finishing in a little over 2:23, just ahead of Mota in third.

If a single race captures the brilliance of Benoit's running even better than the Olympics, it is Chicago 1985. She started fast—irrationally, suicidally so—and forced the pace for the entire grinding, exhausting effort. She concentrated her focus to such a degree that she might as well have been on a dirt road in rural Maine, in the dark of a brutally cold morning that keeps everyone else inside. She blocked out her competitors—much more difficult to do when they are sitting on your shoulder than when they are almost two minutes behind. She pushed herself past her own breaking point, and held on until the last of her rivals had succumbed. She kept her wits about her enough to strategize for the endgame. And she was on the edge of failure from the beginning. As a race, it was a gift, one not to be taken for granted.

***

After Chicago, Kristiansen turned her attention to the track. In July 1985, she lowered the world 10,000m record by fourteen seconds, running 30:59. In July 1986, she lowered it again, this time to 30:13. In August, she won the European Championships 10,000m by more than thirty seconds. A month later, she lowered the 5000m world record to 14:37. Though she won the London Marathon again in 1987, running 2:22, she still focused more on track events, winning the 1987 world championship 10,000m in a relatively pedestrian (for her) time of 31:04. Her stretch of running from 1985 to 1987 rivals what Waitz accomplished from 1978 to 1980. Kristiansen became the only person, male or female, to hold the 5000m, 10,000m, and marathon records simultaneously. Her marathon record wasn't broken until 1998. She held the 5000m until 1995. The 10,000m record remained until 1993, when it was broken by Wang Junxia.[2] No one else touched Kristiansen's 10,000m time until Paula Radcliffe ran 30:01 in 2002.

In February 1986, Benoit won the Sullivan award, awarded by the AAU to the top "amateur" athlete in the nation (though amateur had come to be defined as athletes competing in Olympic or collegiate sports). She wanted to run Boston in 1986, but foot surgery derailed that plan. In 1987, she again planned on running Boston, though this time, she would be two months pregnant. A thigh strain kept her from the starting line. Her daughter, Abby, was born in October. As the next Olympic buildup began, in 1988, Benoit found herself starting from near-zero, having not raced a marathon since 1985.

Waitz battled injuries as well. She won New York in 1985, though her time, 2:28, hardly earned a mention after the Benoit-Kristiansen duel a week earlier. In the spring of 1986, she won the London Marathon in 2:24.54, despite having had to miss considerable training due to a knee injury that winter. In the fall, she went back to New York and won again. Though she was still among the elite, she did not inspire the same fear she had earlier in her career; her competitors were no longer racing for second place. She was no longer the face of women's distance running but one among many. And by 1987, sports media tended to view her as a living legend, with all that the term implies about being on the downhill side of one's career.

But she still had her sights on testing herself against the best, and as she prepared for 1987 World Marathon Championships in Rome, her training runs were faster than ever, faster even than in 1983 and 1984 when she'd been at her peak. Kristiansen was running the 10,000m, and Benoit was seven months pregnant. Only Mota, who had run 2:23 in 1985, could boast a faster time than Waitz; Lisa Martin, one of the other prerace favorites, said Waitz was the one she was most worried about at Worlds. Ten days before worlds, Waitz ran a 10,000m time trial and felt great. The next morning, she woke up with a limp. Waitz watched the World Championships on crutches, having suffered a stress fracture, and could only wonder what might have been. "Lisa had every right to be worried," said Waitz with a sad smile.

Mota, meanwhile, remained as far under the radar as possible for someone who won big races so consistently. She won Chicago in 1984, finished third in 1985, then won Euros in 1986, the Tokyo International in the fall of 1986, and Boston in the spring of 1987. That summer at the World Championships, she won in 2:25.21, seven minutes ahead of second place finisher Zoya Ivanova.

Heading into the Olympic year, Benoit, Waitz, Mota, and Kristiansen were all still active and all among the best in the world—when healthy. But in the months before the Olympic trials, Benoit suffered a hip injury and could not repeat the miracle of 1984. As the Trials approached, she said, "I'm almost in shape," but she chose not to compete: "I have too much respect for the marathon to do that," she said.

Kristiansen chose the 10,000m at the Olympics over the marathon and entered as the overwhelming favorite. But midway through the race, she suffered a fractured bone in her foot and stepped off the track with three thousand meters to go. Perhaps the greatest distance runner of all time, Kristiansen ended her career without an Olympic medal.

Mota and Waitz both returned to the Olympic marathon, though Waitz had suffered a knee injury earlier that summer. She'd had arthroscopic surgery on August 8; she called Benoit to ask for advice on getting back into racing shape quickly. On September 15 she tested her knee in a 15K race and pronounced herself healthy enough to race the Olympics on September 22. Mota was now the one to beat—the runner everyone else keyed on. Conditions favored her: the Seoul Olympic marathon was hot, humid, and smoggy—everything Los Angeles could have been.

The pace remained conservative early on. Mota started to pick it up after halfway. Around mile 15, Waitz fell off; soon she was limping and dropped out. Four athletes remained: Mota, Martin, Katrin Dorre of East Germany, and Tatyana Polovinskaya of the Soviet Union. Polovinskaya made a surge at mile 20, which dropped no one. Mota kept grinding down the pace, and soon Polovinskaya dropped off. Dorre tried to take the lead around mile 23; the others matched. Mota pulled away, but only slightly. She held on for a thirteen-second victory; Martin held off Dorre for silver, thirty seconds behind Mota, and Dorre took bronze.

***

Benoit, Waitz, Mota, and Kristiansen won every global championship on offer in the 1980s. They dominated Boston, New York, Chicago, London, and Tokyo—the major marathons of their era. Over their careers, they collectively lowered the world record a combined six times and a total of thirteen minutes. They transformed women's marathoning from a novelty into one of the marquee events in athletics; they received top billing at major races, pushed the men out of the headlines, and commanded greater prize money. All four have a claim to being the greatest marathoner of their era, perhaps even of all time. Waitz utterly dominated the early years of their shared era; she stood alone and untouchable, winning New York nine times, winning the first World Championship, and lowering the world record nine minutes on her own. Benoit was electric, fearless, a force of nature when healthy: she shattered Waitz's world record in 1983, won the first Olympic gold with a gutsy, dominating performance, and beat Kristiansen both mentally and physically at Chicago in 1985. But Kristiansen posted times that simply defied belief, rewriting the record books and setting a new standard for future generations to try to match.

Mota, though the slowest of the four—the only one never to hold the world record—had the ability to come up big when it counted most. She is the only marathoner ever to hold the World, European, and Olympic crowns at the same time.

There hasn't been a generation like them since. And they stood together on the starting line only once, for a single golden race: the first women's Olympic marathon, the greatest marathon in Olympic history.

CHAPTER 19

Dusk

IN 1990, BOTH MORE OR LESS GLIDING INTO RETIREMENT, BENOIT VISited Waitz in Norway with Scott, their daughter, Abby, and their newborn son, Anders. Benoit wanted to have Anders christened in Norway, and asked Jack and Grete to be his godparents. It was, Benoit said, a way to connect to her own Scandinavian heritage. The christening took place in Balestrand, a stunning village on Sognefjord, Norway's longest fjord. Together, the Benoit Samuelsons and the Waitzes traveled across the fjord on a replica Viking ship to an old wooden church. Naturally, there was a race: a half-marathon; Benoit won, Waitz watched and cheered.

Waitz ran her last marathon in 1992, in New York, in a time of 5:32. As a runner, she'd always seemed to exist in her own world, a place apart from everyone else, but in 1992, she ran stride for stride the entire distance with her old friend Fred Lebow.

As Waitz had set the standard for marathoners, so had Lebow done for race directors. And just as other runners had risen to exceed what Waitz had done, so, too, did Lebow find the New York City Marathon getting outbid by other big city races. But Lebow was still Lebow—one of a kind, a race director like no other, his life still a whirlwind. Until, one day his grip on that life grew shaky. In early 1990, everything slowed down for him—he had to walk more slowly, he became forgetful, he couldn't focus, and he began to have trouble speaking. He went to see an old friend and the 1974 New York City Marathon winner, Dr. Norbert Sander. A biopsy confirmed the worst: a tennis ball-sized tumor in Lebow's brain. He had maybe six months to live.

Treatment began almost immediately, first at Mount Sinai Hospital, later at the Sloan-Kettering Cancer Center in Manhattan. In his darkest moments, lying in bed alone, Lebow had moments of denial, wanting to believe that it was some other Fred Lebow who was too sick and exhausted to move. But Lebow, at his core, was irrepressible. He started walking as often and as much as he could: twelve steps at his weakest; then five minutes, then ten, then up to two miles. At Mount Sinai, he discovered a small rooftop terrace—sixty-seven laps to the mile; at Sloan-Kettering, he counted hallway tiles to figure out how many circuits of his floor made one mile (eleven).

Fred's visitors weren't permitted to sit in his room with him; if they arrived at walking time, they walked the halls with him. And he recruited patients to walk with him, too, starting what amounted to a cancer patient recreation program—which, as so often happened with Lebow, became part of a scheme: "Hospitals need to have more of an emphasis on keeping people active," he said. "They need . . . workout rooms, and they need to get patients into these rooms and make them take care of themselves."

His training had a goal: he'd never run his own five-borough New York City Marathon. By the time the marathon ventured out of Central Park in 1976, it was too big a beast for him to both direct and run; often he ran the Chicago Marathon a week before New York, just so his legs would be tired enough to mitigate his envy of all the runners in his marathon. Impossible as it seemed for a man who could barely walk two miles, running New York became his focus, his reason to get through treatment.

Two and a half years after his diagnosis, Lebow huddled with Waitz on the starting line. Waitz, looking more anxious than she did before any of her previous races, tried to keep Lebow calm. Lebow was still trying to direct the race—trying to move groups of runners, barking out instructions to fix last-minute issues. Fifty-five seconds before the gun was supposed to sound, a group of runners near the front surged across the line—a dreaded false start, a slow-motion stampede with the weight of twenty-six thousand runners behind it, impossible to contain or call back. Lebow was frantic, near tears: "I should never have run this race!" he cried.

Waitz spoke gently in his ear, trying to reassure him, as if he were one of her elementary school students from long ago. She helped him get his jacket off, guided him to their starting position—they would start running with the back of the pack, so as not to get overrun; they still had some time before they'd cross the starting line.

She ran next to Lebow, and they were surrounded by a pack of other close friends and protectors who would try to keep the path clear and the crowds at bay. Still, spectators darted off the sidewalk to shake his hand or snap a photo. Of the two million spectators who lined the streets, nearly all waited for Lebow. Their cheers pushed him down the course; the louder they were, the faster he ran. Waitz kept a tight rein on him, scolding when she had to: "Fred if you don't slow down, you're going to have to walk the last six miles." She enforced walk breaks, made him eat and drink.

Sloan-Kettering stood near the 17-mile mark. Doctors, patients, and children stood outside and cheered him; most held handmade signs for him. His doctors rushed into the street to hug him. By this point, Lebow was exhausted, physically and mentally. His breathing grew ragged. Waitz was the constant voice in his ear, reassuring, encouraging, motivating— and occasionally demanding a rest.

And Lebow, even at the outer edge of his physical limits, remained a mischief maker. Near mile 20, he doubled over, moaning. Grete, heart in her mouth, stopped and leaned over to check on him, and he sprinted away down the course. "Fooled you!" he shouted.

Near the park, the crowds grew bigger and louder—cheering as if their own lives depended on it, as if they needed Fred to finish, as if their voices could carry him the last miles.

And perhaps they did. His stride became a shuffle, steps grew slower, and each one seemed shaky. But he and Waitz reached the park. "New York, New York" blared out of the speakers near the finish. Grete began to cry—she knew they would make it. Fred began to cry, and hand in hand they ran the last steps together. They had won—at least for one day, Fred had beaten cancer, and all the joy and meaning and connection that Lebow had brought to marathoning, all the excitement and toil and support of twenty-six thousand runners, nearly as many volunteers, and two million spectators seemed to lift the two runners shuffling toward the finish more than three hours behind the winners.

Grete stood aside at the finish to let Fred cross alone; he refused, and beckoned to her, and together they broke the tape one last time. Willie Mtolo, the men's winner, had come back out to the course to hold the finish tape for Fred. In the midst of a massive ovation from the gathered spectators, officials, volunteers, and runners, Grete and Fred embraced, and she held onto him as if she were afraid to let him go.

Lebow and Waitz were a symbiotic pair. Fred channeled his competitive streak into making his marathon as big as possible, ensuring that records were set on his course, crowning the top champions with the New York laurel, and exhorting the media to cover his race. He needed stories. Grete understood that she was a story, that publicity was part of her job. She was naturally shy—more so when speaking in her second language—and disliked crowds; nonetheless, she forged genuine connections with both news media and runners who came to hear her speak. "You've got to keep smiling, and be nice to everybody," she said. When she was with Lebow, that was easier. She was more relaxed with him; he drew off much of the spotlight's glare and absorbed the attention of the crowd, made himself the center of it. And he respected her need for privacy away from the race.

In appearance and demeanor, they could not have been more different. Lebow was self-centered in the way that young children are self-centered—completely, earnestly absorbed in the small universe of what mattered to him; he was a wild man on marathon day—raging from place to place around the start, desperately grabbing volunteers to fix last-minute problems. There was no checklist of what had to get done, one close colleague observed, save for what was in Lebow's head. He exhibited what she came to think of as a heart-on-sleeve American personality, shouting to the world both his joys and frustrations. Waitz, on the other hand, was all Norwegian cool, outwardly composed, her nerves bottled up.

But they shared an obsession with being the best and understood how it marked them as different from most others. Lebow sought to share the joy he found in running with the rest of the world; Waitz, as a matter of national constitution, would not effusively share the joy like Fred, but she needed running the same way he did. Further, though New York was the site of some of their greatest triumphs, they were both far from home. Lebow made himself a New Yorker, and the city would claim him as one of its own; Waitz was a "New Yorker by adoption," according to New York media, or "the New Yorker from Norway," according to mayor Ed Koch. But she and Fred were still both foreigners, outsiders in America.

Brain cancer finally claimed Lebow in 1994. The night before he died, Waitz was there with him. He hardly stirred in his last days, but he perked up in her presence. At the 1994 New York City Marathon, the New York Road Runners unveiled a bronze statue of Lebow, in a running suit, trademark cap on his head, beard slightly scraggly, looking down at his stopwatch. Although there was a moratorium on erecting new statues within Central Park, Lebow now resides at the Park's edge, 90th Street and East Drive, steps from the Reservoir path he loved. And every year, he travels by pickup truck to the finish line of the marathon near the Tavern on the Green. To honor Lebow in 1994, Waitz and twenty-two other former champions gathered at the marathon; Waitz offered to shepherd Lebow's family around for the weekend.

Professional running is a selfish sport; while training, preparing, and racing, one must often push aside the concerns of others, keep one's world as small as possible. In retirement, freed of her relentless focus on becoming the best, Waitz found more time and space to let her natural kindness show through. She was still as private as always, but she no longer seemed aloof and apart; instead, she became more willing to make a gift of herself. Running became her way to connect with others.

And running became a way for others to reach out to her, to spend time in her world. In 1984, she helped start the Grete Waitz Run, a 5K in Oslo, to encourage women to be more active and competitive. One of the women who took the message to heart was her mother, Reidun. She'd never understood her daughter's obsession with running; though she'd made peace with it and supported Grete's career, she'd also hoped to raise a more traditional girl—dresses, piano lessons, and all. By 1989, the Grete Waitz Run had had tens of thousands of women participating—it was the largest women's-only race in the world—and Reidun half-joked that if these women could do it, she should, too.

Grete gave her mother a pair of running shoes. Soon, they were walking and jogging together—and talking. "For the first time," Grete wrote, "my mother opened up to me, and we showed each other our emotional sides." Their runs together became a vital bond, especially as Grete's father fell terminally ill. The two women who had circled each other warily in Grete's youth, who never fully understood each other—"I was the apple that fell very far from the tree," wrote Grete—became each other's closest, most vital supporters. They ran together at the 1990 Grete Waitz Run, and at the end, the daughter gently encouraged her mother—"Mom, you want to finish running, don't you?"—and after they circled the track at Bislett Stadium and crossed the finish line together, they shared the kind of hug they'd never shared after Grete's great victories.

Waitz also devoted more and more time to charitable work, to supporting running for all women—more and more, she embraced the role of public figure. But "for such an introvert," said Waitz's friend and collaborator Gloria Averbuch, "it must have been exhausting and horribly difficult to be so kind and gracious constantly."

Sometime in 2005, her feeling of exhaustion grew to the point that it was clearly more than just the emotional toll of spending so much time in the public eye. Her doctor's diagnosis seemed impossible: as it came for Lebow, cancer came for Waitz. And as with Lebow, friends and competitors found it hard to reconcile such a ravaging disease with such a vibrant, active person. She refused to dwell on it publicly—she viewed her battle "as something that concerns me and my family and no one else . . . the day that I beat it, then I will talk about it."

Even as she refused to talk about it, she used it to help others. In 2007, two years after her diagnosis, she founded a charity, Aktiv mot kreft—Active Against Cancer—which helps cancer patients stay active and positive, to feel fully human rather than merely like a patient. Like Lebow, she felt that the worst possible thing for her was to merely lie in bed and rest during treatment—it made her feel like an invalid. Being active helped her feel more like herself. Her public role expanded, from legendary athlete to legendary athlete and cancer fighter; and when she talked about cancer, she used it to forge a connection and to buoy others. She still came to the New York City Marathon every year, now as both honored guest and charity spokesperson. Shay Hirsch, wife of *Runner's World* publisher George, was in her own fight against cancer at the same time; it became her point of connection with Grete: they could commiserate over treatments, but mostly Grete tried to lift Shay's spirits. They talked about wigs—all styles and colors, and Grete made a point of showing up each year at the New York City Marathon with a new one. When a fan sent Waitz a quilt she had made, Waitz called her personally and had a long conversation about her cancer treatment and her plan to beat it.

"She wanted the least possible attention to her own illness," said Helle Aanesen, the director of Aktiv mot kreft, "but worked tirelessly to the end to help others."[1] When she died, on April 19, 2011, the running world mourned. New York remembered her as one of their own. Waitz had specified her desire for a very small, private, quiet funeral. And it was exactly so: on April 28, she was laid to rest, surrounded only by family and a few very close friends. But she acquiesced to the need for the public to gather as well, to remember their Grete. Outside of Bislett Stadium, the spiritual home of track and field in Norway, there stands a statue of Waitz. It was half-buried in flowers and wreaths after her death. On May 11, there was a public memorial for Waitz at Bislett. The memorial had the feel of a state funeral; royalty and other influential figures, from the running world and otherwise, attended: Crown Prince Haakon, Prime Minister Jens Stoltenberg, Oslo Mayor Fabian Stang; a full delegation from the New York Road Runners; hundreds of cancer survivors and patients; volunteers with Aktiv mot kreft; and old rivals Mota and Benoit. When Benoit spoke to the crowd, her voice caught, and she blinked away tears. "I grew up with three brothers," she said. "Grete was the big sister I never had."

Benoit and a small group of friends visited Jack at the condo he and Grete had shared. Together they basked in the glow of memories of Grete's spirit, competitive fire, kindness, and love. Jack pulled out a soft felt bag that contained Grete's Olympic silver medal. Benoit picked it up and looked at it closely, turning it in her hands. "It's amazing how alike we are," she said. "We both live on the water, both keep our medals hidden away in a drawer."[2]

Benoit raced with an almost primal, ferocious, animalistic energy; Waitz was methodical and calculated, though no less competitive and ruthless. Waitz plotted out a strategy, figured out the splits; Benoit tended to throw herself into a race with desperate abandon, only to settle in and think through tactics on the fly. At the finish, Benoit's celebrations were an unrestrained release of emotion, a letting go of her intense focus; even in victory, Waitz was typically controlled. Benoit's smile, acknowledging the crowd, came on in a radiant flash, a thousand watts of pure joy and intensity; Waitz's smiled as if slightly embarrassed by the attention. Benoit would dance the night away after a race, sometimes before—once, when the Falmouth Road Race fell the morning after a friend's wedding, Benoit said (mostly joking) that she won the race fueled by vodka and wedding cake. Waitz, if she went out at all, went for a quiet dinner with Jack and her brothers. Benoit admitted to living with a little bit of clutter; Waitz's shoes were always lined up just so by the backdoor, and a writer who once peeked into Grete's silverware drawer declared that she'd never seen cutlery aligned so neatly. Benoit's uniforms always seemed to billow about her, and she favored a hat that seemed three sizes too big; Waitz favored a trim-fitting kit and pulled her hair into a tight bun. On the run, Benoit raced with force, constantly driving, pressing forward; Waitz seemed to skate across the surface of the roads.

But they shared the same commitment to transcendent greatness. And each, through a combination of will, ability, focus, and pain tolerance, achieved it. And each understood the other's journey; few others, not even their spouses, could fully appreciate the crucible of physical and emotional trials that marked their path. Both would have lived a more private existence if they could, would have preferred a near monk-like pursuit of running perfection; both accepted their roles—as public figures, as symbols of women's running, as inspiration to millions—with sincerity and seriousness. Both unflinchingly faced the added scrutiny and pressure that came with wanting to be the best, and both have a fair claim to the title. And each would probably say the other is more deserving.

It is a tragedy that Kristiansen and Waitz, two others who could have shared such a bond, were perhaps too much the other's opposite ever to acknowledge it. Kristiansen is much more outgoing—profiles early in her career described her as bubbly or carefree—and perhaps wanted a type of friendship that Waitz couldn't offer. Kristiansen was looking for a teammate; Waitz had never been that type of person. Kristiansen needed Waitz to be something she was not; Waitz couldn't find a way to connect with Kristiansen on a level she was comfortable with. Kristiansen didn't attend Waitz's memorial, which was widely seen as a sign of disrespect or enmity toward Waitz. But however complicated Kristiansen's feelings toward Waitz are, it was never that. Rather, she found the public spectacle—the concentration of politicians and the media—distasteful. On that, she and Waitz would have seen eye to eye.

***

Waitz lowered the world record nearly ten minutes on her own; it has only been lowered another ten minutes since her retirement. She broke barriers in the obvious way: the first woman under 2:30, the first female world marathon champion. But she also broke barriers in a fittingly understated way: Waitz, without saying a word, made it impossible to talk about women's running as something different from men's running. She didn't demand attention or ask for equal billing with the male runners, but the way she ran insisted on it; for the media to treat her differently from the male stars would have made them seem patently ridiculous. She was too good, too dominant, too unflappable; she ran in a way that put a halt to the "for a woman" qualifier that often attached itself to expressions of women's greatness. She was the greatest champion in New York's history, full stop. She set an even higher standard with her grace, kindness, patience, humility. Other stars have come and gone, but none has shone brighter than Waitz, the first great star of the women's marathon.

If no star shone brighter than Waitz, none has endured longer than Benoit. She is still one of the most recognized and beloved figures in running. Understandably, she has grown weary of recounting the stories of her past heroics, but she remains gracious in doing so for each new generation. She prefers to look ahead, vocally supporting the runners who have come after her, enthusiastically applauding each time her records are broken. Parts of her body have grown worn and frayed by the tens of thousands of miles she's run, but she's still out on the roads as often as she can be, and she continues to break new ground, setting new goals in running and pursuing them with the same passion she had in her twenties.

Benoit's retirement has been a moving target. Initially, perhaps, it was in 1988 after missing the Olympic Trials. But then she qualified for the 1992 Olympic Track Trials in the 10,000m. Then in 1996, she came back to run the Olympic Marathon Trials again at age 39. That seemed like her swan song, until she returned to the Trials in 2000, and again in 2008, at age 51—where she ran 2:49.08, an American record for the 50–55 age group. "All I wanted was to break three hours and finish," she said, though her competitive nature had her picking off runners in the latter stages as the crowd cheered her around the course.

Retirement still isn't something Benoit is yet ready to contemplate. After experimental knee surgery in 2021, she ran the 2022 London Marathon in 3:20.20, winning the 65–69 age group by seven minutes. Running is her message. Decades ago, she helped redefine how fast women could run and how they could race; now, she continues to push the limits of what's possible, and to redefine in the public consciousness what women can do as they age. Recently, she became a grandmother, and she says her new goal is to race a 5K with her granddaughter. No doubt Benoit will take the race out hard and dare the little girl to keep up.

Postlude

Cambridge, Massachusetts, August 12, 2019, 2:30 p.m.: *Three-time Boston Marathon champion Bobbi Gibb walks unannounced into the home of three-time Boston Marathon champion Sara Mae Berman—she's visiting her son, who rents an upstairs apartment in the Bermans' house. Gibb pokes her head into the living room to say hello to Sara Mae, who explains that she's in the middle of an interview for a book about the first women's Olympic marathon.*

"Oh," says Gibb. She pauses. "I would've liked to run in the Olympics." There is another, longer moment of silence. "Oh, well," she says.

Berman nods. "Oh well."

There is a statue of Bobbi Gibb in Hopkinton, commissioned by the 26.2 Foundation, a nonprofit devoted to promoting and supporting the marathon. The artist they chose for the project? Bobbi Gibb. Originally, she wanted to sculpt a generic everywoman, someone to symbolize all the runners who followed her; the foundation's board convinced Gibb that she was the best possible symbol for the rise of women's running. The commission is part of a larger effort in the running world to properly acknowledge the pioneer generation. The accolades have a bittersweet tinge: the pioneers are glad to be recognized, glad that women's running is finally being granted its rightful place on the world stage. But as competitive athletes, they can't help but feel that change came a generation too late.

Occasionally, members of the pioneer generation still gather in Boston, with Berman's home in Cambridge serving as a central hub. It is an extraordinary group: Gibb; Berman; Hansen; Cheryl Bridges Treworgy, who set a world marathon record of 2:49.40 in 1971 (and whose daughter, Shalane Flanagan, won an Olympic silver in the 10,000m in 2008); and Julia Chase, the first woman to run an AAU-sanctioned road race, in 1961. Nina Kuscsik comes up to see them all when her health allows.

Patti Catalano, now Patti Dillon, seems to have found a connection with these early pioneers. More so than the generation of runners Catalano competed against, these women understand being an outsider. Dillon came through more hard times than any of them: She's battled bulimia—her fixation on weight and fitness took a destructive turn at times in her career. She spent time living out of her car, destitute, seeing no future ahead. But she's come out the other side; a happy marriage, kids, a healthier relationship with running. She coached youth cross-country when her children were interested in running, and instilled in her charges the same tough-mindedness that helped her succeed. When her children moved on to other things, she happily moved on with them. She has fully embraced her Mi'qmak heritage, speaks to groups of Native American youth and aspires to speak at every reservation in the country. She is coaching a Native American running group based in New Mexico.

When the pioneers gather, their laughter is easy and they exude the contentment of people who charted their own course in life, who have been resolutely true to themselves. The strength of their bond is clear—a shared history, forged in the pursuit of something that they could only find in running. They were told no in many different ways: doctors said they wouldn't be able to bear children; well-meaning friends said nobody would want to date them; Treworgy's school required female PE majors to wear dresses at all times on campus. They couldn't escape the message that they had to choose between being a proper woman and following their passion. It didn't matter: "I knew in my heart I was a runner . . . we did not need encouragement—it was inside us the whole time," says Treworgy. Running, says Gibb, is about "Human endurance, human courage—what it takes to live a life."

They are rebels and exemplars—the spiritual descendants of Emma Sharpe, the pistol-carrying pedestrienne. They cleared the way for runners like Benoit, Waitz, and all the great athletes who came after them. They created opportunities that didn't exist during their own careers. The sport is still far from perfectly equitable—running still needs its Emma Sharpes—but they set it on the right path. The triumphs of each successive generation belong in part to them.

Acknowledgments

Something I've always loved about runners: we support each other whenever we can. We're competitive, of course, but we also want others to succeed. Without exception, when I reached out to someone in the running community, they were encouraging of this project and offered to help. The list of people who helped me better understand what I was trying to write about is impossibly long, and I am especially grateful to the following individuals:

Erin Dromgoole, who shared with me her wonderful unpublished thesis on the early history of women's track and field; the late great Gloria Ratti, whose nearly fifty years of service to the BAA made her an invaluable resource, and whose kindness will be sorely missed; Steve Vaitones, who let me ransack the USATF-New England archives; Chris Turner, librarian at World Athletics; Gwendolyn Swift, archivist at the USOC; Chris Lotsbom, director of race communications and media at the BAA, who answered every question and ran down every request for information; Michael Salmon at the LA84 foundation, whose persistence and patience yielded treasure after treasure; Jennifer Parks, who shared mountains of minutes from the IOC; Jorg Krieger, who helped me understand the IAAF's inner workings (and who also shared mountains of minutes with me).

Tom Ratcliffe helped connect me with a number of important figures in the running world; Amby Burfoot and George Hirsch have been incredibly gracious in their encouragement of the project and offered invaluable help and insights; Toni Reavis, the voice of American road racing, was there when most of the big events happened and shared his perspective on the races and racers at the heart of this story; Jeff

Benjamin offered a wealth of insight and connections; Tom Derderian, quasi-official historian of the Boston Marathon, is a walking reference for the past sixty years of New England running and helped me with some important details from the 1970s; Jack Fultz, whose enthusiasm is infectious, shared his personal journey through the sport, which intersected with many of the characters in this book; Anne Roberts at the New York Road Runners helped me better understand elite athlete coordination (and Fred); Gloria Averbuch, friend of and collaborator with Grete Waitz, gave me a better understanding of Grete as a person; Jacqueline Gareau and Lorraine Moller, incredibly talented Olympians, helped me understand the world of the elite marathoner.

To Bobbi Gibb, Kathrine Switzer, Sara Mae Berman, Eleonora Mendonça, Julia Chase, Jackie Hansen, Doris Brown Heritage, Joan Ullyiot, Cheryl Treworgy, and other members of the "pioneer generation" who shared their stories with me: Your talents are many, and your lives beyond running—as artists, scientists, researchers, lawyers, doctors, photographers, writers, and activists—are just as inspirational as what you contributed to the sport.

Much appreciation to the runners who became main characters in the book, especially Patti Catalano Dillon, for your honesty and frankness; Ingrid Kristiansen, for giving me so much of your time and insight. Above all, thank you to Joan Benoit for your graciousness. I know you've been through your story so many times, with so many people. Thank you for doing it again with me.

To Jack Waitz, thank you for your openness, for providing me with so much information, for your ever-patient responses to all my questions, for your general positivity. It is easy to see why Grete took such comfort in you.

To the wonderful people at Lyons: running and the outdoors are in your DNA, and I'm glad my book found a home with you. Thanks especially to Gene Brissie—your experience and professional judgment have given me so much confidence throughout this project; Jehanne Schweitzer, for your patience, sharp eye, and stylistic grace; Joanne Foster, for making my manuscript read so smoothly; Justine Connelly and the rest of the team, for turning the manuscript into a truly beautiful book.

It may be a breach of protocol to thank an editor who ultimately passed on this project, but to Jamison Stoltz: thank you for your thoughts on how to structure the story—as you can see, I stole some of your ideas.

To my agent, Amaryah: it is hard to believe we started talking about this project in the fall of 2019—it's been a long road, one I could not have traveled without your advice, editing skills, persistence, and relentless positivity. Thank you, thank you, thank you!

A big thanks to my dear friends, especially Battle, for your encouragement and offers to help; Lee Kiechel Koles, for reading early (and very rough) chapters; Jenny, for your patience and thoughtful advice; and Ben—words cannot adequately express the impact of your suggestions.

To Jess: You are the inspiration for this project, and the one who made it possible in so many ways—I was always afraid to try to become a writer until we began our journey together. You make scary things easier. Thank you for your advice, support, space, and belief; thank you for picking up the slack when I could not. Speaking of: thank you to Elliot and Emma, the delights of my life and the ones who remind me that writing a book is nowhere near as cool as trains or crayons or socks.

Notes

Prelude

1. Coubertin, "Les Femmes Aux Jeux Olympiques," *La Revue Olympique*, July 1912, 109–11. Quoted in Mary Leigh, "The Evolution of Women's Participation in the Summer Olympic Games, 1900–1948" (PhD diss, Ohio State University, 1974), 75.

2. Race description is based on footage from the race.

3. Leigh, "The Evolution of Women's Participation in the Summer Olympic Games, 1900–1948," 185.

Chapter 1

1. In the aftermath of Gibb's first marathon, newspaper reports speculated that she had jumped into the race midway.

2. Though such an outcome may seem unlikely, Cloney and Semple followed rules to the letter: The Reverend O'Neil Shannon, a Boston legend who coordinated programs for inner-city youth, ran Boston almost twenty times in the 1950s and 1960s and was a beloved figure at the marathon. But he never ran with a number: in his youth, he'd been a professional boxer, and by rule amateurs who competed against professionals—even middle-aged, retired ones—would lose their Olympic eligibility.

1. Bruce Hamilton and Greg Ryan, "Drugs, Denial, and Deflection," *International Journal of the History of Sport*, 36, https://www.tandfonline.com/doi/full/10.1080/09523367 .2019.1696312?scroll=top&needAccess=true.

Chapter 3

1. Jane Leavy and Susan Okie, "The Runner: Phenomenon of the '70s," *Washington Post*, September 30, 1979, https://www.washingtonpost.com/archive/sports/1979/09/30 /the-runner-phenomenon-of-the-70s/ba9e2a3d-a353-4f89-a3ba-b8c38b354034/?utm _term=.1313fab57542.

2. Leavy and Okie, "The Runner: Phenomenon of the '70s."

3. Joe Falls, *The Boston Marathon: The Incredible, Zany Story of America's Greatest Footrace and the Men and Women Who Have Run It* (New York: MacMillan, 1977).

4. Fred Lebow with Richard Woodley, *Inside the World of Big-Time Marathoning* (New York: Rawson Associates, 1984).

5. Jim Fixx, "Code of the Crazies," Running Times, June 1978, 27. Quoted in Aaron L. Haberman, "Thousands of Solitary Runners Come Together: Individualism and Communitarianism in the 1970s Running Boom," Journal of Sport History, vol. 44 no. 1 (Spring 2017).

6. Thaddeus Kostrubala, The Joy of Running (Philadelphia, PA: Lippincott, 1976), 145.

7. Both Andrews and Henning are quoted in Patti Hagan, "How They Run On," New York Times, December 24, 1978, https://www.nytimes.com/1978/12/24/archives/how-they-run-on.html.

8. Quoted in Neil Amdur, "A Marathon Man from Red Bank," New York Times, April 16, 1978, https://www.nytimes.com/1978/04/16/archives/new-jersey-weekly-a-marathon-man-from-red-bank-sports.html?searchResultPosition=3.

9. "A Modest Proposal for Joggers," Letter to the Editor by Herman H. Spitz, New York Times, June 3, 1979, sec. 4, 18.

10. Pamela Cooper, The American Marathon (Syracuse, NY: Syracuse University Press, 1998), 60.

11. Quoted in Joe Falls, The Boston Marathon: The Incredible, Zany Story of America's Greatest Footrace and the Men and Women Who Have Run It (New York: MacMillan, 1977).

12. Erika Powers, "From Boston to Los Angeles: Women Marathoners' Changing Perspectives from Pleasure to Empowerment and the Establishment of the Women's Olympic Marathon" (master's thesis, University of Wisconsin-Eau Claire, 2017).

13. Quoted in Cooper, The American Marathon, 168.

14. Ron Rubin, Anything for a T-Shirt: Fred Lebow and the NYCM, The World's Greatest Race (Syracuse, NY: Syracuse University Press, 2004), 93.

15. Neil Amdur, "Politicians Jump Marathon Gun," New York Times, September 17, 1976, 90, https://www.nytimes.com/1976/09/17/archives/politicians-jump-marathon-gun.html?searchResultPosition=272.

16. Darcy C. Plymire, "Positive Addiction: Running and Human Potential in the 1970s," Journal of Sport History 31, no. 3 (Fall 2004): 297–315.

17. Leavy and Okie, "The Runner: Phenomenon of the '70s."

18. "Run for Your Life" documentary, https://www.youtube.com/watch?v=CMK7e7uP-TY; Judd Erhlich, filmmaker, 2008 Brooklyn Film Networks.

19. https://more.arrs.run/race/16010.

20. Original idea first expressed by theoretical physicist Max Planck; this phrasing is from economist Paul Samuelson in Newsweek, June 16, 1975.

21. Switzer, Marathon Woman, (Philadelphia: Da Capo Press, 2009), 332.

22. As relayed by Dr. David Martin, who was on the organizing committee for the race, and was one of the leaders of the Atlanta Track Club, https://germanroadraces.de/?post_eng=a-pioneering-project-dr-david-martin-recalls-in-distance-running-how-an-extraordinary-race-staged-in-atlanta-30-years-ago-eventually-won-olympic-status-for-marathon-runners-25-years-avon-frauenl.

23. Miss Cooksey Foils Marathon Favorites," New York Times, March 20, 1978, C6.

24. Kenny Moore, "Ready to Run a Long Way," Sports Illustrated, March 20, 1978, https://vault.si.com/vault/1978/03/27/70773#&gid=ci0258c130500926ef&pid=70773---025---image.

25. Switzer, *Marathon Woman*, 343.

Chapter 4

1. "New York City," *Runner's World*, December 1978.

2. Waitz and Averbuch, *World Class* (New York: Grand Central Publishing, 1986), 129–30.

3. "Marathon Review," *Runner's World*, February 1979.

4. Waitz and Averbuch, *World Class*, 13.

5. Christal Saneh, "Grete Waitz, First Lady of the Marathon," Museum of World Athletics, https://www.worldathletics.org/heritage/news/grete-waitz-new-york-city -marathon-comic-feature?fbclid=IwAR08qiiVx_rZl_m8jMnJIg_gfvyI_SijdVOma3YM Cml4Ht7fJoJzWbB7yQE.

6. Non-Eastern Bloc athletes fared slightly better, percentagewise, in field events: Italy's Sara Simeoni won gold in the high jump, and Brigitte Holzapfel won bronze; Tessa Sanderson of Great Britain earned silver in the javelin.

Chapter 5

1. Excerpt from Phil Stewart's *Running Times* coverage of the race, https:// www.runnersworld.com/advanced/a20800356/running-times-1979-boston-marathon -coverage/.

Chapter 6

1. Neil Amdur, "Some Are Troubled by Lebow's Moves," *New York Times*, October 20, 1981, A27, https://www.nytimes.com/1981/10/20/sports/some-are-troubled-by-lebow-s -moves.html?searchResultPosition=527.

2. Amby Burfoot, "A Marathon with Heart," *Runner's World*, October 1978.

Chapter 7

1. Neil Amdur, "Issue and Debate: Are Women Geared for Distance Running?," *New York Times*, April 25, 1978, 33, https://timesmachine.nytimes.com/timesmachine/1978 /04/25/110843807.html?pageNumber=33.

2. Letter from J. B. Holt to Arpad Csanadi, December 6, 1979, World Athletics archives.

3. Letter from Richard Sargent to Jon Wigley (cc'd Holt and Csanadi), February 4, 1980. World Athletics archives.

4. Letter from Richard Sargent, director, sports, to Barbara Palm, Chair Women's LDR TAC, June 16, 1980. World Athletics archives.

5. It wasn't until after the 1984 Games that television revenue became such a massive windfall for the IOC.

6. Minutes of Meetings 22, no. 16 (April 16, 1980) USOC House of Delegates Session. USOC archives.

7. Kenneth Reich, *Making It Happen: Peter Ueberroth and the 1984 Olympics* (Santa Barbara, CA: Capra Press, 1986).

8. Reich, *Making It Happen*, 15.

9. That became unsustainable as the Games approached.

10. Reich, *Making It Happen*, 176, 71.

11. Reich, *Making It Happen*, 40.

12. IRC Newsletter, March 1980.

13. Letter from S. E. Strauzenberg to J. B. Holt, June 16, 1980. World Athletics archives.

14. Anita DeFrantz, "An Olympian's Oral History—Interview with Monique Berlioux," May 31–June 1, 2013, LA84 Foundation.

CHAPTER 8

1. Amby Burfoot, "Grete," *Runner's World*, March 1981. It is worth noting that although she was undefeated on the roads, she did lose on the track to the Soviet Union's Svetlana Ulmasova in the World Cup 3000m in August 1979.

2. This probably was a short course; Lebow admitted that the course at that time was closer to six miles than ten kilometers, which is 6.2 miles.

3. Charles Butler, "From Out of Nowhere," *Runner's World*, November 2011.

4. Waitz and Averbuch, 29.

5. Burfoot, "Grete."

6. Interview with Jack Waitz, 2019.

7. Burfoot, "Grete."

8. https://www.nytimes.com/1981/05/27/sports/grete-waitz-ready-for-toughest-mile .html.

9. Burfoot, "Grete."

10. Lesley Visser, "Waitz and Salazar Go the Distance," *Boston Globe*, April 18, 1982.

11. Robert Breer, "Running for Her Life," *Boston Globe*, November 30, 2003. Reprinted at https://howtobefit.com/patti-catalano.htm.

12. In his book about the Boston Marathon, Tom Derderian, who was working in Exeter at the time and claims to have been running thirty-one minutes in 10K races at the time, recalled getting dropped by Benoit and having to hitchhike back home.

13. Interview with Jack Fultz, June 2022.

CHAPTER 9

1. In 2021, the average times were 4:26 and 4:54.

2. Chris Rattue, "Weekend Profile: Allison Roe," *New Zealand Herald*, April 24, 2006, https://www.nzherald.co.nz/sport/weekend-profile-allison-roe /57UXOGHC2TCPZE2BHWBFBNWQ6A/.

3. https://www.letsrun.com/forum/flat_read.php?thread=1104591.

4. Roger Robinson, "Allison Roe Stays in Shape," *Runner's World*, April 14, 2012, https: //www.runnersworld.com/races-places/a20803035/allison-roe-stays-in-shape/.

5. Roger Robinson, "Allison Roe," https://athletics.org.nz/legends/allison-roe/.

6. Robinson: "Allison Roe."

7. Jane Leavy, "Seko Wins Marathon, Roe Fastest Woman," *Washington Post*, April 21, 1981, https://www.washingtonpost.com/archive/sports/1981/04/21/seko-wins -marathon-roe-fastest-woman/db6c575d-7f89-42ec-9c05-c40e8e279737/.

8. Robert Creamer, "Of Greeks and Russians," *Sports Illustrated*, February 5, 1956, 30–56.

9. Lisa Lindell, "Cuckoo Collins: The Crooked Path of a Nineteenth Century Sprinter," *Journal of Sport History* 45, no. 3 (Fall 2018): 334–51.

10. Lindell, "Cuckoo Collins."

11. Simon Trumbull, "A Triumph over Adversity: Audain's Life and Running Career," *World Athletics Heritage*, https://worldathletics.org/heritage/news/anne-audain-distance -runner-new-zealand.

12. The trust accounts, Cassell has stated, were always meant as a temporary bridge to a completely open professional model.

13. If it seems remarkable that so many records were set at New York in the early 1980s, it is a little too remarkable. Years later, the course was measured and found to be some- where between 80 and 150 meters short. This was not unusual—many courses in those years weren't precisely measured. Still, since Roe's record, and Waitz's before hers, were both minutes ahead of the second best marks, and because 150 meters is a little more than thirty seconds, it is fair still to credit them with being the world's fastest marathoners.

14. Judy McGregor, "Allison Roe's Double Blow for Feminism in a Troubled Arena," *New Zealand Herald*, September 18, 2018, https://www.nzherald.co.nz/ sport/judy-mcgregor-allison-roes-double-blow-for-feminism-in-troubled-arena /5KPXZ26O57NVUABA5TOXBY3QPY/.

Chapter 10

1. Lesley Visser, "Waitz and Salazar Go the Distance," *Boston Globe*, April 18, 1982.

2. She actually ran 1:09.

3. Boston was, however, behind the times: Will Cloney insisted that Boston would never pay athletes—they had never even paid travel expenses. Boston remained "The most stubbornly amateur event in the world," and as a result had lost some of its luster.

4. Joe Concannon, "Rating the Runners," *Boston Globe*, April 15, 1983.

5. Lesley Visser, "I was Running Very Fast," *Boston Globe*, April 20, 1982, 1.

6. From Indro Neri, *Dante Was a Runner (Dante Era Una Podista)*, Florence, Neri Editore, 1995. Reprinted and translated at http://www.worldwiderunning.com/palio_del _drappo_verde.php.

Chapter 11

1. Michael Strauss, "Waitz Wins Race for 4th Time," *New York Times*, June 1, 1982.

2. Joe Concannon, "Benoit's Back in the Running," *Boston Globe*, September 30, 1982, https://www.proquest.com/docview/294278020/FDD406AF92974E2FPQ/8?accountid =9675.

3. Roy Johnson, "Her Victory Is Fourth," *New York Times*, October 25, 1982.

4. Johnson, "Her Victory is Fourth."

5. Waitz's time, 2:25.28.66, was, in fact, just better than Roe's time from New York in 1982, 2:25.28.8. Further, there was already speculation that the New York course was short, which was confirmed in 1985, New York's course was somewhere between 70 and 150 meters short of the official distance. So, Waitz's London time did become, after the fact, the world record. Briefly.

6. Ian Thomsen, "Benoit Shatters the Record," *Boston Globe*, August 16, 1982.

7. "Top Woman is Hailed," *New York Times*, April 19, 1983.

8. Joe Concannon, "Her Opposition Is an Ocean Away," *Boston Globe*, April 17, 1983.

9. Joe Concannon, "For Kristiansen, the Waitz Is Over," *Boston Globe*, October 13, 1985.

10. Concannon, "For Kristiansen, the Waitz Is Over."

11. Neil Amdur, "Women Make Big Gains in Marathon," *New York Times*, April 20, 1983, https://www.proquest.com/docview/122279044/9E9F4CB63FE34A0FPQ/41?accountid=9675.

12. Kenny Moore, "Splendor and Agony in Helsinki," *Sports Illustrated*, August 15, 1983.

CHAPTER 12

1. Marlene Cimons, "For Joan Benoit, the Road to LA Goes Through an Island off the Coast of Maine," *Los Angeles Times*, December 26, 1983, C1.

CHAPTER 13

1. Puica was the world-record holder in the mile, having run 4:17.44, and she would win Olympic gold in the 3000 meters in Los Angeles.

2. Roger Underwood, "Joan Benoit Refuses to Let Olympic Dream Die," *The Olympian*, May 13, 1984, D1.

CHAPTER 14

1. *The Olympian*, May 12, 1984, A7.

CHAPTER 18

1. It's hard to know what she means exactly. She ran NYC in 1979, though she didn't finish. In 1980 she finished third, and second in 1981. She also ran in 1982, just six months after the European Championship. In 1983, she was still coming back from giving birth to Gaute. But in 1985, she swore she'd never run New York. In other interviews, Kristiansen has suggested that Lebow protected Waitz, or that Waitz demanded that Kristiansen and other potential challengers be kept out of New York; Grete said it would be ludicrous to think she'd limit the field, and Jack to this day argues that they never told Lebow who to invite or not. Given Waitz's oft-stated desire to race the best, and given that she had no problem taking on Roe in 1981 even though she was hurting, it seems unlikely that she ducked challengers. It is certainly the case that Waitz was always the number one star in New York, a fan favorite and, of course, Lebow's favorite.

2. Junxia was part of an impossibly fast group of women who trained under Ma Junren. Junxia and nine other Chinese athletes later signed a letter saying they were forced to take "large doses of illegal drugs" while training under Ma.

CHAPTER 19

1. George Hirsch, "The Humanity of the Long Distance Runner," *New York Times*, April 24, 2011.

2. Toni Reavis, "Celebrating Grete," https://tonireavis.com/2011/05/11/celebrating -grete/.

Index

39, 97–98; Mota in, 103–4, 142–43; after 1984 Olympics, 219–23; in Olympics, 80, 131–32, 201–7, 230–31, *p3*; organization of, 44; Pioneer Era in, 17–21; psychology of, 128–32, 207–14, 236–37; Roe in, 116–17, 127, 147–53, 175–76; sexism and, 103–4; spectators of, 54–55, 206–7, 210; strategy in, 107; training for, 13, 18–19, 145–46, 234; ultramarathons, 123–24; in United States, 28, 44–48; to USSR, 88–89; water stations in, 25, 45, 74–75, 157, 202–7, 211; women in, 39–43, 48–52, 82–83, 93, 119–22, 225–28, *p7*; World Marathon Championships, 229–31; world records in, 2; before World War II, 25–26. *See also specific topics*
marketing: AAU in, 124; culture, 87; for distance running, 49–50, 62, 122–23; for New York City Marathon, 44–45, 53–54; by Nike, 81, 163; Roe and, 119–22; sponsorship and, 48–49, 52, 222; to Switzer, 39; for women, 30–31
Martin, David, 250n22
Martin, Lisa, 229–30
Masuda, Akemi, 103, 133
May, Carey, 154
McClure, Nikki, 196
McGregor, Judy, 131

McKay, Jim, 130
media: Boston Marathon in, 116–17, 151; Cooksey in, 53; culture in, 41; in Eastern Europe, 60; economics of, 125–28; fame in, 221–22; gender in, 14–16, 19–20, 45; Gibb in, 249n1; IOC and, 125, 251n5; Kuscsik in, 28, 52; in Los Angeles, 196–97; marathons in, 39, 97–98; at New York City Marathon, 79–80; at 1984 Olympics, 215–16; 1976 Olympics in, 58; at Olympic Trials, 184–85; Semple in, 17–18, 27–28; sexism in, 53–54; Switzer in, 32–33, 185, 212, 216; track and field in, 92; violence in, 35–36; Waitz, G., in, 55–56, 120, 143, 190; women in, 103–4, 147–48
Melpomene, 3
Merrill, Jan, 106
Merrill, Sam, 43
Mexico, 4, 90
Meyer, Greg, 139
Michaels, Al, 103, 212
Miller, Don, 93
Miller, Glen, 195
Miller, Tom, 18–19
Miller Lite, 163
Milliat, Alice, 5–7, 36, 95–96
Milvy, Paul, 40
Mission Bay Marathon, 46
Moller, Lorraine, 97, 128, 175–76
Moon, Aubrey, 18

Moore, Kenny, 149
Mota, Rosa: Benoit, J., and,
133, 239; career of, 225–27,
229–31, 239, *p4*, *p6*; in Chicago
Marathon, 221; in cross
country running, 173; Fogli
and, 157; in marathons, 103–4,
142–43; at Olympics, 201–11,
213; psychology of, 168, 219;
reputation of, 2, 169, 190
Mtolo, Willie, 236
Muhrcke, Gary, 33
Muhrcke, Jane, 43
Murdoch, Rupert, 131

National Jogging Association,
45–46
Native Americans, 113, 244
NBC Sports, 97–98
Ndereba, Catherine, *p7*
nervousness, 135–36
Netherlands, 35
New Year's Day Welly to the Elly
race, 44
New Year's Eve race, 77–78
New York: distance running in,
29–33; landscapes of, 44–45;
L'Eggs Mini-Marathon, 30–33,
50, 106, 112, 117, 146, 190, *p3*
New York City Marathon: AAU
and, 43; Boston Marathon and,
80–81, 119–20; celebrations
at, *p5*; Chicago Marathon
and, 226, 234; competition
in, 78–79; eligibility for,

127–28; history of, 22, 30–31,
105–6; Kristiansen, I., in,
129, 141–42, 255n1; Lebow
to, 237; London Marathon
and, 254; to Manufacturers
Hanover, 49; marketing for,
44–45, 53–54; media at, 79–80;
records in, 55–56, 149, 253n13;
sponsorship for, 61; Waitz, G.,
and, 53–56, 60–62, 146–48,
167, 230, 239, 241; women in,
128–32
New York Road Runners, 28–29,
40, 79, 127, 130, 237, 239
New Zealand: Amateur Athletics
Association, 127–28; Aukland
marathon in, 121; Australia
and, 81; Board of Tourism,
149; culture of, 131; distance
running in, 3–4, 26–27; Nike
and, 82; Olympics to, 175;
Waitakere Range in, 121
Nike: Athletics West and, 180;
Blue Ribbon Sports and, 87;
labs at, 116; marketing by, 81,
163; OTC marathon, 129,
145–46; research lab, 135;
sponsorship with, 176; women
to, 81–82, 88, 96
Nixon, Richard, 40, 90
North Carolina State, 66–69, 82
Norway, 56–60, 77–78, 168, 190,
200, 220, 237–39. *See also*
Waitz, Grete

I., and, 133, 178–79, 241;
Lebow and, 233–37, 255n1,
p5; in media, 55–56, 120, 143,
190; New York City Marathon
and, 53–56, 60–62, 146–48,
167, 230, 239, 241; at 1984
Olympics, *p3*; psychology of,
77–80, 219–20; records by,
71, 105–6, 117, 189, 241–42;
reputation of, 2, 168–69, 201–7,
254n12; Roe and, 122, 128–32,
253n13, 254n5; Samuelson
and, *p6*; training by, 106–10;
USSR and, 252n1; in World
Cross Country championships,
172–73
Waitz, Jack: Benoit, J., and, 233,
239–40; as spectator, 105,
108, 140, 148, 154–55, 255n1;
support from, 55–56, 60–62,
77–78
Waldniel International Marathon,
47, 50, 88–89
Walters, Kay, 164
water stations, 25, 45, 74–75, 157,
202–7, 211
weather, 58–59, 142–43, 167,
185, 207
Weisfield Jewelers, 163–64
Wigley, Jon, 92
Williams, Michael, 50
Winter, Liane, 47–48, 145
Wolper, David, 197

women: to AAU, 85–89, 243;
activism for, 16–17, 19–20,
28–29; AIAW for, 66, 68; in
athletics, 53–62, 65–66, 191,
230–31; Berman, S. M., for,
21–23; in Boston Marathon,
48–49; in college athletics,
65–70; in culture, 27–28, 122–
23; in distance running, 77–83,
152–55, 228–30; in European
Athletics Championship, 140–
43; field hockey for, 18, 63–66,
68; Gibb for, 11–17, 243–44;
Grete Waitz Run for, 237–38;
in history, 41–43; in IAAF, 36;
in marathons, 39–43, 48–52,
82–83, 93, 119–22, 225–28,
p7; marketing for, 30–31; in
media, 103–4, 147–48; in New
York City Marathon, 128–32;
to Nike, 81–82, 88, 96; in 1984
Olympics, 73–75, 193–200,
207–14; in 1972 Olympics,
32–33, 35–37; in 1928
Olympics, 5–7; in Olympics,
3–4, 47–48, 81, 95–96, 98–100,
125–26; in Olympic Trials,
161–67, 170; prejudice against,
50–51; recognition of, 72;
records for, 3–4; sexism and,
44–48, 140–41; sponsorship
with, 49–50, 125, 174; in
Tokyo Marathon, 88–89; in
track and field, 60; Women